MW00679212

DECENTRALIZING HEALTH SERVICES IN MEXICO

U.S.-Mexico Contemporary Perspectives Series, 25
CENTER FOR U.S.-MEXICAN STUDIES
UNIVERSITY OF CALIFORNIA, SAN DIEGO

Contributors

Raquel Abrantes Pêgo

Javier Alagón

Sofía Arjonilla Alday

Anne-Emanuelle Birn

Miguel González-Block

Núria Homedes

René Leyva

Ricardo Loewe

Lucila Olvera Santana

Antonio Ugalde

Óscar Zapata

DECENTRALIZING HEALTH SERVICES IN MEXICO

A CASE STUDY IN STATE REFORM

edited by

Núria Homedes and Antonio Ugalde

LA JOLLA, CALIFORNIA

Center for U.S.-Mexican Studies, UCSD

© 2006 by the Regents of the University of California. Published by the Center for U.S.-Mexican Studies at the University of California, San Diego. All rights reserved under International and Pan-American Conventions. No part of this publication may be reproduced or transmitted in any form or by any means, electronic or mechanical, including photocopy, recording, or any information storage or retrieval system, without prior permission in writing from the publisher.

ISBN-13: 978-1-878367-56-3 (paper)
ISBN-10: 1-878367-56-0 (paper)
ISBN-13: 978-1-878367-57-0 (cloth)
ISBN-10: 1-878367-57-9 (cloth)
Printed in the United States of America

Cover art © Eric Westbrook/Images.com.

Library of Congress Cataloging-in-Publication Data

Decentralizing health services in Mexico : a case study in state reform /
edited by Núria Homedes and Antonio Ugalde.
    p. cm. -- (U.S.-Mexico contemporary perspectives series ; 25)
Includes bibliographical references and index.
ISBN-13: 978-1-878367-56-3 (pbk.)
ISBN-13: 978-1-878367-57-0 (cloth)
1. Health services administration--Mexico. 2. Health care reform--Mexico.
3. Public health--Mexico. I. Homedes, Nuria. II. Ugalde, Antonio. III. Series.

RA395.M6D43 2006
362.1'04250972--dc22

                                                2006012427

To the memory of President Salvador Allende,
a life ruthlessly cut short by those who value profit
above health and human dignity.

CONTENTS

Preface

The quality of health care and the coverage of health care services in Latin America do not correspond to the level of expenditures in this sector, a fact that has long been acknowledged. Poor planning and investments, physicians' promotion of excessive and unnecessary high-tech tertiary care, an uncommitted labor force, corruption, and the concentration of resources in urban areas are only a small sampling from a long list of ills affecting the health sector.

Most Latin American countries suffered a severe economic downturn beginning at the end of the 1970s. Facing large public debts that had accumulated over decades, Latin America's governments found themselves without the resources to meet their financial commitments. The International Monetary Fund and World Bank came to the "rescue" and offered new loans tied to the acceptance of structural adjustments that demanded a significant contraction in social expenditures, including health. It was expected that savings from these adjustments would free up public funds and that the savings would be used to pay down the public debt.

It was the deplorable state of health services, the result in part of these structural adjustments, that led the World Bank to embark on formulating health care policies to promote efficiency, equity, quality, and user satisfaction—praiseworthy objectives that are hard to oppose. The model of health reform that the World Bank produced had three key policies: decentralization of services, privatization, and a package of basic services that would be available to the poor without cost. With various degrees of success, the World Bank has promoted these three policies in most developing countries of the world, including in Latin America. Of the three, decentralization has been the most universally and most readily accepted.

The purpose of this book is to verify—through fieldwork-based qualitative and quantitative data gathered in several Mexican states—whether, after twenty years of decentralization in Mexico, the objectives promised by the policy's promoters have been attained. The study of Mexico's decentralization is of particular relevance to the ongoing debate on the advantages and disadvantages of decentralization in different political, cultural, and economic contexts. Mexico is a very large country, and, with 100 million people, it is one of the most populous in the world. Politically, it is a federation of thirty-one states and a Federal District, with a political system modeled on that of the United States. In other words, Mexico has ideal traits to justify the decentralization of health services.

The first chapter in this volume offers a comprehensive review of the literature on decentralization. It briefly discusses the reasons given to justify decentralization of various economic sectors in various political and historical contexts, and it analyzes the role of supranational organizations in promoting the recent drive to decentralize the health sector. The chapter then presents the conflicting definitions of decentralization that experts have developed and the difficulties that these definitions create when one attempts to measure the degree of decentralization that a country has achieved. A decentralization matrix is offered as an alternative to a decentralization scale.

The review of the health decentralization literature suggests that decentralization in other Latin American countries has not achieved efficiency, equity, and community participation, nor has it improved the quality of services. The authors conclude that the main purpose behind the recent health decentralization drive—in addition to reducing central government expenditures—has been to facilitate the privatization of health services.

A detailed history of health decentralization in Mexico is presented in chapter 2. After the Mexican Revolution of 1910–1917, the federal government, facing regional power elites that could potentially subvert the construction of a unified modern state, engaged in a steady and successful process of centralization that relegated federalism to symbolic status. However, after several decades of building a centralized health system, authorities began to question its benefits. The first earnest effort to return to a federal health system coincided with the economic recession of the 1980s. Chapter 2 analyzes the characteristics of this first decentralization attempt (implemented between 1983 and 1988), the hiatus that followed during the presidency of Carlos Salinas de Gortari (1988–1994), and the changes introduced during the second decentralization (from 1994 to 2004). In 2004, President Vicente Fox officially began implementing a new health model that had been approved by Congress in 2003.

During the first decentralization, only fourteen states answered the federal government's call to decentralize. Between 1997 and 1999, all states and the Federal District responded to the federal request, signing agreements that defined the responsibilities of both the states and the federal government. Decentralization was still an unfinished project in 2004, when the new model was introduced, extending access to health services to the uninsured poor through the People's Health Insurance Program (Seguro Popular de Salud). While it is too early to forecast the success of the new health model, chapter 2 analyzes its potential impact on decentralization and concludes that Mexican health policymakers have de facto reverted to a policy of centralization.

The second and third parts of the volume (chapters 3 through 9) present case studies of decentralization in ten states. These studies provide a comprehensive and critical analysis of Mexico's decentralization, its accomplishments, and its shortcomings. It should be emphasized at this point that this volume is more than a thematic collection of works written by different authors. While a number of scholars, including the editors, have contributed to the case studies, all of the studies follow a similar format in examining the transfer of authority over fiscal, human, and physical resources, and all combine qualitative and quantitative data to provide a wealth of information far greater than could have been compiled by a single author. In all of the case studies, the in-depth interviews were unstructured and open-ended to allow a free flow of communication. The occupational characteristics of the persons interviewed in the various states are similar; the interviews include officials of the departments of public health, political and labor leaders, personnel in nongovernmental organizations, and academicians. The studies have purposely been selected to create the unity of focus that the reader will find in this volume.

Shortening the distance between decision makers and users requires transferring resources and responsibilities to local governments. This has not occurred in Mexico, but an intermediate policy has been the creation of health districts as administrative units under the authority of the state health secretariats. It was understood that the health districts would also be decentralized. Most states have advanced little in this respect; as a result, the number of independent studies of health districts is extremely limited. Nevertheless, we have been able to include one study that examines this important aspect of decentralization; chapter 9 presents the results of fieldwork conducted in the health districts of Nuevo León, a state that had shown a firm determination to delegate some authority to the districts.

It is important for readers to know the outcome of the first decentralization, why so little was accomplished, and why its consequences were contrary to those sought by the policy's proponents. There are very few independent studies of the first decentralization, but we were fortunate to locate two outstanding pieces that apply a political economy perspective to the process and results of decentralization in five states.

The first of these two studies was conducted by a team of researchers from Mexico's National Institute of Public Health. Miguel González-Block and his colleagues present findings from their comparative study of two of Mexico's poorest states, Oaxaca and Guerrero, and clearly document the political underpinnings of decentralization. Oaxaca, in an attempt to co-opt escalating social movements for political autonomy in the face of excessive centralization, was the first state scheduled for decentralization. The federal government used decentralization as a political tool to provide the governor with the resources and authority to win over rebellious local leaders. The intent was to show Oaxacans that there had been a transfer of authority and decision-making power to the region and that this signaled the beginning of the end of the excessive centralism that had characterized Mexico's political system for seven decades. Apparently the strategy failed, and political violence escalated in the state. The federal government concluded that in Oaxaca decentralization was more a political risk than an asset, and decentralization was aborted.

González-Block and colleagues made the startling discovery that decentralization in Guerrero—despite having been very limited—brought about a 180° change in service distribution, moving from a pattern of equity to one of inequity. In the case of personnel management, the transfer of authority did not extend beyond some controls over professional behavior, and practically all decisions continued to be made at the federal level. In contrast, in Oaxaca, where decentralization had been halted, inequity did not increase.

In chapter 4, Anne-Emanuelle Birn presents findings from a study sponsored by the Inter-American Development Bank to assess progress in the decentralization of social services. She examined decentralization in three states—Jalisco, Morelos and Hidalgo—and concluded that decentralization did change the organization of medical care in these states but "largely for the worse." The cost was not negligible. From official estimates, Birn found that the decentralization of fourteen states in the first decentralization cost 140,000 million pesos.

Chapters 3 and 4 also touch on decentralization—or its absence—under President Salinas. Most analysts of Mexican politics agree that Salinas put the brakes on decentralization and engaged instead in a policy of recentralization. It is not clear to what extent the failure of the first decentralization influenced Salinas's decision to reverse course. Nevertheless, the policy of health services decentralization continued to appear in official documents, even though it had been replaced by the SEDESOL social development program, in which funds were distributed to municipalities directly from the Office of the President. SEDESOL was presented to the World Bank as a policy of decentralization, whereas it was in fact an instrument for centralizing political power in the presidency, doling out World Bank loan funds directly to local elites in exchange for their help in weakening the political base of states' elected political leaders.

Decentralization got renewed impetus under President Ernesto Zedillo (1994–2000). Chapters 5 though 9 discuss the implementation of decentralization from 1996 to the end of the twentieth century in Baja California Sur, Sonora, Guanajuato, Tamaulipas, and Nuevo León.

Lucila Olvera Santana, a researcher at Mexico's National Institute of Public Health at the time of the study, allowed respondents to voice their thoughts about the implementation of health services decentralization in Baja California Sur. The many quotations in her chapter are eloquent testimony to the incomplete and imperfect nature of the process. Like the authors of other chapters in this section, Olvera Santana examines the decentralization of fiscal, personnel, and physical resources to the state. She also discusses in some detail the extent of community participation, an important point since, as indicated earlier, community involvement is one of decentralization's stated objectives. Her research confirms that the transfer of authority has been very limited. Her findings reveal that Baja California Sur was not ready for decentralization, and the state's health-sector debt continues to rise. Because of this indebtedness, Baja California Sur could not provide sufficient resources, supplies and medicines became increasingly scarce, and, consequently, the quality of services was compromised. Olvera Santana did not find any evidence of efficiency improvements or efforts by health authorities to involve the community.

Raquel Abrantes Pêgo, also a researcher at the National Institute of Public Health at the time of the study, observed the uncertainty that decentralization generated among health personnel in Sonora. State officials saw decentralization as a policy defined by federal health authorities, with very little input from the state. Budget allocations continued to be determined in Mexico City, and the resources transferred from the center were insufficient to cover the state's newly acquired responsibilities. The decentralization of human resources was, as one respondent phrased it, merely "a virtual change," and community participation was reduced to contributions through user fees and volunteer work during immunization campaigns. Abrantes Pêgo also found that medical associations had a negative reaction to decentralization. Their members resented the fact that they were not consulted on the policy or given sufficient information about the reform. They also saw a potential opening of the health care market to privatization, which could jeopardize their jobs.

Abrantes Pêgo found that the rhetoric of decentralization had unintentionally changed the nature of the relationship between state and federal authorities by easing the subordination of governors and state political forces to the federal government. This is an important development even though, after twenty years of decentralization, it is not yet clear to what extent the new power alignment has improved the quality, efficiency, and equity of health services.

The title of chapter 7, "Guanajuato: Invisible Results," denotes the outcome of decentralization in this state where President Vicente Fox previously held the governorship and other political positions. Sofía Arjonilla Alday presents findings from her fieldwork that formed part of a broader study of Mexico's health reform, financed by Canada's International Development Research Centre. As in the other case studies presented in this volume, Arjonilla Alday found in Guanajuato that the limited decision-making power transferred from the federal government to the states was centralized in the State Health Secretariat. Health districts continued to be managed by the State Health Secretariat, and transfers of authority to the municipalities were limited to oversight of a few sanitary programs.

While Guanajuato's contribution to its state health budget has not risen since 1994, the federal government has increased its funding substantially and does not appear willing to relinquish control over the transferred funds. The Guanajuato case adds credence to the view that decentralization by itself does not increase the productivity of personnel, given that the state's physicians fail to meet federal guidelines for the number of consultations to be provided per hour.

There is one more important finding from Guanajuato. Transferring power to the states does not guarantee the adoption of policies that are more appropriate for meeting local needs. Arjonilla Alday finds that state policymakers use their newly acquired decision-making power poorly, spending most of the state funds on the construction and rehabilitation of hospitals rather than on preventive programs and on primary care facilities, where 80 percent of health problems are resolved. Moreover, she argues, investing collected user fees in urban hospitals increases inequity because this practice represents a transfer from the poor, who are the principal users of health clinics, to urban hospitals to which the poor lack access, for both cultural and economic reasons.

Chapter 8 includes research from Tamaulipas and Nuevo León. The findings are part of a project that examined decentralization's impact on health relations between Mexico's northern border states and their U.S. counterparts. Nuevo León is one of Mexico's wealthiest and most urbanized states. It enjoys good health care infrastructure and has better health indicators than most other states in the nation. While very aware of the limitations of the transfer of power from the federal government to the state, particularly with respect to personnel and cost increases, officials at the Nuevo León State Health Secretariat maintained a positive outlook toward decentralization. They have taken advantage of the window of opportunity opened by decentralization and have found new sources of income through contracts with municipalities and the Mexican Social Security Institute; under these contracts they offer medical services to municipal employees and IMSS beneficiaries who, because of distance, cannot access the services provided by their respective social security institutes.

In Nuevo León we found that user fees were extracted from the poor who utilize health centers, and a substantial portion of these fees were allocated to health professionals and staff of the health districts. This financial transfer from the poor to middle-class personnel suggests a lack of concern for equity issues; in effect, it allows health policymakers to impose a regressive tax. On the other hand, Nuevo León's governor had mandated that user fees not be levied in the state's poorest health district. The data also show that productivity was very low and had not increased with decentralization, a point that the state secretary of health acknowledged and for which he had no short-term solution.

Nuevo León is a very powerful state, both economically and politically; consequently, it has more leverage at the national level than do most other states in Mexico. Because of Nuevo León's heavy industrial base, federal authorities and national political elites pay more attention to the state's demands, giving it the kind of advantage that can increase existing inequities among the states.

The Tamaulipas study confirms the findings in other states regarding the incomplete nature of decentralization. Tamaulipas presents an interesting variation because, unlike other states in Mexico, prior to decentralization it had developed a network of autonomous hospitals funded by the state and governed by community boards presided over by the governor but independent from the State Health Secretariat. Ironically, with decentralization, these hospitals lost their autonomous status and became part of the State Health Secretariat.

Chapter 9 discusses the transfer of decision-making authority to the district level in Nuevo León. The organization of the health districts, the use of their newly acquired authority, the advantages and shortcomings of decentralizing to the district level, and the complex relations between health districts and municipalities are analyzed in some detail. District officials agreed that decentralization had allowed them to organize services in ways that they deemed advantageous. For example, health districts could use collected user fees to purchase drugs and sundries directly from wholesalers and pharmacies. Health districts did not consider that community participation was a component of decentralization; as they understood it, communities participate through the Healthy Municipalities Program, which, as discussed elsewhere in the volume, is not a very significant program and does not have a measurable impact on the health status of the population.

Decentralization of some administrative functions at the district level could have very positive consequences provided that inequities among districts do not increase, that the State Health Secretariat organizes an efficient supervisory system, and that abuses and corruption are controlled.

The chapters in this volume provide a comprehensive view of twenty years of decentralization in Mexico. It is an unfinished story with a long way to go before completion, a goal that may never be reached. The new People's Health Insurance Program for those not covered by social security plans, which the federal Ministry of Health began as a pilot program in 2002, was approved in 2003 by the federal Congress as the cornerstone of the new health reform. Officially, the implementation of the new reform was begun in 2004. It is too early to predict whether it will be a success story or one of those programs that, dotting the history of Mexico, end or languish at the end of the administration that launched them. However, this much can be said: its characteristics and some declarations by top health policymakers suggest that the new reform and Seguro Popular will probably devolve to the federal government the little power that was transferred to the states over the last twenty years. The Seguro Popular has been entirely designed at the top, is centrally administered, and will deprive the states of the financial resources, including user fees, that allowed them to gain some decision-making authority.

We hope that Mexico's experience with decentralization will be a valuable contribution to policymakers in other countries that are considering or implementing decentralization of health services, to technical experts who are advising nations, and to academicians who are pursuing research on the topic.

Antonio Ugalde, Austin, Texas
Núria Homedes, Houston, Texas

Acknowledgments

This volume has benefited from the openness of many health professionals, including managers of Mexico's Ministry of Health and state-level health secretariats, political and labor leaders, and faculty of several universities. All selflessly shared their thoughts and time with the authors of the various chapters. They are so many that we cannot list them individually; our sincere thanks to each of them. We have striven to represent their views and opinions accurately, and we hope that the time they spent conversing with us and the trust they placed in us have not been in vain.

We are particularly indebted to Dr. Jesús Zacarías Villarreal, health secretary in the state of Nuevo León at the time of the research, who made our stay in Monterrey fruitful and enjoyable. He provided an open door to the Nuevo León Health Secretariat and encouraged his staff to share their knowledge and decentralization experiences with us.

Special thanks go to Ana María Salinas and Cecilia Montemayor for coordinating our fieldwork in Nuevo León and Tamaulipas, respectively; their assistance was essential to make our fieldwork efficient and pleasant. Cecilia provided many useful insights about the distinctiveness of Tamaulipas and helped gather pertinent documents and reports.

Lucila Olvera Santana, Raquel Abrantes Pêgo, and Sofía Arjonilla Alday, who contributed chapters to the volume, deserve particular recognition. From the beginning they saw the need to give unity to the book. We will always remember with gratitude their patience and understanding during the many revisions the chapters underwent. Raquel generously offered her home in Mexico City for informal meetings during the process of making this book a reality.

Dr. William Glade, director of the Institute of Latin American Studies of the University of Texas at Austin at the time of the research, helped us find funding for our fieldwork in Nuevo León and Tamaupilas and, most importantly, always provided encouragement to us in our academic effort.

We also wish to express our appreciation to Sandra del Castillo for her thorough editing of this volume, and to Olive Roen for improving the English version of the manuscript.

PART I

Decentralization: Theory and History

1

Decentralization: The Long Road from Theory to Practice

ANTONIO UGALDE AND NÚRIA HOMEDES

The current trend toward the decentralization of health sectors is justified under the assumption that it will improve the quality, equity, and efficiency of health systems and increase satisfaction for the users of services. In addition, advocates of decentralization expect that it will increase community participation in health decision making and democracy.

BACKGROUND: UP AND DOWN THE LADDER OF POWER AND CONTROL

A brief review of world history reveals that tensions between central, regional, and local authorities have been a constant. Empires were created by force and collapsed or were destroyed with the passing of time; kingdoms were enlarged by marriages; nations expanded and were often partitioned through treaties, wars, or the purchase of territories. Unions of independent states or the founding of a commonwealth of nations introduced new political arrangements. With all these territorial and legal changes, there were changes in the locus of decision making; in some instances, decisions were centralized; in others, decentralized.

Countries joining the European Union (EU) surrendered some national sovereignty and decision-making power to a supranational organization. Over the course of more than forty years, the European Union has carefully defined which policies in each sector—and under what arrangements, which differ substantially from sector to sector—are the responsibility of supranational organizations (United Nations Department of Economic and Social Affairs 2000). At the same time, within the EU there are regions and groups that demand greater decentralization. In the United Kingdom, Scotland regained its Parliament in 1999 after 292 years of governance from

London. Spain, a country that was heavily centralized, has become one of the most decentralized nations within the Union. Starting in 1978, Spain's new constitution created sixteen autonomous regions that have progressively acquired more policymaking powers in various sectors of the economy. Tensions between the center and the periphery continue in Spain and elsewhere in the European Union. For example, Catalonia and the Basque Country demand to be considered nations while remaining part of Spain, there is pressure from the Northern League to gain autonomy from Italy (a nation only since the end of the nineteenth century), and the situation in Northern Ireland remains unsettled. Czechoslovakia—created in 1918 from the ashes of the Austro-Hungarian Empire—broke apart in 1993; and twelve years later, with their accession to the European Union, the two new republics found themselves surrendering part of the autonomy they had acquired after partition, now sharing common laws, regulations, and directives imposed by the EU. Slovenia is an example of secession and accession—seceding from Yugoslavia and joining the European Union thirteen years later, at which time some of the autonomy previously gained was lost. The European Union illustrates the complexity of the process of centralizing and decentralizing decision making, the time required to "succeed," and the unfinished nature of the process.

Examples of tensions between central and regional powers from other parts of the world include the threat by the province of Santa Cruz in Bolivia to declare autonomy/independence, the fierce and destructive wars in Africa to reconfigure the arbitrary national boundaries set by former colonial powers, the violent efforts by Chechnya to secede from Russia, the history of Crimea's Autonomous Republic, Taiwan's refusal to return to China, the threats by French provinces to break away from Canada, and the independence movement in Puerto Rico.

Free market blocs, free trade agreements, and World Trade Organization membership also limit the decision-making power of the signatory states. Nations that join free market blocs relinquish some important financial, environmental, and labor decision-making power. Adherence to international treaties is a voluntary limitation of national power, in accordance with national goals or values. When borrowing from the International Monetary Fund (IMF) or World Bank, nations and communities surrender some economic decision-making power to these institutions. Thus Mario

Tema, a Guatemalan indigenous leader, reminded then-director of the World Bank Paul Wolfowitz and other top officials that they should get the consent of those who live in an area before launching major projects that affect their lives—such as the open-pit mine located ten miles from his community of Sipacapa (Oxfam America 2005).

In sum, relations between central and regional powers are seldom smooth. Some regions may request more autonomy or seek secession, while others may refuse to accept additional power to make decisions, particularly when the acceptance implies a financial cost or increased responsibility. There are many forces behind centralizing and decentralizing power in decision making. Centralization and decentralization could take place in a country simultaneously as national reforms decentralize decision making within the country and international agreements transfer some decision making to supranational organizations or trading groups. Improving efficiency, equity, quality, and citizens' satisfaction has never been the driving force behind centralizing or decentralizing shifts of decision-making power (Sandiford 1999). Ethnic intransigence, religious fundamentalism, and political and economic ambition have been the primary motivations for such changes. In this chapter we analyze the forces that have led to the current decentralization movement and the impact that decentralization has had in the performance of the health sector.

THE ROLE OF SUPRANATIONAL AND BILATERAL ORGANIZATIONS IN THE GLOBAL DRIVE FOR DECENTRALIZATION

The previous discussion suggests that centralization and decentralization have taken place in countries at different historical times and in response to a variety of motivations. During the last twenty-five years, we have witnessed calls for decentralization in many countries as a part of state reform. The coincidence in the timing, the commonality of reasons given to support decentralization, and the organizations behind its thrust raise questions about the real motivation underlying the decentralization drive.

A close examination reveals that the driving ideology is neoliberalism. Neoliberals have exercised decisive control of the U.S. government since President Ronald Reagan came to power in 1980. As the world's largest economy and the nation with the most destructive military arsenal, the United States has imposed its policies on key supranational organizations;

under its influence, the International Monetary Fund, the World Bank, multilateral regional banks, the Organisation for Economic Co-operation and Development (OECD), and other supranational institutions embraced neoliberal policies.

The goal of neoliberalism is to concentrate capital worldwide in a few hands—that is, to centralize economic power in the super rich. It is not surprising that in 1992 Prud'homme viewed decentralization as "a political strategy by ruling elites to retain most of their power by relinquishing some of it" (cited in Dillinger 1994: 8). Neoliberalism has been very successful in increasing wealth disparities. Wealth concentration has taken place everywhere, and the gap between the rich and the poor has grown steadily during the last twenty-five years. According to the United Nations Development Programme, a small percentage of the world's population owns a very large percentage of the world's wealth (UNDP 2005).

To achieve their objective, neoliberals have created an ideology based on two simple principles: (1) the private sector is more efficient than the public sector, and (2) big government corrupts.[1] Therefore, the role of the state needs to be reduced and that of the private sector enlarged. This can be accomplished by privatizing activities that, in most nations, traditionally have been carried out by the public sector. Examples are the mail service, education, law enforcement (including prisons), health, roads and railroads, communications, energy and natural resources, and an increasing number of activities in the defense sector. The state's presence in the production of goods and services is anathema to neoliberals. In their view, the role of the state is to regulate the private sector to control abuses. The connection between privatization and decentralization has been made by a number of experts and will be discussed later.

Without empirical evidence on the adequacy of these policies, the World Bank has spent considerable human and financial resources to promote privatization and decentralization. Between 1988 and 1998, the World Bank prepared ninety-three reports on decentralization (Litvack, Ahmad, and Bird 1998). The World Bank's Flagship Program has promoted decentralization and other policies among key public civil servants. Through thousands of fellowships financed directly or indirectly by the World Bank,

[1] As will be discussed in a later section of this chapter, the failure of the Soviet Union was used to reinforce the neoliberal ideology.

selected candidates attend workshops given by World Bank personnel, like-minded faculty from prominent U.S. universities, and consultants who support the World Bank's ideology.

Early reports acknowledged that the World Bank did not have expertise in decentralization (Litvack, Ahmad, and Bird 1998) and that it was ill prepared to monitor its implementation. Thus in 1994 Ball noted that "the Bank's experience with developing and implementing projects in decentralized countries is still relatively new.... [A]s decentralization occurs Bank staff from many sectors ... may provide inconsistent advice ... and policy statements" (Ball 1994: 21–22). Nevertheless, World Bank economists and consultants have attempted to demonstrate the benefits of decentralization in studies that use questionable methodologies and language. For example, without providing supporting data, a 1994 consultant's report affirmed: "Decentralization in Latin America has been accompanied by a number of striking innovations in demand expression. These range from systematic use of public referenda and demand surveys to *cabildos abiertos* and other devices for collective expression of priorities" (Peterson 1994: 3) and "the current wave of decentralization has produced a remarkable variety of local experiments in citizen participation in governance" (Peterson 1997: 31).

Contrary to the perception that citizen participation was weak in the region before decentralization, Latin American social scientists have documented that the region's history is full of social movements that for decades forcefully voiced the need for education, health and potable water, housing, decent salaries, land for the peasants, and affordable prices for food staples. For doing this, leaders of social movements, labor unions, and political parties were killed, disappeared, or imprisoned by the military with the support, arms, and funding of the United States. Democratically elected political leaders of the left who promoted popular participation were deposed and sometimes killed—with the acquiescence and/or support of the United States. Allende in Chile, Arbenz in Guatemala, Aristide in Haiti, Bosch in the Dominican Republic, and Goulart and Quadros in Brazil were all democratically elected Latin American presidents who were killed, deposed, or pressured to resign by the United States, only to be replaced by dictatorial regimes. It should be remembered that the World Bank cut loans to Allende because of his programs to help the poor. The same has happened in other parts of the world. The World Bank's suggestion that decentralization has promoted participation and democracy has no historical foundations and is ludicrous.

The United States Agency for International Development (USAID) has financed without reservations the drafting and implementation of decentralization policies in many Third World countries. USAID responds to the priorities set by the U.S. Department of State and, therefore, to the political and economic interests of the U.S. government (Department of State and USAID 2003). Echoing the World Bank's view that decentralization is an instrument for fostering democracy and citizen participation, USAID has financed projects and studies of decentralization in many countries, supported the Health Reform Initiative, and financed the Partners for Health Reform Plus program, which includes decentralization projects and is implemented by a private consultancy firm.

USAID has taken the initiative to decentralize health systems in developing nations without considering the need for decentralization or the presence of enabling conditions, including the political will to decentralize. An example is the health decentralization project in Paraguay. With USAID funding, an American university entered into the politics of the country. Despite considerable investments of local and U.S. financial resources and time, the initiative accomplished little. Without supporting evidence, the project members concluded that: "it is quite evident that many more Paraguayans are now much more involved in and concerned about their national health-care system than was the case a few years ago" (Rosenbaum, Rodríguez-Acosta, and Rojas 2000), a statement reminiscent of the conclusions of the reports prepared for the World Bank cited above.

The pretense that a few faculty members from a U.S. university who have limited health care expertise could change a country's health care delivery system reflects the arrogance of the U.S. government. Its self-imposed duty to extend its neoliberal ideology globally, through supranational organizations and USAID, has produced global outrage and has not yielded the promised results. According to an editorial in the *New York Times*: "Two decades of Washington-recommended economic and trade policies have not done much for millions of urban and rural poor" (*New York Times* 2005).

The Soviet Union's Demise and Decentralization

Neoliberals seized upon the collapse of the Soviet Union in 1991 to support the validity of their two basic principles. For neoliberals, the Soviet Union and its satellite countries had demonstrated beyond reasonable doubt the inefficiency of the public sector and central planning. At the same time, neoliberal ideologues ignored the economic success of central planning and strong central authorities elsewhere. In China, the public sector's control of the economy was as strong as in the Soviet Union, and to date strategic industries and services continue to be centralized and run by the public sector; it would be hard indeed to deny China's impressive economic growth over the last twenty years. In 1961, Korea was one of the poorest countries in the world, deprived of natural resources and good agricultural land. Yet within a few years, Korea had, through central planning and the government's creation and control of mega-corporations called *cheabols*, surpassed the wealth of many middle-income countries and had joined the club of wealthy democratic nations. Dictator Park Chung Hee (1961–1979) had taken notice of Japan's Meiji's policies, the benefits of a strong central government, and the *zaibatsu* system, and had adapted them to the Korean context. The year 1868 is considered the beginning of Japan's economic transformation under the Meiji dynasty: "The [Japanese] state took a hand not only in creating the 'social overhead' of railroads, irrigation canals, and roads but also as the initiator of directly productive enterprises" (McCord 1965: 60). Strong government control and central planning are behind the most successful development stories, including those of Singapore, Taiwan, and Malaysia.

After years of domination by the Soviet Union, Central and Eastern European states were ready to break away from Moscow's heavy governing hand. Armed with advice and loans from the World Bank and International Monetary Fund, the former satellites moved rapidly to privatize services and industries and to implement decentralization. In Central and Eastern Europe, as in other parts of the world, the model of reform suggested by the supranational organizations included financial decentralization and regional/local autonomy.

The United Nations endorsed the decentralization trend—with reservations. In 1996 the UN General Assembly recommended, where appropriate (an important caveat), the decentralization of public institutions and services. In 1997 and 1998, the meetings of experts of the UN Program in Public Administration and Finance emphasized the importance of decentralization, but "warned against the pitfalls of hastily conceived and poorly implemented decentralization programs, which not only failed to achieve the hoped-for results, but sometimes had been known to favor corrupt practices ... and the power of local elites" (UN 2000: 1).

By 1999 many political leaders in Eastern Europe and the Commonwealth of Independent States (CIS) were aware that decentralization was not producing the promised results (UN 2000). The UN Department of Economic and Social Affairs, in cooperation with the UN Development and Governance Division, held a conference to assess the results of decentralization in the CIS and in the former Soviet satellites. An important contribution of the conference was identification of the requisite conditions for a successful implementation of decentralization—including legislation to avoid negative consequences such as regional public debts that could put a country's economy at risk, increase inequities among and within regions, or even provoke political disintegration.

The justification for decentralization that neoliberal organizations have offered has not been grounded in any theoretical principle. The hidden objective behind the promotion of decentralization is the privatization of resources and services previously owned by the state to facilitate capital concentration in the hands of a small transnational elite. Modernizing the state may or may not require decentralization; as discussed above, states have modernized under centralized powers. Before examining the impact of decentralization of the health sector in Latin America, we must first examine the meaning of decentralization.

THE MEANING OF DECENTRALIZATION

Decentralization implies a transfer of decision-making authority from a higher political or administrative level to a lower one. As Monrad Aas (1997) suggests, decentralization and centralization are opposite ends of a scale. The end points are ideal constructs that do not exist; at one end of the scale, all tasks are performed by one person (a chief or possibly a dictator); at the other end is anarchy. What we have found in the literature is a lack of agreement about the meaning of decentralization and an absence of guidance on how to measure the degree of decentralization that a country may have achieved. The World Health Organization's regional office for Europe noticed this confusion when it affirmed that "the term 'decentralization' is often used very loosely in the literature, despite the existence of several well-established approaches to its definition" (WHO-Europe 2005: 7).

The European Observatory on Health Care Systems and Policies (2000a) defines decentralization as "changing relations within and between a variety of organizational structures/bodies, resulting in the transfer of the authority to plan, make decisions or manage public functions from the national level to any organization or agency at the sub-national level." For the World Bank, decentralization includes one very different dimension. In a leading document, the Bank affirms that "a country is not decentralized unless it has a locally elected sub-national government" (Burki, Perry, and Dillinger 1999: 3). This link between decentralization and local elections contrasts with prior World Bank experience. The World Bank has always pointed to the success of decentralization in Chile under the government of dictator Augusto Pinochet (1973–1989), and other authors have noted that local elections have little to do with the efficiency of the public sector. Tanzi, of the International Monetary Fund, and others have argued that centralized countries such as France, Italy, and Chile assign people to local offices who could be more capable than elected officials and who "closely follow local developments and assess local needs" (Tanzi 1995: 9).

The Decentralization Scale

In an effort to distinguish degrees of decentralization, authors, following Cheema and Rondinelli's lead (1983), have distinguished four types of decentralization: deconcentration, delegation, devolution, and privatization. However, there is no consensus about the meaning of some of these terms. Some writers, particularly in Latin America, view the typology as the scale to measure the degree of decentralization that a country has achieved (Flamand 1998; Nigenda et al. 2002).

Deconcentration is defined as a transfer of administrative authority from central to regional offices (Cheema and Rondinelli 1983; European Observatory on Health Systems and Policies 2000a). But for Cohen et al. (1981), deconcentration could imply a considerable transfer of authority or none at all; the latter would be the case when the central authority simply creates more offices but does not transfer power. This is also Ball's (1994:

26) understanding; he affirms that with deconcentration, "a central government retains responsibility for service delivery, but establishes regional or local branch offices and charges them with day-to-day management." Despite the ambiguity, those who use the typology as a scale place deconcentration at the scale's lower end.

Some define delegation as a transfer of decision-making and administrative authority over specific functions to organizations that are under the control of the local government. For Hunter et al. (1998), delegation is giving an authority the right to plan and implement decisions relating to particular activities without direct supervision by a higher authority. Others define delegation as the transferring of responsibilities to local offices or organizations outside the structure of the central government—such as quasi-public (nongovernmental) organizations—but with the central government retaining indirect control (European Observatory on Health Care Systems 2000b; Witter and Ensor 1997). The European Observatory's definition contains a dimension of privatization since it includes nongovernmental organizations (NGOs) such as associations of providers or sickness funds. For Silverman (1992) and Bossert (1995), delegation also takes place when responsibility is transferred to semi-autonomous institutions.

Devolution is considered to be the most extreme type of decentralization. For Cheema and Rondinelli (1983), devolution is the handing over of functions and resources from the center to autonomous local governments, which assume responsibility for the funding, administration, and provision of services. The European Observatory has a different understanding; it defines devolution as passing responsibility and a degree of independence to the regional or local government, with or without financial responsibility (that is, the ability to raise and spend revenues) and refers to it as political decentralization. Unlike deconcentration, with devolution, regional and local governments are generally independent of the national government with respect to their functions and responsibilities. For Hunter et al. (1998), devolution implies that governments relinquish certain functions to new or different organizations outside their direct control. According to this understanding, devolution means the creation or strengthening of subnational levels of government that are substantially independent of the national level with respect to a defined set of functions. Bossert (1995: 147) defines devolution as a shift of responsibility and authority from the central offices of a ministry to separate administrative structures still within the public administration (such as provinces, states, or municipalities), and Ball (1994: 26) simply states that, with devolution, "responsibility of service delivery is passed to a lower level of government."

According to Burki (a former World Bank vice president for the Latin American region) and colleagues, decentralization also takes place "through the sale of assets, the granting of concessions, and through public-private alliances" (Burki, Perry, and Dillinger 1999)—that is, by privatizing. However, the view that privatization is a type of decentralization is not accepted by other scholars (see, for example, Collins and Green 1994), while others clearly state that decentralization is an excuse to privatize health services (Zamora 2001; Castro Valverde and Sáenz 1998). Some authors have added a fifth category—regionalization—to the decentralization typology. Nigenda et al. (2002) indicate that regionalization occurs when resources or activities are dispersed but the central authority keeps a strong control.

Other Approaches to Decentralization

Other authors have approached decentralization differently. Rodríguez (1997) separates types and modes of decentralization. Within the types, she includes political, spatial, administrative, and market decentralization or privatization.[2] According to Rodríguez, the decentralization modes include deconcentration, devolution, and delegation.

For economists, there is an important difference between fiscal and administrative decentralization. Fiscal decentralization exists when subnational governments have the power to raise taxes and spend funds within the limits established by law. Administrative decentralization occurs when funds are collected by the central government and subsequently distributed to decentralized entities to be spent under guidelines established by the central government (Tanzi 1995).

We like to distinguish between administrative and political decentralization. The transfer of authority to make administrative decisions from

---

[2] Spatial decentralization refers to the dispersal of urban populations and economic activities among settlements to avoid concentration in large metropolitan areas (Rondinelli 1990).

higher to lower levels in an organization is justified when the concentration of power at the center deprives the institution of the flexibility it needs to efficiently achieve its objectives. We can distinguish three types of political decentralization: (1) when new political subdivisions are created with their own legislative branch, such as the case of the autonomies in Spain; (2) when previously appointed heads of political divisions such as states, provinces, or municipalities are now elected by the citizens of the divisions, as, for example, in Colombia; (3) when administrative entities such as ministries are created in political divisions, the provincial minister is appointed by the governor, and the ministry is under the authority of the provincial government, as, for example, in Argentina. Administrative decentralization may or may not require political decentralization. Generally, the decision to decentralize politically is not intended to achieve administrative efficiency. The two decentralizations are independent of each other and need not take place at the same time.

When the sixteen autonomic regions were created in Spain in 1978, not all of them decentralized under the same conditions and degrees of autonomy. The forces behind the political decentralization in Spain were historical and unrelated to the need for democratization or an increase in public-sector efficiency. Understanding the advantages and limitations of decentralization in Spain is important for Latin America because Spain has often been held up as a decentralization model (for an account of the decentralization of Spain's health sector, see Rey del Castillo 1998). It should be noted that the OECD criticized the funding model in decentralized Spain for reducing the fiscal responsibility of the autonomic regions and creating a tendency to overspend and create large deficits (Aizpeolea 2000). More recently, some segments of Spanish society have expressed concern that political decentralization could lead some autonomic regions to secede, a fear that has also been expressed in Bolivia.

Administrative decentralization could take place in specific institutions, as, for example, in the parastatals or in hospitals. The literature on institution-specific decentralization in Third World countries is almost nonexistent. Even in developed societies, empirical investigations on the impact of decentralization for hospitals are few (Monrad Aas 1997). There is a clear difference between decentralizing the administration of hospitals and creating autonomous hospitals, but this has not been acknowledged in the decentralization literature. Neoliberal reform has promoted the latter (Ministerio de Salud de la Nación 1994) because, when hospitals are given autonomy, it is independent boards, foundations, or corporations that make the decisions. From the decentralization point of view, whether those entities hold for-profit or not-for-profit status is unimportant. The management of autonomous hospitals can contract with the private sector for a large number of activities, such as diagnostic tests, maintenance of infrastructure and equipment, and food and laundry services.[3] For neoliberals, it is fundamental that public hospitals, where the largest amount of the health care budget is spent, become autonomous and, where possible, that private hospitals provide hospital care. In countries where private hospitals provide care, the beneficiaries have been the transnational health corporations (Stocker, Waitzkin, and Iriart 1999).

Given differences in interpretation, a lack of precision, and ambiguity in definitions, it is clear that Rondinelli's typology cannot be used as a scale to measure levels of decentralization. The lack of agreement in the use of basic terms poses a significant obstacle to meaningful discussions. For

---

[3] World Bank economists give a different justification for the transformation of public hospitals into autonomous institutions. For these economists, in addition to increasing management efficiency and flexibility, the independence of autonomous hospitals subsidizes the demand for services rather than supply, a change that also allows the introduction of accountability and competition. The user can choose the hospital that offers better services at a better price.

These arguments can be easily rebutted. First, health planning can estimate demand with some accuracy, and funding can be adjusted accordingly. Second, a user's choice among hospitals is a myth. Hospitals are generally chosen by the physician, and, as the case of Colombia suggests, hospitals that cater to the wealthy and middle class exclude the poor majority. Third, the idea that there could be competition among hospitals is also a myth. Only in very large metropolitan areas is there some competition, in part because distance is a deterrent to choice and in part because hospitals are specialized. The United States' health care system shows that choice and competition do not exist in the private market and that privatization does not increase efficiency or quality. Finally, private hospitals cannot take advantage of the benefits of economies of scale, and outsourcing often increases costs. There is one reason to privatize hospitals that is not voiced by neoliberals: the desire to destroy labor unions. It is more difficult for workers of private hospitals to organize than it is for public employees.

example, in a letter to the *British Medical Journal*, Sandiford (1999) is not clear in his decentralization/devolution terminology. This situation and the absence of reliable decentralization indicators lead to discussions that are based more on ideological principles than on theory. For example, it has been said that, due to its colonial history, Latin America is excessively centralized, but during the twentieth century the countries of the region created thousands of decentralized institutes and industries or parastatals.

THE DECENTRALIZATION MATRIX

A public organization or ministry performs hundreds of functions that traditionally have been classified under the following categories and sub-categories: fiscal (generation and disbursement of funds), human resources (management that includes supervision and evaluation, training and education), physical resources (selection, procurement, and maintenance of infrastructure and equipment), and programmatic (program design, planning, and evaluation)—categories that can be used to measure decentralization (Ugalde and Homedes 2002). Hutchinson and LaFond (2004) also use a listing of functions to assess the implementation of decentralization.

The functions and the transfer of authority by levels can be displayed in a large matrix because the authority to decide on each function and each subcategory can be transferred to one or several administrative levels. The horizontal axis displays the location of decisions starting at the central government, beginning with the central planning agency, then the ministries, and moving progressively to local offices. Depending on the function, the horizontal axis may include private for-profit or not-for-profit organizations. The transfer of authority from a higher administrative level to a lower one generally will be contingent upon having fulfilled certain conditions, which may be different at each level of administration. The headings on the horizontal axis need not coincide with the politico-administrative levels of the country. A Ministry of Health could have a number of malaria regions that correspond, not to any politico-administrative division, but to the epidemiological geography of malaria, or it could have a number of hospital regions or health districts each of which serves several municipalities.

The vertical axis presents the functions by categories and subcategories. Each cell of the matrix will include different conditions limiting the transfer of authority. We can illustrate the transfer of authority using the human resources function and the management subcategory. In one Health Ministry, the minister had to personally approve vacation dates for each of the Ministry's more than one hundred thousand employees. Even if the minister was only signing the permits, this practice reflected a very poor use of the minister's time. The decentralization of this activity could be achieved in a variety of ways, and a variety of conditions could be imposed. The minister could transfer or delegate the approval authority to any of the following: the deputy minister, the director of human resources, a staff member of the Office of Human Resources, the provincial/municipal director of health or a member of his/her staff, or the directors of hospitals or health units. The minister or the person appointed by him or her may retain the power to approve the vacation dates of some personnel, such as the directors of the divisions of the Ministry or directors of provincial health services. A similar situation may exist if the directors of provincial health services received the authority to give the approvals. In sum, the decentralization of this simple function can exhibit many variations.

The minister or the directors of the various offices of the Ministry may want to delegate other functions such as approvals to purchase office or medical supplies, to repair and maintain infrastructure and equipment, to determine the schedule of services to the public, the supervision of personnel, promotions, performance evaluations, or personnel transfers. These activities could be delegated to different levels of the Ministry, to private organizations, or to mixed committees with private and public representation, and different restrictions could be established. For example, the schedule of services could be decided by the clinic director, but the Ministry may require that the decision be made with the approval of the health committee or after hearing the community, that services should be offered eight hours per day and Saturday mornings, and that one physician always be on call. In this case, some decision authority has been transferred, but with conditions that limit it. If supervision of personnel is transferred to lower administrative levels, there will be a need to decide who selects or appoints the supervisors of the supervisors and to whom they report. The delegation of supervision could be different for each health activity—immunizations, medical care, or environmental health, for example—as could be the participation of the community or private sector.

The decentralization matrix provides a view of the complexity of decentralization, an understanding that administrative decentralization can occur without political decentralization, and an awareness that decentralization is a process and, consequently, implies continuous changes rather than reforms.

STATE REFORMS, DECENTRALIZATION, AND PRIVATIZATION

Two basic components of reforms to modernize the state are privatization and decentralization. Advanced Western economies have divested themselves of a number of government monopolies, such as flagship airlines, toll roads, telecommunications and energy corporations, and state corporations that produced a large variety of industrial products (steel, ships, aircraft, tobacco, and so on). Yet social services, including health and education, continue to be financed and managed by the public sector. Few in the advanced economies heeded the call for decentralization. Some nations were satisfied with their level of decentralization, and those few that decentralized did so for reasons other than those advanced by the IMF and World Bank.

In other areas of the world, governments responded to the call for privatization and decentralization, in part because the supranational organizations imposed these policies as a condition for receiving loans and grants. In Russia, in the Commonwealth of Independent States, in Latin America, and in other regions, a large number of state industries, telecommunications and utility companies, and oil, gas, and mining corporations were rapidly privatized, in some cases with tragic results. Transnational corporations and a few citizens with close connections to political elites were able to purchase many of the public corporations at bargain prices. Argentina is a prime example of the catastrophic economic consequences of following IMF advice. Mexico privatized hundreds of state enterprises, including fisheries, cement plants, airlines, telecommunications, and so on, but has maintained the oil industry as a public monopoly.

Health Delivery Inefficiencies and Structural Adjustments

In Latin America, as in other parts of the world (Segall 2003), the inefficiencies of the public health services have been known for decades. A partial list of causes for the poor performance of the public health services includes lack of basic supplies, poor maintenance of infrastructure and equipment, political interference in personnel appointments, inappropriate use of resources and the stealing of supplies, absenteeism (particularly among physicians), excessive control of decision making by physicians, lack of midlevel technicians, and a poor mix of professionals (Fernández 1998; World Bank 1997, 1996, 1992, 1987; Angell and Graham 1995; ANSAL 1994; Ugalde and Homedes 1994; Sanguinetty et al. 1988; Gagliano, Rosenfeld, and Tillea 1988; Becht and Bravo 1984). Political leaders, users, providers, and researchers were all aware that changes were needed to address the users' dissatisfaction, reverse the low efficiency and quality of care, improve accessibility, and reduce inequity.

Some of the deficiencies could have been caused by excessive administrative centralization, but certain reports indicated that some deficiencies were attributable to decentralization and that the structural adjustments the IMF and World Bank imposed to solve the Latin American financial crisis of the 1980s exacerbated the problems of health care delivery (CEPAL 1994). In the 1960s, Colombia's minister of health decided to centralize private hospitals that received public funding (which were the majority) in order to improve the quality of services and use of resources. An assessment of El Salvador's health system for USAID reported that decentralization and hospital autonomy were the most severe obstacles to an adequate use of hospital resources and the quality of hospital care (Ruiz, Askin, and Gibb 1978). More recently, Argentina's Health Ministry launched a national program to distribute basic medicines to an estimated sixteen million people who could no longer afford them following the 2001 economic depression. Health services decentralization was singled out as one impediment to the otherwise relatively successful program (Homedes and Ugalde 2006). The experience of this program raised questions among health administrators about the need to organize a national health system. It should also be pointed out that those countries that decentralized health care before the current trend got under way did not improve efficiency and quality of care, nor did they foster community participation and democratization. For example, Paraguay decentralized its Health Ministry in 1940, and fifty years later its health system continued to suffer deficiencies similar to those in other Latin American countries (Veldhuyzen van Zantes and Semidei 1996).

The 1980s financial crisis was caused by central governments' inability to service their accumulated public debt. It was imperative for these governments to reduce spending and free up funds to pay down the debt. The IMF and World Bank found that the most expedient way to achieve this was to reduce social spending—that is, spending on health and education. The spending reduction could be achieved by transferring responsibility for financing social services to the states and provinces, a process that was also called decentralization. Officially, supranational organizations and USAID have not stated that reducing central outlays is a prime reason for decentralizing (World Bank 1993), but decentralization researchers (Collins 1989), World Bank economists (Griffin 1999), and consultants (Peterson 1994) have acknowledged that this is so. In the case of Argentina, the provinces in turn faced the consequences of the economic crisis and, following the central government's example, decentralized by transferring responsibility for funding social services to the municipalities (Ase 2005).

In Colombia, municipal decentralization has resulted in many municipalities contracting out the delivery of health care to NGOs. Although NGOs and cooperatives generally are nonprofit, their personnel may obtain financial benefits. This is the case for the health cooperatives in Costa Rica, where professionals who work at the cooperatives serve simultaneously as officers of the cooperatives. If expenses are less than income, the surplus is distributed among the professionals in the form of salary increases. The same can be applied to NGOs. Decentralization, if implemented according to neoliberal principles, allows local authorities to establish a system of recovery fees, which is a way of partially privatizing health financing. The World Bank began promoting recovery fees in the late 1980s and continued to support them, even though reports indicated that the fees were a barrier to access for the poor (World Bank 1993). When evidence demonstrated that recovery fees created inequalities (Segall 2003), the World Bank changed course and decided not to recommend them (World Bank 2001). In the interim, many suffered and died.

EVIDENCE-BASED RESULTS OF LATIN AMERICA'S HEALTH DECENTRALIZATION

As health economists have noted, the health care industry is an imperfect market, and some health services (such as immunizations and the control and treatment of infectious diseases) have large externalities and are considered public goods. Thus the provision of health services cannot be privatized as easily as other sectors of the economy. The determination to decentralize and/or privatize health systems appears to be more heavily influenced by the ideology of the "scientist" than by any evidence-based knowledge.

Even while large numbers of experts questioned the wisdom of a wholesale or global health decentralization that failed to take a country's political and cultural context into account, and despite multiple reports documenting the deleterious results of decentralization (De Groote, De Paepe, and Unger 2005; Ugalde and Homedes 2002; Ramiro et al. 2001; Zamora 2001; Campos-Outcalt, Kewa, and Thomaso 1995; Collins and Green 1994), the World Bank and other transnational agencies forge on, advising, demanding, and financing health decentralization. It should be noted that several staff at the World Bank identified some requisite conditions for decentralization to be successful (Burki, Perry, and Dillinger 1999) and, after reviewing the literature, other World Bank economists reached the conclusion that "decentralization is neither good nor bad for efficiency, equity, or macroeconomic stability.... [T]he primary measures for local and central accountability assumed in most discussions of decentralization may not hold or are different in many developing countries" (Litvack, Ahmad, and Bird 1998: viii).

The lack of congruence between the work of some World Bank staff and the institution's policies may be surprising, but, as we have shown elsewhere, it is not rare (Homedes, Ugalde, and Rovira 2005). A close examination of World Bank documents also uncovers some cynicism. Thus Litvack, Ahmad, and Bird (1998: 3) affirm that "the debate on whether decentralization is 'good' or 'bad' is unproductive since decentralization is a political reality worldwide," ignoring that this political reality is the result of pressures exercised by the World Bank, USAID, and other agencies that followed their lead. These agencies have not yet reversed their policy of promoting decentralization.

Table 1.1 presents neoliberals' theoretical foundations for promoting decentralization, along with the findings of field researchers working in Latin America. Qualitative studies, relying on participant observation and in-depth interviews, have provided a wealth of information and detail that could not be captured using quantitative research methods. Most of the

Table 1.1. Reasons Given for Decentralizing, Rationales, and Evidence-based Results

Reason 1: To Improve Community Participation

Rationales	Evidence-based Results
1. It is important to incorporate the community in decision making. By empowering citizens to participate in planning, services are more adequately targeted to local needs and will be better used. This leads to efficiency gains and less waste, facilitates access, and improves quality. 2. It is easier for users to demand accountability because supervision and control are closer.	Decentralization has not increased community participation (De Groote, De Paepe, and Unger 2005). According to Ase (2005: 19), in the province of Córdoba (Argentina) the results of decentralization in getting the community to participate in health decision making "have been frankly a total disappointment." Explanation: 1. Communities may not respond to calls to participate because they have learned from experience that authorities do not take their input into account (Ugalde 1985). 2. Local elites are not willing to share decision making with the population. Decentralization cannot by itself change power relations. "True decentralization rarely results because it threatens dominant-class interests at the local level" (Scarpaci 1992: 236). Local elites use decentralization to increase their own power, and according to Prud'homme (1994) and Tanzi (1994) they could be more corrupted than central elites. 3. When state/provincial governments receive decision-making authority from the central government, they tend to centralize power at the state/provincial level (Del Valle López 1998). 4. Local politicians tend to make decisions to satisfy the local elites, and frequently these decisions are not those that produce the best health care for the majority. They seldom take into account the health needs of the population (Holley 1995).

Table 1.1, continued

Reason 2: To Promote Democracy

Rationale	Evidence-based Results
1. The top-down decision model in Latin American public institutions has had negative consequences for democracy. It is important to stimulate local participation in health care planning and delivery in order to improve democracy in the region. According to the Pan American Health Organization, decentralization "should be viewed as part of the process of democratic development which is under way in most of [Latin America]" (PAHO 1988: 13).	Decentralization has not promoted democracy. Explanation: There is no evidence that decentralization has strengthened democracy in Latin America. Methodologically, it will be extremely difficult to prove the cause-effect relationship between decentralization and democracy. Dictator Augusto Pinochet promoted decentralization, but nobody claims that Chile's return to democracy was instigated even partially by the decentralization of health services. In Brazil, decentralization was initiated after the restoration of democracy.

Reason 3: To Increase Efficiency

Rationales	Evidence-based Results
1. Local decision makers know better the needs of the local population, respond more efficiently to community needs, and avoid costly errors made by distant bureaucrats who tend to be ignorant of local health conditions. Needs may vary by epidemiological and demographic differences, and by socioeconomic classes and cultural differences. Decentralization gives decision makers more flexibility to plan and organize more efficiently services that fit local needs than can distant decision makers.	1. A study carried out in several developed societies concluded that the larger the participation of decentralized/privatized entities in the financing of a health system, the lower the efficiency and ability to control costs (Economic Council of Canada 1991).

Table 1.1, continued

Reason 3: To Increase Efficiency, continued	
Rationales	Evidence-based Results
2. Local decision makers know better the infrastructure and supplies that are required locally, and therefore they can more efficiently use available resources to build, maintain, and purchase supplies to satisfy local health needs. 3. Large complex organizations such as Ministries of Health and social security programs suffer from authority leaks as instructions are passed down along the many bureaucratic levels. Authority leaks have a negative impact in the implementation of programs and lead to a waste of resources. 4. If the product and the process of production are standardized and the external context is stable, hierarchical organizations can respond adequately to population demands. However, if the product is not sufficiently standardized and there are changes in the external context, then the organizations need agility to respond to the changes. This is achieved by transferring decision-making power and the authority to respond swiftly to changes to lower levels of the hierarchy.	2. The Latin American experience also suggests that decentralization has not increased efficiency. In a number of cases it has increased inefficiencies (Gershberg 1998). In other cases, as reported by Atkinson and Haran (2004: 826) in their study in Ceará, Brazil, the results are mixed: "Does decentralization improve system performance? No, not per se. Importantly, decentralization was never associated with worse performance." We have found that health reforms that include decentralization have in some countries required large increases in health funding (Jaramillo 2002); in Chile the health budget doubled in real terms between 1990 and 1997 (Titelman 1999), but outputs did not. In Colombia, despite large increases in health funding, inefficiency increased due to a lack of managerial capacity and information flows (Plaza, Barona, and Hearst 2001). There are some exceptions. In some instances when decentralization has been privatized through nonprofit agencies with foreign support, pilot experiments suggest that efficiency has improved (Lavadenz, Schwab, and Straatman 2001). However, the additional costs and technical support that projects such as this receive questions if the model is viable at a national scale or if it will survive once foreign support is withdrawn.

Table 1.1, continued

Reason 3: To Increase Efficiency, continued	
Rationales	Evidence-based Results
5. Civil servants in large bureaucratic organizations tend to create a culture of complacency and defend their interests even if it creates some problems in the delivery of services. This is one of the main sources of inefficiencies. The large size of their unions makes it difficult to carry out necessary changes to improve efficiency. Decentralization is a partial solution to the problem.	Explanation: 1. In poorer states/regions/provinces and municipalities there is a scarcity of qualified personnel (Prud'homme 1994). It is difficult to recruit experienced public health personnel to work in decentralized entities; therefore, training is essential. Decentralization has been carried out without sufficient training (Rosenbaum, Rodríguez-Acosta, and Rojas 2000; Homedes, Ugalde, and Rovira 2005). Costly errors have been committed as a result. 2. Economies of scale are lost with decentralization. Frequently, there are higher prices for the purchase of drugs and equipment. The economies of scale also apply to management functions. After decentralization, each decentralized unit has to take time to prepare bids, norms and manuals, and to reorganize the services, all of which require resources (Homedes and Ugalde 2006; Ase 2005; Sandiford 1999; Barillas 1997; Veldhuyzen van Zantes and Semidei 1996). 3. Local politicians tend to make appointments based on patronage rather than technical qualifications. Decisions are not based on technical needs, and errors are costly. 4. Presidents of small municipalities have little knowledge of public health matters and may make expensive and wrong decisions. It has been reported in several countries that earmarked funds for health have been diverted to other programs (Ase 2005; Ruiz Mier and Giussani 1996).

Table 1.1, continued

Reason 3: To Increase Efficiency, continued	
Rationales	Evidence-based Results
	5. Communities may prefer more visible programs that are less desirable from a cost-efficiency perspective—for example, building a hospital instead of expanding immunization or clean water programs, or buying expensive equipment that cannot be used because the hospital lacks technical personnel (Ase 2005; Altobelli 2000; Ugalde 1999; La Forgia and Homedes 1992).
	6. Decentralization creates problems of coordination between administrative levels and unnecessary referrals from lower to higher levels of technical complexity, which reduces the efficiency of services (Ase 2005; Larrañaga 1999; Duarte 1995; Veldhuyzen van Zantes and Semidei 1996). In the cooperative of Tibás in Costa Rica, there were twice as many referrals as in the social security health centers, and the cost per capita was 3 to 5 times higher (interview with the cooperative's medical director, April 2000).
	7. Decentralization of health services inevitably creates intermediate service levels between political divisions. Hospitals, labs and diagnostic centers, and specialty ambulatory care centers may have to serve and be financed by several municipalities, by more than one political division (for example, several municipalities and the province), and have to account to all of them (Acevedo Mercadante, Yunes, and Chorny 1994). Organizationally, this system seldom works efficiently.

Table 1.1, continued

Reason 3: To Increase Efficiency, continued	
Rationales	Evidence-based Results
	8. The bureaucracies of the decentralized political divisions grow, but there is no reduction of personnel at the central bureaucracy. It is not possible to reduce the salaries of personnel that worked at the central level when they were transferred to lower levels; local personnel had demanded that their salaries be harmonized with those of the transferred personnel. More personnel and salary increases have not been accompanied by increased outcomes. In Colombia at the beginning of decentralization (1994), hospital personnel costs represented 50% of all hospital costs. By 1997 they had increased to 70% (Departamento Nacional 2002). In this country, an analysis of the production of the first and second levels of autonomous public hospitals showed that, between 1996 and 1998, operational costs grew by 24% in real terms, while production grew by only 4% (Ministerio de Salud Pública 1998). In Chile, increased health expenditures were destined to salary increases and hospital rehabilitation (Oyarzo 2000), but there were no improvements in service provision (Barrientos 2002).
	9. Contracting out is inefficient (De Groote, De Paepe, and Unger 2005).

Table 1.1, continued

Reason 4: To Better the Quality of Care

Rationales	Evidence-based Results
1. As indicated above, the proximity of community to decision makers allows members of the community to demand quality services. Otherwise, political leaders will not be reelected. 2. In decentralized health systems, workers have more flexibility to organize their work; as a result, their morale and responsiveness increase. Morale is also increased because their demands for needed supplies can more easily be satisfied by closer access to authorities who better understand their needs. Satisfied workers tend to produce better-quality services.	We have not found any studies that present measurable information demonstrating that quality has improved with decentralization. Methodologically, it will be very difficult to attribute quality improvements to decentralization. Even if users' satisfaction increases, satisfaction should not be confused with quality of care. The study by Ase (2005) concludes that quality of care has deteriorated with decentralization. When decentralization has been privatized through non-profit agencies, pilot experiments suggest that quality improves (Lavadenz, Schwab, and Straatman 2001). See the comment in the discussion of efficiency above, but the experience in Colombia is mixed. Explanation: 1. Users of services do not have the technical knowledge to evaluate the quality of services they receive. It has been documented that low-income patients do not even know the surgery that they receive, and in Brazil most Caesarean deliveries are for the convenience of the hospitals (which make more money from Caesarean than from vaginal deliveries) and physicians (who can schedule the deliveries) than because of medical need.

Table 1.1, continued

Reason 4: To Better the Quality of Care, continued	
Rationales	Evidence-based Results
	2. Decentralization alters the organization of services and personnel. In particular, those in administrative positions are given new/different responsibilities. New responsibilities include planning, supervision, evaluation, data collection, new accounting procedures, and so on, that previously were carried out by the higher levels of the bureaucracy. Without adequate training, performance may be of poor quality and faulty.
	3. Autonomous hospitals tend to cut costs, a situation that may directly affect the quality of care unless other changes occur (Molina de Salazar 2002; Gómez 2002). The market approach creates stress and job dissatisfaction, which have a negative effect on the quality of care (Guevara and Mendias 2002). According to an evaluation of autonomous hospitals in Brazil: "quality remains the 'forgotten component' of health care delivery. In some aspects, the situation may have worsened:… low quality of care in birthing rooms and neonatal units that contribute to infant and maternal mortality … occurrence of avoidable deaths … high hospital-acquired infection rates" (La Forgia 2003: 10).
	4. Fragmentation of health policymaking and diversion of funds to medical care have resulted in a decrease in the quantity and quality of public health interventions (De Groote, De Paepe, and Unger 2005; Sarmiento 2000; Sandiford 1999).

references included in table 1.1 address only a few health reform issues in one country, although a limited number used a global or regional approach. The quantity of references is limited because, as indicated by Atkinson and Haran (2004: 822), "empirical studies assessing whether the promise of decentralization has been realized are surprisingly rare and mostly depict the variations in the formal structures implemented from the national scale (Mills et al. 1990)."

We have cited all the articles we identified in our comprehensive literature review, but for reasons of space we do not assess their methodology or the quality of the information gathered. An additional comment is pertinent. Frequently, studies include several aspects of the reform, and it is sometimes difficult to tease out the consequences of the various components—for example, decentralization, privatization, and free trade agreements. We have tried to present the consequences of decentralization only, but we are aware that inefficiencies may have multiple causes linked to the reforms and/or factors exogenous to the health sector.

With a few exceptions (Crook and Sverrisson 2001), findings from other regions are strikingly similar (see, for example, Mutemwa 2006; Chowdhury 2004; Segall 2003; Bossert and Beauvais 2002; Collins, Omar, and Tarin 2002; United Nations Department of Economic and Social Affairs 2000; Collins and Green 1994; Kolehmainen-Aitken 1992). In their study of the Philippines, Ramiro et al. (2001: 68) concluded: "the results of this study corroborate past observations that … the objectives of decentralization cannot be obtained by simply changing the system of governance. A more thoughtful groundwork for devolution is necessary before broadened participation and empowerment of the community can be attained." Campos-Outcalt, Kewa, and Thomaso (1995: 1096) found in their study of health districts decentralization in Papua New Guinea that "opinion was nearly unanimous among provincial and health center staff that the health services were worse.… The objective evidence that does exist provides a mixed picture with a general trend towards fewer services and a mixed performance on population coverage [after decentralization]."

Decentralization and Equity

An increase in geographical and social inequity has been an additional undesired outcome of decentralization in several countries (Ase 2005; Barrientos 2002; Hernández 2002). Collins, Araujo, and Barbosa (2000: 125) cite data from local studies in Brazil and conclude that decentralization there "is reproducing and reinforcing inequalities," and they ask for additional analysis to better understand the causation of inequities. It is easy to understand that wealthy states/provinces and large municipalities can dedicate more resources to health care than can poorer states/provinces (Duarte Quapper and Zuleta Reyes 1999). Users of services in wealthy provinces and municipalities can afford higher recovery fees than can users in poor ones, increasing the variation in funds available to health centers and hospitals across provinces and municipalities. Recovery fees create inequities. In cities with several municipalities, as is common in many Latin American megalopolises, decentralization will increase urban health inequities due to differential recovery fees imposed by the municipalities. Social inequities have increased with decentralization as autonomous hospital pricing and legal loopholes allow patient selection; the best hospitals will care for the wealthiest clients, and rural zones within municipalities will receive fewer resources than urban ones (Holley 1995). Decentralization also produces a segmentation of health insurance plans, with the best and most expensive plans used by the wealthy and plans that cover only very basic services used by the poor (Barillas 1997).

There are remedies that can reduce inequity. Two obvious ones are the allocation of national funds on the basis of need rather than population, and the transfer of solidarity funds from the wealthier political divisions to the poorer. Most countries have not been able to use these common-sense solutions because they are politically difficult and technically complex. Wealthy provinces and municipalities have more political clout and are not willing to share resources; in fact, they use their political power to obtain more funds per capita than what is available to those with less influence. To devise a formula for distributing a health budget unequally in order to reduce health inequity is not easy. In addition to the demographic and epidemiological variables, many other factors—such as population dispersion, health status, availability of personnel, and poverty distribution—have to be taken into account as well.

In the few countries that have closely followed World Bank policy recommendations and have decentralized—such as Chile, Colombia, and Nicaragua—and have also implemented solidarity transfers, the formula and the quantity of the transfers have not been sufficient to reduce the health inequity gap. Chile's Health Ministry acknowledged that the country's health system was "extremely inequitable" (Ministerio de Salud 2003).

The Colombia case is interesting because studies present contrasting views regarding the reform's impact on equity. The central government distributed health funds more equitably, with poorer departments receiving a higher allocation than wealthier ones. The central government also considerably increased its allocation to health. With these additional financial resources, there was a dramatic expansion of health insurance coverage among the lowest income decile. Based on these facts, Bossert et al. (2003), Jaramillo (2002), and Hincapié Correa, Mesa Ochoa, and Rhenals (1998) affirm that decentralization has increased health equity. However, De Groote, De Paepe, and Unger (2005), Holguín Zamorano (2004), Castaño et al. (2001), and Céspedes et al. (2000) hold a contrasting view. For them, co-payments have created access barriers among the poor. In Colombia, health insurance does not guarantee access to needed services. The data suggest that health insurance for the poor has not increased the demand for services (McPake, Yepes, and Sánchez 2003). Thus, prior to the reform, 61.7 percent of those needing health care were seen by a physician, but in 2000 the share dropped to 51.1 percent (World Bank 2002) despite the very large funding increases. Additionally, a more equitable allocation of health resources to municipalities has not resulted in a more equitable availability of services; in Bogotá, 78 percent of health providers are located in the northern part of the city, where the more affluent class resides (Alcaldía Mayor de Bogotá 2004). At the same time, the coverage gap between rural and urban dwellers has not been reduced (Flórez and Tono 2003; Gonzáles 2000). In Colombia, all out-of-pocket expenses have been reduced, but the percentage of the reduction has been significantly higher for the wealthiest than for the poor (Grupo de Economía de la Salud 2003). Finally, before accepting that a more equitable distribution of resources produces equity, it is necessary to determine how funds are spent, for they could be used to purchase inadequate technologies, to pay higher salaries to middle-class health providers, or for other uses that do not promote equity.

In Colombia some authors list as one of the benefits of decentralization the disproportional increase in the health budget. This is wrong. More funds can be allocated to health care with or without reforming a health system. The two are independent political decisions.

It is unfortunate that decentralization has not reduced health inequities and may actually have increased them. Studies have shown that increasing health equity has a very positive impact on wealth distribution, and, according to most experts, the unequal distribution of wealth is the most severe social problem in Latin America today and the root cause of political instability.

DISCUSSION

Political decentralization may foster competition among decentralized provinces or states or facilitate experimentation with new forms of organization, but a growing number of studies are concluding that decentralization has failed to achieve its overt goals. Referring to decentralization in general in Latin America, Finot (2002: 140, 144) summarized this view as follows: "After ten years [of decentralization] … the progress made in participation is uneven, we still do not see conclusive results regarding efficiency, and income gains continue to be concentrated in some regions. Coverage in social services has increased but disparities between geographical regions continue to rise. The system of transferring funds does not promote fiscal efficiency, and the excessive debt accrued by subnational governments is a cause of macroeconomic imbalances (CEPAL 1998)..... It has not created important and persistent improvements in public efficiency and reduction of corruption."

The fact that decentralization has failed does not mean that decentralization should not take place. The decision to decentralize or not to decentralize, the type of decentralization, and how to achieve it—if policymakers consider it desirable—depend on the historical, cultural, geographical, political, and economic characteristics and the size of the country. There is no generic formula for decentralization.

The United Nations in 1962 understood that some countries could profit from decentralization to achieve flexibility and speed up the bureaucratic resolution of administrative bottlenecks. The UN also favored political decentralization to bring the commons closer to citizens and encourage community participation (United Nations Technical Assistance Program 1962). This position is very different from the last twenty-five years of wholesale support for decentralization among supranational and bilateral agencies. Even if one nation on its own, without outside influences, would reach the decision to decentralize, its authorities have to understand that some forms of decentralization may have negative side effects. For example, political decentralization could lead to fragmentation of the health system or even the state (Barillas 1997), and if the enabling factors are not present to make implementation successful, the result may be worse than what existed before. Dilla Alfonso (1997), in an insightful analysis of decentralization, concurs with Conyers (1986: 97) when she declares: "most of the objectives which decentralization is supposed to achieve—such as efficiency or coordination, national unity or popular participation—are themselves complex issues for which there are no easy or obvious recipes, and which cannot be achieved by decentralization whatever form it takes. The most obvious implication is the need for a realistic approach to decentralization, one which does not regard it as a panacea for all evils … but which recognizes that in many situations some form of decentralization can go some way in helping to achieve certain development objectives, although it may also make it more difficult to achieve others." The results presented in table 1.1 are not surprising if we consider that decentralization has been pressured and hastily implemented.

The failures of the current trend of improvised decentralization have had credibility costs. When new attempts are made to decentralize, political leaders need to be aware that there will be more resistance from the population and civil service. Evidence-based analysis suggests that decentralization has also had high financial costs, and attempting to implement it without assuring that enabling factors are in place is a waste of scarce resources. The health sector has some specific characteristics that set it apart from other services and industries. Decentralizing a process such as energy production is very different from decentralizing health services. The characteristics of the health sector need to be studied in detail (Collins, Araujo, and Barbosa 2000; Segall 2000) to determine the specific enabling factors needed to facilitate decentralization's success. Some studies suggest that the process has to be reversed, that first there must be efficient management and then decentralization (Atkinson and Haran 2004). While genuine democracy generates participation, health care decentralization cannot promote democracy by itself. To try to invert the process reflects historical unawareness. We should ask, perhaps rhetorically, what would have been the results for health care delivery if the budget increases associated with decentralization and health reform had been directed to overcome the decades-known health systems' deficiencies?

Some authors are beginning to suggest that there is a need for a stronger central government role in the health sector. Barrientos (2002) and Segall (2000) remind us of the positive aspects of centralized policies. Past experience shows, for example, that vertical programs have been particularly effective in fighting—sometimes eradicating—communicable diseases. Anton Kruiderink, assistant administrator and director of the Regional Bureau for Europe and the Commonwealth of Independent States, reminded participants in a conference held to assess the results of decentralization in the CIS and former Soviet satellites that "the ideology of shrinking the State followed in the region, instead of promoting an 'activist State', may well prove the biggest departing mistake of this millennium" (United Nations Department of Social and Economic Affairs 2000: 9). The conference underlined that decentralization is a very complex process, one that takes time and needs to be implemented in stages with important legal, political, and cultural components, and that each country needs to choose a model and decide how to proceed with its implementation.

While each country's context is different, there is much for policymakers to learn from studying the implementation process of decentralization elsewhere. The twenty years of experience in Mexico offer a large store of information that can provide valuable feedback, help identify errors to be avoided, present ideas on how to overcome obstacles, and shorten the distance between theory and practice.

References

Acevedo Mercadante, O., J. Yunes, and A. H. Chorny. 1994. "Descentralización y municipalización en Sao Paulo, Brasil," *Boletín de la Oficina Panamericana de la Salud* 126: 381–96.

Aizpeolea, L. R. 2000. "Un informe de la OCDE critica el modelo de la financiación autonómica," *El País*, April 10.

Alcaldía Mayor de Bogotá. 2004. "Un modelo de atención primaria en salud para garantizar el derecho a la salud en Bogotá." Santa Fe de Bogotá: Secretaría Distrital de Salud de Bogotá.

Altobelli, L. 2000. "Community Management of Health Facilities." Paper presented at the meeting "The Challenge of Health Reform: Reaching the Poor," organized by the World Bank, San José, Costa Rica, May 24–26.

Angell, A., and C. Graham. 1995. "Can Social Sector Reform Make Adjustment Sustainable and Equitable? Lessons from Chile and Venezuela," *Journal of Latin American Studies* 27, no. 1: 189–210.

ANSAL. 1994. "Health Sector Reform in El Salvador: Towards Equity and Efficiency." Executive summary. San Salvador: USAID.

Ase, I. 2005. "La descentralización de servicios de salud en Córdoba." Unpublished.

Atkinson, S., and D. Haran. 2004. "Back to Basics: Does Decentralization Improve Health System Performance? Evidence from Ceará in North-east Brazil," *Bulletin of the World Health Organization* 82, no. 11: 822–27.

Ball, G. 1994. "Implementation of World Bank Projects and Public Sector Decentralization: The Lessons from Latin America." Draft report, May 11.

Barillas, E. 1997. "La fragmentación de los sistemas nacionales de salud," *Revista Panamericana de Salud Pública* 1, no. 3: 246–49.

Barrientos, A. 2002. "Health Policy in Chile: The Return of the Public Sector?" *Bulletin of Latin American Research* 21, no. 3: 442–59.

Becht, J., and J. Bravo. 1984. "Evaluation Report: Project Concern International. Bolivia Primary Health Care Development and Training." USAID document PDAAT 884. Washington, D.C.: USAID.

Bossert, T. 1995. "Decentralization." In *Health Policy and Systems Development: An Agenda for Research*, ed. K. Janovsky. Geneva: World Health Organization.

Bossert, T., and J. C. Beauvais. 2002. "Decentralization of Health Systems in Ghana, Zambia, Uganda and the Philippines: A Comparative Analysis of Decision Space," *Health Policy and Planning* 17: 14–31.

Bosset, T., O Larrañaga, U. Giedion, J. J. Arbeláez, and D. M. Bowser. 2003. "Decentralization and Equity of Resource Allocation: Evidence from Colombia and Chile," *Bulletin of the World Health Organization* 91, no. 2: 95–100.

Burki, S. J., G. Perry, and W. Dillinger. 1999. *Beyond the Center: Decentralizing the State*. Washington, D.C.: World Bank.

Campos-Outcalt, D., K. Kewa, and J. Thomaso. 1995. "Decentralization of Health Services in Western Highlands Province, Papua New Guinea: An Attempt to Administer Health Service at the Subdistrict Level," *Social Science and Medicine* 40, no. 8: 1091–98.

Castaño, R. A., J. J. Arbeláez, U. Giedion, and L. G. Morales. 2001. "Evolución de la equidad en el sistema colombiano de salud." Series Financiamiento y Desarrollo, no. 108. Santiago de Chile: CEPAL.

Castro Valverde, C., and L. B. Sáenz. 1998. *La reforma del sistema nacional de salud: estrategias, alternativas, perspectivas.* San José, Costa Rica: Ministerio de Planificación y Política Nacional.

CEPAL (Comisión Económica para América Latina y el Caribe). 1994. "Salud, equidad y transformación productiva en América Latina y el Caribe." Documentos Reproducidos, no. 41. Washington, D.C.: Pan American Health Organization.

————. 1998. *El pacto fiscal: fortalezas, debilidades, desafíos.* Santiago de Chile: CEPAL.

Céspedes, J. E., C. M. Almeida, I. Jaramillo, et al. 2000. "Efectos de la reforma de la seguridad social en salud en Colombia sobre la equidad en el acceso y la utilización de los servicios de salud," *Revista de Salud Pública* 2, no. 2: 145–64.

Cheema, S. G., and D. A. Rondinelli. 1983. *Decentralization and Development: Policy Implementation in Developing Countries.* Beverly Hills, Calif.: Sage.

Chowdhury, M. 2004. "Community Participation in Health Care," *Bulletin of the World Health Organization* 82, no. 11: 881.

Cohen, S., et al. 1981. "Decentralization: A Framework for Policy Analysis. Project on Management Decentralization." Berkeley, Calif.: Institute of International Studies.

Collins, C. G. 1989. "Decentralization and the Need for Political and Critical Analysis," *Health Policy and Planning* 4: 118–71.

Collins, C. G., J. Araujo, and J. Barbosa. 2000. "Decentralizing the Health Sector: Issues in Brazil," *Health Policy* 52: 113–27.

Collins, C. G., and A. T. Green. 1994. "Decentralization and Primary Health Care: Some Negative Implications in Developing Countries," *International Journal of Health Services* 24: 459–76.

Collins, C. G., M. Omar, and E. Tarin. 2002. "Decentralization, Health Care and Policy Process in the Punjab, Pakistan in the 1990s," *International Journal of Health Planning and Management* 17: 123–46.

Conyers, D. 1986. "Decentralization and Development: A Framework Analysis," *Community Development Journal* 212, no. 2: 97.

Crook, R. C., and A. S. Sverrisson. 2001. "Decentralization and Poverty-Alleviation in Developing Countries: A Comparative Analysis or Is West Bengal Unique?" Brighton: IDS, University of Sussex.

De Groote, T., P. De Paepe, and J. Unger. 2005. "Colombia: In Vivo Test of Health Sector Privatization in the Developing World," *International Journal of Health Services* 35, no. 1: 124–41.

Del Valle López, A. 1998. "Descentralización de los servicios de atención primaria de salud a nivel municipal." Paper presented at the II CLAD International Congress on State Reform and Public Administration, Madrid, October 14–17.

Departamento Nacional de Planeación. República de Colombia. 2002. "Política de prestación de servicios para el sistema de seguridad social en salud y asignación de recursos del presupuesto general de la nación para la modernización de hospitales públicos." Documento Compes 3204. Bogotá: Departamento Nacional de Planeación, November 6.

Department of State and USAID. 2003. "Security, Democracy and Prosperity. Strategic Plan 2004–2009. Aligning Diplomacy and Development Assistance." Washington, D.C.: U.S. Department of State.

Dilla Alfonso, H. 1997. "Political Decentralization and Popular Alternatives: A View from the South." In *Community Power and Grassroot Democracy*, ed. M. Kaufman and H. Dilla Alfonso. Ottawa: IDRC.

Dillinger, W. 1994. "Decentralization and Its Implications for Service Delivery." Urban Management and Municipal Finance, no. 16. Washington, D.C.: World Bank.

Duarte Quapper, D. 1995. "Asignación de recursos per cápita en la atención primaria," *Cuadernos de Economía* 32, no. 95: 117–24.

Duarte Quapper, D., and M. S. Zuleta Reyes. 1999. "La situación de salud primaria en Chile." Manuscript.

Economic Council of Canada. 1991. "Regulatory Mechanisms in the Health Care Systems of Canada and Other Industrialized Countries: Description and Assessment." Ottawa: Economic Council of Canada.

European Observatory on Health Systems and Policies. 2000a. "The Observatory's Health Systems Glossary." Copenhagen: World Health Organization Regional Office for Europe. www.euro.who.int/observatory/glossary/toppage, accessed December 26, 2005.

———. 2000b. "Health Care Systems in Transition (Hit)-Template." Copenhagen: World Health Organization Regional Office for Europe.

Fernández, Y. 1998. "El proceso de descentralización y la autonomía hospitalaria: caso del hospital Rísquez en Venezuela." Paper presented at the II CLAD International Congress on State Reform and Public Administration, Madrid, October 14–17.

Finot, I. 2002. "Descentralización y participación en América Latina: una mirada desde la economía," *Revista de la CEPAL* 78: 139–49.

Flamand, L. 1998. "Las perspectivas del Nuevo Federalismo: el sector salud. Las experiencias de Aguascalientes, Guanajuato y San Luis Potosí." Working Document No. 55. México, D.F.: Centro de Investigación y Docencia Económicas.

Flórez, C. E., and T. Tono. 2003. "Inequities in Health Status and Use of Health Services in Colombia: 1900–2000." Paper presented at the 2003 Hawaii International Conference on Social Sciences, Honolulu, June 13–15.

Gagliano, E., A. Rosenfeld, and T. Tillea. 1988. "Fundamentos de la propuesta de descentralización y desconcentración de la atención estatal en salud en Córdoba." Paper presented at the VIII National Congress of Public Administration, Córdoba.

Gershberg, A. I. 1998. "Decentralization and Recentralization: Lessons from the Social Sectors in Mexico and Nicaragua." RE2/SO2. Final report submitted to the Inter-American Development Bank, January 15.

Gómez, L. F. 2002. "Atención médica, salud, pobreza y Ley 100," *Acta Médica Colombiana* 27, no. 4: 235–44.

Gonzáles, J. I. 2000. "Eficiencia horizontal y eficiencia vertical del Sistema de Selección de Beneficiarios (SISBEN)." Draft document. Bogotá: Departamento Nacional de Planeación, Misión Social.

Griffin, C. 1999. "Empowering Mayors, Hospital Directors or Patients? The Decentralization of Health Care." In *Beyond the Center: Decentralizing the State*, ed. S. J. Burki, G. Perry, and W. Dillinger. Washington, D.C.: World Bank.

Grupo de Economía de la Salud. 2003. "Resultados económicos de la reforma a la salud en Colombia," *Observatorio de la Seguridad Social* 3, no. 7: 1–10.

Guevara, E. B., and E. L. Mendias. 2002. "A Comparative Analysis of the Changes in Nursing Practice Related to Health Sector Reform in Five Countries of the Americas," *Revista Panamericana de Salud Pública* 27, no. 4: 235–44.

Hernández, M. 2002. "Reforma sanitaria, equidad y derecho a la salud en Colombia," *Cadernos de Saúde Pública* 18, no. 4: 991–1001.

Hincapié Correa, A. L., S. Mesa Ochoa, and M. R. Rhenals. 1998. *Desenvolvimiento, tendencias y perspectivas del proceso de descentralización colombiano*. Medellín: Corporación para el Desarrollo de la Investigación y la Docencia Económica.

Holguín Zamorano, G. 2004. *La bolsa y la vida*. Bogota: Misión Salud.

Holley, J. 1995. "Estudio de descentralización de la gestión de los servicios de salud. Territorio de Capinota, Bolivia." Latin American Health and Nutrition Sustainability Project. Washington, D.C.: University Research Corporation.

Homedes, N., and A. Ugalde. 2006. "Improving Access to Pharmaceuticals in Brazil and Argentina," *Health Policy and Planning* 21, no. 2: 123–31.

Homedes, N., A. Ugalde, and J. Rovira. 2005. "The World Bank, Pharmaceutical Policies, and Health Reforms in Latin America," *International Journal of Health Services* 35, no. 4: 691–717.

Hunter, D., et al. 1998. "Optimal Balance of Centralized and Decentralized Management." In *Critical Challenges for Health Care Reform in Europe,* ed. R. B. Saltman et al. Buckingham: Open University Press.

Hutchinson, P. L., and A. K. LaFond. 2004. *Monitoring and Evaluation of Decentralization Reforms in Developing Country Health Sectors.* Bethesda, Md.: Abt Associates.

Jaramillo, I. 2002. "Evaluación de la descentralización de la salud y la reforma de la Seguridad Social en Colombia," *Gazeta Sanitaria* 16, no. 1: 48–53.

Kolehmainen-Aitken, R. L. 1992. "The Impact of Decentralization on Health Work Force Development in Papua New Guinea," *Public Administration and Development* 12: 175–91.

La Forgia, G. M. 2003. "In Search of Excellence: Strengthening Hospital Performance in Brazil." Unpublished concept paper. LCHSHH. Washington, D.C.: World Bank, March 19.

La Forgia, G. M., and N. Homedes. 1992. "Decentralization of Health Services in Colombia: A Review of Progress and Problems." Unpublished report prepared for the World Bank. Washington, D.C.

Larrañaga, O. 1999. "Eficiencia y equidad en el sistema de salud chileno." Financiamiento y Desarrollo Series. Proyecto Cepal/GTZ Reformas Financieras al Sector Salud en América Latina y el Caribe. Unidad de financiamiento. Santiago de Chile: Ministerio de Salud/FONASA.

Lavadenz, F., N. Schwab, and H. Straatman. 2001. "Redes públicas, descentralizadas y comunitarias de salud en Bolivia," *Revista Panamericana de Salud Pública* 9, no. 3: 182–89.

Litvack, J., J. Ahmad, and R. Bird. 1998. *Rethinking Decentralization in Developing Countries.* Washington, D.C.: World Bank.

McCord, W. 1965. *The Springtime of Freedom: The Evolution of Developing Societies.* New York: Oxford University Press.

McPack, B., F. J. Yepes, and L. H. Sánchez. 2003. "Is the Colombian Health System Reform Improving the Performance of Public Hospitals in Bogotá?" *Health Policy and Planning* 118, no. 2: 182–94.

Mills, A., J. P. Vaughan, D. L. Smith, and I. Tabibzadeh. 1990. *Health Systems Decentralization: Concepts, Issues and Country Experiences.* Geneva: World Health Organization.

Ministerio de Salud. República de Chile. 2003. "Reforma de salud." Santiago de Chile.

Ministerio de Salud de la Nación. República de Argentina. 1994. "Proyecto de reforma del sector salud PRESSAL. Hospital público de autogestión. Anexo

A. Términos de referencia, organización y gestión. Hospital Central y Teodoro Schestakow de la Provincia de Mendoza." Buenos Aires.

Ministerio de Salud Pública. República de Colombia. 1998. "Programa de apoyo a la reforma. Análisis de las tendencias de ingresos, gastos, y producción de hospitales de I y II nivel, 1996–1998." Bogotá: Ministerio de Salud Pública.

Molina de Salazar, D. I. 2002. "Salud gerenciada y ética: ¿son compatibles?" *Acta Médica Colombiana* 27, no. 6: 433–39.

Monrad Aas, I. H. 1997. "Organizational Change: Decentralization in Hospitals," *International Journal of Health Planning and Management* 12: 103–14.

Mutemwa, R. I. 2006. "HMIS and Decision-making in Zambia: Re-thinking Information Solutions for District Health Management in Decentralized Systems," *Health Policy and Planning* 21, no. 1: 40–52.

New York Times. 2005. Editorial: "A Different Latin America," December 23.

Nigenda, G., R. Valdez, R. Ávila, and J. A. Ruiz. 2002. *Descentralización y programas de salud reproductiva.* México, D.F.: Fundación Mexicana para la Salud.

Oxfam America. 2005. "Guatemalans Go to the Top of the World Bank. Meeting with President an Opportunity to Voice Concerns about Mining Project." www.oneworld.net, December 14, accessed December 19, 2005.

Oyarzo, C. 2000. "La descentralización financiera en Chile en el marco de los noventa," *Pan American Journal of Public Health* 8, nos. 1/2: 72–84.

PAHO (Pan American Health Organization). 1988. "Developing and Strengthening of Local Health Systems in the Transformation of National Health Systems." Document CD33/14. Washington, D.C.: PAHO.

Peterson, G. E. 1994. "Decentralization Experience in Latin America: An Overview of Lessons and Issues." LACTD Dissemination Note. Washington, D.C.: World Bank, May.

———. 1997. "Decentralization in Latin America: Learning through Experience." Latin American and Caribbean Studies. Washington, D.C.: World Bank.

Prud'homme, R. 1994. "On the Dangers of 1994: Decentralization." Policy Research Working Paper No. 1252. Washington, D.C.: World Bank.

Ramiro, L. S., F. A. Castillo, T. Tan-Torres, et al. 2001. "Community Participation in Local Health Boards in a Decentralized Setting: Cases from the Philippines," *Health Policy and Planning* 16 (Suppl. 2): 61–69.

Rey del Castillo, J. 1998. *Descentralización de los servicios sanitarios: aspectos generales y análisis del caso español.* Granada: Escuela Andaluza de Salud Pública.

Rodríguez, V. E. 1997. *Decentralization in Mexico: From Reforma Municipal to Solidaridad to Nuevo Federalismo.* Boulder, Colo.: Westview.

Rondinelli, D. 1990. "Decentralizing Urban Development Programs: A Framework for Analyzing Policy." Washington, D.C.: USAID.

Rosenbaum, A., C. Rodríguez-Acosta, and M. V. Rojas. 2000. "Decentralizing the Health Service Delivery in an Emerging Democracy: A Case Study of Organizational Change, Civil Society Participation and Local Institutions Building in Paraguay," *International Review of Administrative Sciences* 66: 655–72.

Ruiz, A., P. W. Askin, and D. C. Gibb. 1978. "Health Sector Assessment. El Salvador." Washington, D.C.: USAID.

Ruiz Mier, F., and B. Giussani. 1996. "Descentralización y financiamiento de la provisión de servicios de salud en Bolivia." Report to CEPAL, ACDI, and ODA.

Sandiford, P. 1999. "Devolution in Latin America Has Had Poor Effects on Health Care," *British Medical Journal* 319: 55.

Sanguinettty, J., et al. 1988. "Informe final. Estudio sectorial de salud." Manuscript. San José, Costa Rica: Detec.

Sarmiento, M. C. 2000. "Enfermedades transmisibles en Colombia: cambios ambivalentes," *Revista de Salud Pública* 2, no. 1. http://www.revmed.unal.edu.co/revistasp/v2n1/Rev2171.htm.

Scarpaci, J. L. 1992. "Primary-care Decentralization in the Southern Cone: Shantytown Health Care as Urban Social Movements." In *Health and Health Care in Latin America during the Lost Decade: Insights for the 1990s*, ed. C. Weil and J. L. Scarpaci. St. Paul: University of Minnesota.

Segall, M. 2000. "From Cooperation to Competition in National Health Systems—And Back? Impact on Professional Ethics and Quality of Care," *International Journal of Health Planning and Management* 15, no. 1: 61–79.

———. 2003. "District Health Systems in a Neoliberal World: A Review of Five Key Policy Areas," *International Journal of Health Planning and Management* 18: S5–S26.

Silverman, J. M. 1992. "Public Sector Decentralization, Economic Policy and Sector Investment Programs." World Bank Technical Paper No. 188, Africa Technical Department Series. Washington, D.C.: World Bank.

Stocker, K., H. Waitzkin, and C. Iriart. 1999. "The Exportation of Managed Care to Latin America," *New England Journal of Medicine* 340, no. 14: 1131–36.

Tanzi, V. 1994. "Corruption, Government Activities and Markets." IMF Working Paper No. 99. Washington, D.C.: IMF.

———. 1995. "Fiscal Federalism and Decentralization: A Review of Some Efficiency and Macroeconomic Aspects." Paper prepared for the World Bank's annual Bank Conference on Development Economics. Washington, D.C., May 1–2.

Titelman, D. 1999. "Reformas al financiamiento del sistema de salud en Chile," *Revista de la CEPAL* 69: 181–94.

Ugalde, A. 1985. "Community Participation in Latin American Health Programs," *Social Science and Medicine* 21, no. 1: 1–53.

———. 1999. "Un acercamiento teórico a la participación comunitaria en la atención de la salud." In *Participación social: metodología, problemas y expectativas: el caso de Nicaragua 1978–1989*, ed. E. L. Menéndez. México, D.F.: Instituto Mora.

Ugalde, A., and N. Homedes. 1994. "Physicians and Underutilization of Primary Rural Health Services: The Case of the Dominican Republic." In *Physicians and Health Care in the Third World*, ed. A. Ugalde and O. Alubo. Studies in Third World Societies, no 55. Williamsburg, Vir.: College of William and Mary.

———. 2002. "Descentralización del sector salud en América Latina," *Gaceta Sanitaria* (Spain) 16, no. 1: 18–29.

UNDP (United Nations Development Programme). 2005. *Human Development Report, 2005.* New York: Oxford University Press.

United Nations Department of Economic and Social Affairs, Division for Public Economics and Public Administration. 2000. *Decentralization: Conditions for Success: Lessons from Central and Eastern Europe and the Commonwealth of Independent States.* New York: United Nations.

United Nations Technical Assistance Program. 1962. *Decentralization for National and Local Development.* New York: United Nations.

Veldhuyzen van Zantes, T., and C. Semidei. 1996. "Assessment of Health Sector Decentralization in Paraguay." Technical Report No. 1. Washington, D.C.: University Research Corporation.

WHO-Europe. 2005. "What Evidence Is There about the Effects of Health Care Reforms on Gender Equity, Particularly in Health?" Copenhagen: WHO, November.

Witter, S., and T. Ensor. 1997. *An Intro to Health Economics for Eastern Europe and the Former Soviet Union.* Chichester, N.Y.: John Wiley and Sons.

World Bank. 1987. "Argentina. Population, Health Sector Review." Report 6555-AR. Washington, D.C.: World Bank.

———. 1992. "Venezuela. Health Sector Review." Report 10713-VE. Washington, D.C.: World Bank, August.

———. 1993. *World Development Report 1993: Investing in Health.* New York: Oxford University Press.

———. 1996. "Panama. Health Sector Study." Report 6225. Washington, D.C.: World Bank, May 30.

———. 1997. "Health Care in Rural El Salvador." Report 16768-ES. Washington, D.C.: World Bank, June 25.

———. 2001. "The World Bank and User Fees." Washington, D.C.: World Bank.

———. 2002. "Colombia Country Management Unit, PREM Sector Management Unit." Colombia poverty report. Latin America and the Caribbean Region. Washington, D.C.: World Bank.

Zamora, J. 2001. "Descentralización en el Instituto Salvadoreño de Seguro Social (ISSS)." Unpublished.

2

Decentralization of Health Services in Mexico: A Historical Review

NÚRIA HOMEDES AND ANTONIO UGALDE

THE DEVELOPMENT OF THE MEXICAN HEALTH SYSTEM, 1910–1940

At the time of Mexico's independence in 1821, the provision of medical services in the country, as in many other countries, was through autonomous municipal or charity hospitals, private allopathic physicians, and traditional healers. Over time, this fragmented system of health care became less and less manageable, and in 1861 the government transferred the administration of the majority of hospitals to state authorities. A few years later, in 1876, General Porfirio Díaz led a successful revolt against President Sebastián Lerdo de Tejada, paving the way for thirty-five years of dictatorship and centralization known as the Porfiriato (Krauze 1997).[1] The first steps toward centralization of health services took place in 1887 with the creation of the General Directorate of Social Welfare (Dirección General de Beneficencia Pública) (Cardozo Brum 1995: 40; see also table 2.1).

The Mexican Revolution ended the Porfiriato in 1910. It then took another seven years for the revolutionary leaders to frame a new constitution that established a federal system[2] with three levels of government (federal,

---

[1] Díaz did not run for president in 1880 and appointed Manuel González, one of the most corrupt and incompetent of his close allies, as his successor. The González presidency was such a disaster that Díaz had no problem returning to the presidency and remaining in power until 1910.

[2] The Federal District, Baja California Sur, and Quintana Roo at that time had a special legal status and were not affected by the new constitution. They created their own separate health systems. These special territories were incorporated into the federation in 1974.

state, and municipal).[3] According to Article 73 of the 1917 Constitution, Congress would pass legislation regulating public health matters, and the three levels of government would provide sanitation and medical services in accordance with national laws and the regulations issued by the High Council of Public Health (Consejo Superior de Salubridad).

The 1917 Constitution, influenced by the progressive spirit of the Revolution, defined the rights of labor in Article 123. Years later this article was used to organize the social security system (Gutiérrez Arriola 2002: 79). The federal Department of Public Health (Departamento de Salubridad Pública) was created in 1917 with responsibility for coordinating public health activities, administering resources for the control of epidemics, and finding solutions to urban sanitation problems. The Department relied on the municipalities to execute most programs (Flamand Gómez 1997: 9).

The framers of the 1917 Constitution believed that a federal system would help to distribute public responsibilities among the three politico-administrative levels of federation, state, and municipality (Barraca 2001). This did not happen, and political power continued to be concentrated at the federal level. One of the social causes that had triggered the Revolution was the abuses and crimes of regional bosses known as caciques (Ross 1955; Kern 1973), and centralism was justified in part by the need to overcome the dominance of those caciques who had survived the Revolution and continued to hold power in many parts of the country. Their presence was considered to be inimical to the formation of a modern state.

The National Revolutionary Party (PNR) was created in 1929. It later became the Institutional Revolutionary Party (PRI), which remained in power until 2000 and fostered the centralization of political and decision-making power in Mexico City. The PRI transformed Mexico into a centralized authoritarian political system (Linz and Stepan 1996), divesting the states of the possibility of organizing their own health services.

The Great Depression had severe impacts on Mexico's economy. During the 1930s there was mounting criticism of the rising centralization that

---

[3] The political and financial autonomy of the municipalities was very limited until recently. There are 2,412 municipalities in Mexico, and they vary widely in type and importance. A municipality may include rural communities; on the other hand, there are large metropolitan areas (such as Mexico City, Guadalajara, and Monterrey) that embrace several municipalities.

was affecting all sectors, from public security and transportation to education. In the health sector, the federal government's response was the 1934 Law for Coordination and Cooperation in Public Health Services (Ley de Coordinación y Cooperación de Servicios de Salubridad). This law made possible the signing of cooperation agreements between the Department of Public Health and the states and, if allowed by state legislation, with municipalities; and it established the foundation for all subsequent health codes (*códigos sanitarios*). According to the cooperation agreements, the Department of Public Health would provide technical guidelines, and the federal and state governments would contribute financial and human resources (Flamand Gómez 1997: 10).

During the same year, the Department of Public Health opened Coordinated Health Services offices (Servicios Coordinados de Salud) in all of the states. Their mission was to carry out public health interventions in the states as representatives of the federal government and to act as intermediaries between the federal executive and the state government. The director of the Department of Public Health, based in Mexico City, named the state directors of the Coordinated Health Services.

In the 1930s, agriculture was the backbone of the Mexican economy. The Department of Public Health understood the economic importance of maintaining a healthy agricultural workforce and allocated significant resources toward that goal. One of the most creative initiatives, later adopted by many countries in Latin America and still operating today, was the organization in 1936 of a mandatory social service (*pasantía* or *servicio social*) to assure the presence of health professionals in rural areas. Ever since, all graduates from medical, dental, and nursing schools must spend a specified period (between six months and two years) practicing their profession in underserved communities before receiving their licenses to practice.

SETTING THE FOUNDATIONS OF A MODERN HEALTH SYSTEM, 1940–1982

During World War II, as the Mexican economy grew and industrialized, the health sector received more resources and was reorganized. In 1943 the General Directorate of Social Welfare, in charge of hospital services since 1877, merged with the Department of Public Health and became the Ministry of Health and Welfare (SSA), and the Coordinated Health Services

Table 2.1. Highlights of the History of the Mexican Health System

← CENTRALIZATION →	
1887	Creation of the General Directorate of Social Welfare
1917	Mexican Constitution: • Federal system of government. • Health is an individual right. • Creation of the Department of Public Health. • Labor rules defined (later influence the development of social security).
1926	Health Code establishes that public health is a federal responsibility.
1918–1929	Yucatán, Puebla, Campeche, Tamaulipas, Veracruz, Aguascalientes, and Hidalgo establish voluntary social security schemes. In 1929, the first social security bill is written but is not approved.
1934	Law for Coordination and Cooperation in Public Health Services. Creation of Coordinated Health Services.
1942	Enactment of Social Security Law.
1943	The General Directorate of Social Welfare merges with the Department of Public Health to become the Ministry of Health and Welfare or SSA. Creation of the Mexican Social Security Institute (IMSS).
1959	Creation of Social Security Institute for State Employees (ISSSTE).
1973	New health code specifies the elements to be included in coordination agreements between the federation and the states.

Table 2.1, continued

	DECENTRALIZATION
1970–1977	Need to decentralize: • Creation of State Development Planning Committees (COPLADEs). • Development of coordination agreements to give more responsibilities for public policies to the states (February 5, 1977). Little success in the health sector.
1974	The Office of the President creates the COPLAMAR program, including IMSS-COPLAMAR (in 1989 renamed IMSS-Solidaridad and in 2002 IMSS-Oportunidades) to foster development in rural areas.
1978	Urban development plan attempts to move people out of the Federal District.
1981	The President's Health Services Coordinating Group: • The SSA needs to define the legal framework that will guide public health and the provision of care. • Need to decentralize the implementation of programs and policies to the states.
1983	The Constitution is modified: • Health is a right. • The public health responsibilities of the federal government and the states will be defined.
1984	Health Law replaces the Health Code of 1973. • Defines public health tasks. • Defines who has public health authority and assigns public health responsibilities. • Announces that the SSA will promote decentralization and the need to develop state health systems. • The SSA is made responsible for coordinating, regulating and evaluating National Health Policies. • Establishes the basis for coordination agreements between the federation and the states.
1986	Presidential decree: IMSS-COPLAMAR is to merge with SSA and form a state system of care for the uninsured. Decentralization starts and, by July 1987 fourteen states have signed decentralization agreements. Creation of the National Health Council.

Table 2.1, continued

		DECENTRALIZATION
1989–1994	State decentralization is reversed. Health districts are strengthened.	
1995	New Federalism Health Reform Program with the intention of: • Expanding coverage. • Ensuring access to a basic package of services. • Decentralizing to the states and strengthening the National Health Council. • Improving quality.	
1996	National Agreement for the decentralization of health services. Strengthening of the National Health Council.	
2001-2006	Cooperative Federalism National Health Program • Complete the formal decentralization of the SSA to the municipal and state level. • Distribute SSA resources in a more equitable manner. • Consolidate the deconcentration of IMSS. • Consolidate cooperation of the states in public health activities. • Strengthen the coordinating role of the National Health Council.	
2003	Approval of amendments to the Health Law by Congress. People's Health Insurance Program (SP). Catastrophic Health Fund. Solidarity Health Fund.	
2004	Official launching of the People's Health Insurance Program.	

offices became the Ministry's representatives in the states. The same year also saw the creation of the autonomous and prestigious National Institute of Cardiology and the Children's Hospital.

The origin of social security programs in Mexico goes back to the years immediately following the drafting of the 1917 Constitution. Between 1918 and 1929, the states of Yucatán, Puebla, Campeche, Tamaulipas, Veracruz, Aguascalientes, and Hidalgo established voluntary social security programs. The first federal social security bill was introduced in 1929 but did not become law until 1942. World War II helped to expand the industrialization of the country and, with it, the formal workforce, and in 1943 the Mexican Social Security Institute (IMSS) was created. *how do I want to say*

Subsequently, a number of social security institutes for special population groups appeared. Thus the Social Security Institute for State Employees (ISSSTE) was organized in 1959, and several state enterprises—such as the National Oil Company (PEMEX), the National Electric Power Company (CFE), and the railroad companies—created separate social security programs. The armed forces have had their own plan since 1979. The banking sector and the Treasury Ministry (SHCP) made other arrangements to ensure benefits for their employees, including an independent health insurance program (Gutiérrez Arriola 2002: 81). However, because social security plans cover a worker and the worker's family,[4] families could be contributing to and be eligible for services from more than one social security network. For example, if one family member is a state employee, s/he would contribute to ISSSTE, while another, employed in the private sector, would contribute to IMSS; therefore, this family would be eligible to receive services from at least IMSS and ISSSTE.

---

[4] Each social security institute offers a different family coverage. For instance, IMSS covers the worker's companion (spouse or someone who has lived with the worker for more than five years or has children with the worker); any person who is economically dependent on the worker (in the case of ISSSTE, if the dependent is male, he must demonstrate inability to work or be over age 55); the worker's parents if they are economically dependent on the worker (in the case of IMSS, they must reside in the same household); and the worker's children (in the case of IMSS, up to age 16, or 25 if they are enrolled in the public education system; ISSSTE covers the spouse's children up to age 18, or 25 if they are studying in the public school system; disabled children are always covered).

During the 1950s the Ministry of Health, responding to public health challenges, created several vertical federal programs that were implemented without the participation of the Coordinated Health Services. Such was the case with family planning, maternal and child health, and environmental health. One example of such a vertical program was the Commission for the Eradication of Malaria (Comisión Nacional para la Erradicación del Paludismo), which was very successful in achieving its mission. The vertical programs expanded the power of the Ministry of Health vis-à-vis the Coordinated Health Services, which were left to provide medical care for the uninsured poor. In addition, some state and municipal governments developed autonomous health care networks for their employees, which occasionally served the uninsured.

The 1960s and 1970s were characterized by industrial expansion and strong economic growth—and a concomitant increase in formal employment (mainly in urban areas) and in the number of social security beneficiaries. As the social security institutes expanded their infrastructure in urban areas, the divide in access to services between urban and rural dwellers widened. Per capita health expenditures among the multiple health plans varied widely, with PEMEX spending the most per beneficiary and SSA the least, a situation that still prevails. The growth of social security coincided with the deterioration of the SSA. Its overall performance worsened as the Ministry lost its sense of direction and mission, was unable to supervise its state offices, and became a residual provider of services (Flamand Gómez 1997: 13).

As in other parts of the world, the 1960s were years of political turmoil and dissent in Mexico. The student and worker movement of 1968 demanded a more equitable distribution of power and resources, members of labor unions expressed dissent with their leadership, and even senior PRI leaders recognized the need for democratic reforms (Rodríguez 1997: 47). The need to decentralize public administration became evident. Under Presidents Luis Echeverría (1970–1976) and José López Portillo (1976–1982), responsibility for implementing federal planning initiatives, but not decision-making authority, was transferred to state-level Development Planning Committees (COPLADEs), and consolidated development agreements (CUDs) were signed yearly between the federation and the states. These coordination agreements covered all sectors and transferred responsibility for the implementation of public policies to the states. According to executives of the Health Ministry, the CUDs were redundant because responsibility for the provision of medical services had been delegated to the states in 1935, as reflected in all coordination agreements written since then.

As noted above, inequities in the health system were profound. In an effort to reduce the gap, the federal government attempted to increase services to the poor by making them eligible for social security, initially through a program called IMSS-CONASUPO, which was defeated by opposition from the autonomous social security institutes. Finally, in 1974, the Office of the President, working through the National Planning Group for Depressed Zones and Marginalized Groups (COPLAMAR), expanded services to rural residents and the poor. In the area of health, the IMSS-COPLAMAR program (later known as IMSS-Solidaridad and, since 2002, as IMSS-Oportunidades) was created to serve the needs of those who were not served by either IMSS or Health Ministry facilities. At the time, the IMSS was under pressure to distribute its considerable financial reserves, and it agreed to administer the financial resources that the federal government allocated to this program and also to contribute infrastructure and personnel.

The IMSS-COPLAMAR program adopted a health delivery model inspired by the Alma-Ata primary-care principles[5] and was judged to be highly successful. It also served to improve the image of IMSS, portraying it as a generous institution willing to share its resources with the poor. By 1981, IMSS-COPLAMAR covered more than ten million persons (out of a targeted population of fourteen million [Birn 1996]) who previously had no access to medical care, and it operated three thousand rural medical units and sixty hospitals (Flamand Gómez 1997: 13).

The onset of economic recession at the end of the 1970s had a negative impact on public services. With the image of government deteriorating, the PRI needed to democratize the decision-making process and be more efficient and more transparent if it wanted to remain in power. In August 1981, President López Portillo accepted the proposal of then Secretary of

---

[5] The International Conference on Primary Health Care in Alma-Ata, Kazakhstan, in 1978 defined and granted international recognition to the concept of primary health care as a strategy to reach the goal of "Health for All in 2000."

Planning and Budgeting Miguel de la Madrid to establish the President's Health Services Coordinating Group (Coordinación de los Servicios de Salud de la Presidencia de la República) to determine how the health system could be streamlined and how the various health networks could be integrated into a national health system with universal coverage. The Coordinating Group emphasized the need for the Health Ministry to define the legal framework that would guide public health interventions and the provision of health services, and it called for decentralizing the implementation of programs and policies to the state level. The proposal advanced by the Coordinating Group anticipated that decentralization would render services more accountable to the needs of states and local communities and that it would lead to greater user satisfaction and less overlapping of services and infrastructure (Soberón Acevedo and Martínez Narváez 1996).

The price collapse in global oil markets in the early 1980s plunged Mexico into a severe recession. By September 1982 the country was on the verge of default, and per capita health expenditures had been reduced by almost half. According to Cornelius and Craig (1984), when Miguel de la Madrid assumed the presidency, the government was near bankruptcy; the Central Bank had exhausted its reserves trying to deal with an unprecedented budget deficit, and in one year some US$23 billion had left the country. Mexico's foreign debt was more than US$82 billion, and there were no funds to pay even the accrued interest. Devaluation and inflation were rampant, at more than 80 and 100 percent, respectively, and the economy had a negative growth rate of –0.2 percent. Over twenty million people, or more than half of the workforce, were unemployed or underemployed, and the country's population was "stunned by the abrupt turn of economic events, and deeply distrustful of public authorities" (Cornelius and Craig 1984: 411).

CENTRALIZED DECENTRALIZATION: DE LA MADRID'S REFORM, 1982–1988

Miguel de la Madrid inherited a country in political and economic turmoil. Having been the main architect of the decentralization studies conducted in 1981, it was natural that he would promote the decentralization of the Mexican administration. Perhaps unaware that his words echoed neoliberal views (Homedes and Ugalde 2005) or perhaps deliberately using the neoliberals' rhetoric, he proclaimed that decentralization increased democracy and justice, eliminated corruption, and increased communities' participation in deciding their future (de la Madrid 1986). For de la Madrid, decentralization was also a means to allow the states and municipalities to develop (Barraca 2001) as well as a response to state and municipal officials' demands for greater autonomy.

De la Madrid viewed decentralization as coherent with the federal system established in the 1917 Constitution, and the Municipal Decentralization Reform of 1983 became a cornerstone of his reform programs (Merino 2003). It included a reform of constitutional Article 115 (Barraca 2001) and the transfer of a significant number of responsibilities to the municipal level, including for potable water, sewerage, public lighting, sanitation, markets and supply centers, cemeteries, slaughterhouses, streets, parks, and public security. However, municipal presidents were disillusioned when they did not see an increase in their budgets and therefore found themselves without resources to satisfactorily carry out their new responsibilities. This reaction confirms the view of those who, as will be discussed below, suggested that decentralization was promoted for economic rather than democratic and participatory purposes.

It was no coincidence that other countries with different political and geographical characteristics also began to decentralize at the same time, presumably following World Bank recommendations.[6] The International Monetary Fund (IMF) was also demanding that Latin American (and other) countries in economic recession implement structural adjustments that required cuts in social spending (Fajardo Ortiz 2002). If they did not reduce social spending, they could not qualify for the short-term IMF loans they needed to refinance their public debt, leading several authors to suggest that the call for decentralization was aimed less at promoting democracy and efficiency and more at reducing federal spending in order to redirect federal resources to debt service (Birn 1996; Griffin 1999; Merino 2003).

In 1983, constitutional Article 4 was amended to guarantee all Mexicans the right to health protection. The same year a new Health Law replaced the Health Code of 1973 and set the framework for the decentralization of health services in Mexico. The 1983 law defined the division of health responsibilities between the federation and the states; established the basis

---

[6] Peru, Colombia, Brazil, Argentina, Costa Rica, Chile, and Venezuela also embarked on administrative decentralization processes around this time.

for health agreements between the states and the federation; specified that, after the president and state governments, the General Health Council (Consejo de Salubridad General) was the main health authority in the country; created the state health systems; and charged the state governments with responsibility for planning, organizing, and developing medical care networks.

After considerable discussion but without consensus among health-sector leaders, de la Madrid decreed on March 8, 1984, that the primary-level and secondary-level services of the Health Ministry and IMSS-COPLAMAR would be integrated into a single state system of care for the uninsured. This process would occur incrementally and would be conducted by a subcommittee of the COPLADE and overseen by a representative of the federal government. Due to opposition from powerful labor unions, the autonomous social security institutes remained outside of the integration plan, as did the very prestigious autonomous tertiary (specialized-care) hospitals, most located in Mexico City. Because the social security institutes and the public tertiary hospitals together represent the lion's share of public health expenditures, it is clear that in terms of geographic scope (only fourteen states decentralized), coverage, and expenditures, this attempt to decentralize health services encompassed only a small part of the Mexican health sector. Furthermore, as will be discussed below, few functions were decentralized, and very little decision-making authority was transferred to the states.

The process of integrating part of the Health Ministry with IMSS-COPLAMAR covered two phases. During the first phase, each state was required to conduct a needs assessment and present a health plan that would: (1) include the incorporation of existing infrastructure into a single network; (2) enact a state health law to define the state's role in health promotion, provision of services, and sanitary regulation; (3) determine the referral system to other levels of care and the contracting arrangements; (4) establish a health information system; and (5) produce procedural manuals for procurement and human resource management. After satisfactorily completing this first phase, a state could sign a decentralization agreement with the federal government and proceed with developing its own state health system (Soberón Acevedo and Martínez Narváez 1996). The decentralization agreements specified that the states had to increase their financial contribution to the health sector by a given percentage, which differed by state but was in the range of 20 to 40 percent of all state health expenditures. It was anticipated that these actions would result in increased coverage for the uninsured, less duplication of infrastructure, and better quality of care (Cardozo Brum 1995: 47–48). Coordination among the states would occur through the participation of all state-level secretaries of health in the National Health Council (Consejo Nacional de Salud), created in 1986.[7]

According to the 1984 presidential decree, decentralization was to be completed by the end of 1986, yet by the end of 1987 only fourteen states had decentralized (see table 2.2). IMSS executives and employees resisted the transfer of IMSS-COPLAMAR, with some justification. IMSS-COPLAMAR had been very successful, enjoyed broad popular support, and had superior infrastructure and better quality of services than what was available through the Health Ministry. The IMSS was concerned, therefore, that the transfer would have negative consequences for the beneficiaries of IMSS-COPLAMAR.

Table 2.2. Dates on Which States Signed Decentralization Agreements

State	Date
Tlaxcala	May 24, 1985
Nuevo León	May 31, 1985
Guerrero	June 11, 1985
Jalisco	July 30, 1985
Baja California Sur	July 31, 1985
Morelos	October 4, 1985
Tabasco	December 6, 1985
Querétaro	December 13, 1985
Sonora	December 17, 1985
Colima	March 7, 1986
Guanajuato	March 7, 1986
México State	March 7, 1986
Aguascalientes	October 19, 1987
Quintana Roo	December 23, 1987

Source: Cardozo Brum 1993a: 369.

---

[7] Initially, state governors were invited to Council meetings.

Several authors have attempted to explain why some states decided to decentralize while others chose not to (Cardozo Brum 1993b; González-Block et al., this volume). They found that the states that decentralized: (1) tended to be wealthier and had the financial resources to increase their contribution to the decentralized health services; (2) had the capacity to expand coverage to all the uninsured; and (3) had relatively few IMSS-COPLAMAR hospitals and clinics and, consequently, met with less opposition. However, not all the states that met these criteria opted to decentralize (such as Sinaloa and Campeche), and some that did not fulfill these conditions did decentralize (Jalisco, México State, and Nuevo León), indicating that a state governor's willingness to support decentralization strongly influenced the decision to move forward.

Functions Transferred under the de la Madrid Decentralization

In accord with the traditional analysis of health systems, we have divided our study of decentralized functions into five areas: the system's organization, physical infrastructure, human resources, financial functions, and programmatic functions.

Decentralizing organizational structure. The decentralized states had to align their organizational structure with their new mission. While there were small and mostly symbolic differences in the way that decentralized states organized their health services, the main change was the transformation of the Coordinated Health Services offices into state health secretariats, which became the ultimate health authority in the states, with responsibility for public health and for the provision of medical services to the uninsured population (see table 2.3). The states of Aguascalientes, Guerrero, and México placed their state health secretariats within the executive branch of state government, although functionally there was no difference between these three states and the others. Two states, Sonora and Baja California Sur, created, in addition to a state health secretariat, a decentralized public agency to provide medical services for the uninsured and to conduct public health activities. In theory, this office would be independent from the state health secretariat, whose main function was regulatory. However, the decentralized public agency never functioned as intended. In practice, the organization of health services in all of the decentralized states was similar, and all the states followed the directives given by the Health Ministry, with very little interference from the state executive and legislative authorities (Flamand Gómez 1997: 22). The Coordinated Health Services offices in the decentralized states were abolished in 1985.

Table 2.3. Organizational Structure Adopted by Decentralized States

Structure	State
Coordinated Health Services units converted into state health secretariats.	Colima Guanajuato Jalisco Morelos Nuevo León Querétaro Quintana Roo Tabasco Tlaxcala
State health secretariats created within the executive branch of state government.	Aguascalientes Guerrero México State
Dual structure: Coordinated Health Services units converted into state health secretariats, and a decentralized public agency created within the state bureaucracy to implement public health activities and deliver health care to the uninsured.	Sonora Baja California Sur

Source: Flamand Gómez 1997: 22.

Decentralizing physical infrastructure. The states were asked to create a unified network for the delivery of medical care to the uninsured, integrating the first- and second-level facilities and the personnel of the Health Ministry and the IMSS-COPLAMAR health units. The states prepared infrastructure development plans and specified the IMSS-COPLAMAR infrastructure that they wanted to incorporate into their networks. After approving the state development plans, the Health Ministry proceeded to buy the requested infrastructure and equipment from IMSS (Cardozo Brum 1995: 51). After decentralization of the fourteen states, IMSS-COPLAMAR retained 50 hospitals and 2,404 health units; it had turned over 23 hospitals and 911 units (Birn 1996). Subsequently, the SSA lent all health infrastructure and equipment to the state health authorities (a practice known as *comodato*). Unfortunately, decentralized states were unable to finance the purchase of needed supplies; did not have the resources to maintain equipment, infrastructure, and vehicles; and did not have the expertise to maintain the quality of services that the IMSS had previously provided. As IMSS professionals had predicted, the COPLAMAR services deteriorated rapidly in the decentralized states (Gershberg 1998).

Decentralizing human resources. Creating a state health system implied that all health workers would eventually be transferred to the state. The reorganization of the labor force was the most controversial and expensive step in the decentralization process because IMSS, the Health Ministry, and state health workers had different labor contracts, salary structures, and benefit packages. IMSS-COPLAMAR employees were governed by Chapter A of constitutional Article 123, while those of the Ministry of Health and the Federal District were covered under Chapter B, and municipal and state employees had still different employment conditions (Ruiz Massieu 1986). Workers under different contracts had varying workloads, vacation allowances, seniority rules, rights and protections, and systems of conflict resolution.

The salaries of Health Ministry employees and state workers were raised to the level of IMSS employees, but equivalence in benefits was not achieved; IMSS workers continued to receive more generous benefits than did SSA or state employees. The cost to the Health Ministry of achieving uniformity in salaries was very high. According to a 1989 Ministry report, the total cost of decentralizing the fourteen states was about 140 billion pesos (Kumate 1989), or approximately US$452 million.[8]

IMSS-COPLAMAR employees were given the choice of remaining within the IMSS or being transferred to the state systems.[9] About 7 percent

---

[8] The exchange rate varied widely during this period. The estimated dollar amount was calculated using the exchange rate for June 1 of each year and the number of states that signed the decentralization agreement each year.

[9] IMSS-COPLAMAR workers who transferred to the state joined the National Union of Health Ministry Employees (SNTSSA). In Mexico's health sector, all workers except political appointees and those in managerial positions are unionized, and all personnel actions such as new appointments, transfers, promotions, benefits changes, and salary increases have to be negotiated with the union leadership in Mexico City, with little or no input from the states. This

remained with the IMSS, leaving the state health secretariats without the personnel needed to operate their services, especially the IMSS-COPLAMAR hospitals.[10] To resolve the problem, the states had to contract personnel, paying their salaries out of their own funds; the states were often unable to offer these workers any benefits.

Financial decentralization. Prior to decentralization, the state health secretariats had little flexibility in the use of federal funds because these monies were earmarked for specific programs. Decentralization did not alter this situation significantly. In the very important area of human resources, the Health Ministry retained full control of the federal budget (Chapter 1000). Further, the Ministry continued to decide the type, salary, and location of new positions; and when a vacancy occurred, a state could only replace the worker after negotiating the new appointment with the union (see note 9). States were not authorized to change the type of appointment; for example, they could not replace a nurse with an x-ray technician even if the change was technically justified.

The decentralized states did, however, gain some degree of financial autonomy. After receiving authorization from the Health Ministry, states could transfer line-item funds within but not across each chapter of the budget (see table 2.4). For example, with authorization they could purchase medicines instead of office supplies, or use funds earmarked for vehicle maintenance to purchase furniture. Additional financial autonomy was to be achieved through the Health Ministry's pledge to increase the allocation of funds to Chapter 4000, the only budget line that states could use at their discretion, though the amounts allocated to the states were very small. The Health Ministry also allowed decentralized states to freely use funds collected through user fees, which previously had to be remitted in their totality to the Ministry of Health. In exchange for these concessions, the states were required to raise their contributions to the state health budget (satisfying the IMF mandate to decrease federal spending).

---

severely limits the ability of the state secretaries of health to make significant changes in the health delivery system.

[10] The vast majority of primary health care clinics were staffed by personnel completing their period of social service.

Table 2.4. Disbursement Categories of the Federal Budget

Chapter 1000 — Personnel services
Chapter 2000 — Materials and supplies (drugs, labs, office supplies, food, uniforms
Chapter 3000 — General services (maintenance, rent, utilities, research, travel)
Chapter 4000 — Transfers
Chapter 5000 — Equipment and furniture (including vehicles)
Chapter 6000 — Public works

Within a few years the Health Ministry acknowledged that decentralized states had gained little control over the budget (SSA 1995). By the end of de la Madrid's presidency in 1988, the decentralized states controlled an average of about 23.4 percent of the budget, or 3 percent more than states that did not decentralize; and most of the funds to be used at the state's discretion were those in Chapter 4000. State contributions to the health budget did not increase as anticipated due, at least in part, to the country's severe economic crisis. According to González-Block et al. (this volume), the decentralized states' average contribution to the health budget prior to decentralization was 17.4 percent of the total budget, and the nondecentralized states contributed 5.6 percent; after decentralization, the decentralized states increased their contribution by 66 percent and the centralized states doubled theirs. However, using a different methodology and including IMSS-COPLAMAR expenditures, Birn (1996) arrived at the opposite conclusion. She documented that, on average, the states' share of total state health expenditures *decreased* by 37.5 percent in the decentralized states and even more in the nondecentralized states (see table 2.5).

Table 2.5. Aggregate State Spending as Proportion of Total Health Budget, 1985–1995

State Contribution to SSA Budget	1985	1986	1987	1985–1987 Avg.	1994	1995	1994–1995 Avg.
Nondecentralized states	13.6%	8.7%	8.0%	10.1%	6.5%	6.8%	6.7%
Decentralized states	26.1%	18.6%	18.9%	21.2%	13.6%	17.3%	15.5%

Source: Birn 1996: 11.

The most significant change in health financing was that decentralized states gained control over user fees, and these became an increasingly important source of funding. Prior to decentralization, states were required to send all funds collected through user fees to the Federal Welfare Agency (Beneficencia Federal), which was part of the Health Ministry.[11] After decentralization, most states required their health units to remit all user fees directly to the state health secretariat or the state treasury, which subsequently developed a system to redistribute those earnings according to the state's health needs. User fees, which in 1994 represented between 2.3 and 16.1 percent of state health expenditures (Birn 1996), allowed states to make a few decisions on their own. In general, the funds generated through user fees were used for some combination of the following: to hire additional personnel, to purchase supplies and medicines, and as personnel incentives to increase efficiency.

Programmatic decentralization. Designing health programs and defining protocols remained the responsibility of the federal government, while the states became responsible for their implementation. States were not allowed to offer services beyond those mandated by the federal government. For example, states had to adhere to the federal protocols for managing tuberculosis patients; that is, even if the states had the resources to offer a different treatment for patients who had developed resistance to traditional drug therapy, they were not allowed to do so. Thus, contrary to the claims of decentralization's promoters, decentralized states did not have the authority to adapt government programs to the needs of their populations. In addition, some states were inadequately prepared or did not have the resources to implement all the priority programs required by the federal level. Evaluations have shown that some health programs, such as vector control and malaria prevention, deteriorated after states decentralized; this occurred, for example, in Jalisco, Tabasco, Guerrero (Birn 1996), and Nuevo León.

The Health Law of 1985 established three categories of sanitary regulations: (1) those that were the responsibility of the federation, such as control of imported and exported products, addiction prevention and organ

---

[11] In some cases (such as Nuevo León), states refused to continue sending funds to the Federal Welfare Agency.

donation programs, and blood banks; (2) twenty-seven programs that were the responsibility of the federal government but were to be implemented by the states, such as control of communicable diseases, environmental health, family planning, occupational health, and social services; and (3) those pertaining to local sanitation, such as control of markets, hotels, restaurants, prostitution, local traffic, farms, swimming pools, and so on, that could be the responsibility of municipalities or states. According to the 1985 law, the decentralization agreements and the state-level consolidated development agreements would specify how and when the states would take responsibility for enforcing the sanitary regulations in category 2; and state health laws and subsequent agreements between states and municipalities would specify how local sanitation programs (category 3) would be managed (Martuscelli Quintana and Sandoval Hernández 1986).

In practice, the changes in sanitary regulation achieved during the first decentralization were minimal. While some decentralized states started taking on their new duties, they acted mainly as intermediaries; most programs were designed at the federal level, and sanctions and fines continued to be imposed and collected by the federal government.

Results of the First Decentralization Attempt

Within the Health Ministry—the only institution in the Mexican health system that was decentralized—decentralization accomplished very little. The states did not gain control over human resources, they had to implement programs dictated at the federal level and in accordance with federal protocols, they did not raise their share of financial allocations to health, and their control over financial resources was limited almost entirely to state contributions and funds collected through user fees.

Cardozo Brum (1995) studied the three official evaluations of the 1985–1987 decentralization attempt and concluded that the decentralized states were financially more dependent on the federal government in 1987 (for 80.7 percent of their funds) than they had been in 1985, when federal funds represented 69.7 percent of all state budgets. This author indicates that the methods used and data presented in these official documents do not provide an adequate basis on which to judge decentralization's net impacts on the accessibility, efficiency, and quality of the system.

In 1992 and 1993, Cardozo Brum conducted her own evaluation of the decentralization process and concluded that decentralization had not had any significant positive impact and that decentralized states had lost the positive advantages that initially had made them suitable for decentralization (Cardozo Brum 1995). Other authors concurred (see chapters 3 and 4 in this volume), asserting that decentralization had not accomplished its objectives and attributing its suspension by the incoming administration of Carlos Salinas de Gortari to the public outcry over the deterioration of the IMSS-COPLAMAR program and other health services.

The deterioration of health services should not be attributed solely to decentralization policy, however. The reform was introduced during a period of severe financial crisis, and the absorption of IMSS-COPLAMAR added a new financial burden to the already impoverished state health secretariats. Federal health expenditures, which equaled about 3.7 percent of GDP during 1977–1982, dropped to 3 percent during 1983–1987. As unemployment figures rose, the social security institutes saw a reduction in the number of their beneficiaries, and the newly uninsured became users of state health secretariat services. The per capita health expenditure for the uninsured between 1982 and 1986 was reduced by over 60 percent (Laurell 1997: 28), meaning that the state health secretariats had to serve more people with fewer resources, and this may explain some of the deterioration in state health services.

The outcome of decentralization could have been different, at least in some states, if the absorption of IMSS-COPLAMAR had not taken place at a time of economic contraction and if the states had maintained their former funding levels. González-Block and colleagues (this volume) have also suggested that the IMSS's reluctance to let the state health secretariats manage the IMSS-COPLAMAR program negatively affected the decentralization process. The World Bank seemed to be oblivious of the failure and affirmed the following in 1991: "The health system has already been decentralized to the state of Guerrero with good results and the process will be completed in Chiapas, Hidalgo, and Oaxaca, monitored under the Basic Health Project (Report No 8927-ME)" (World Bank 1991: 16). As discussed by Anne-Emanuelle Birn in this volume, in Oaxaca decentralization was stopped for political reasons soon after its initiation, and it is difficult to characterize decentralization in Guerrero as successful.

A HIATUS IN DECENTRALIZATION, 1988–1994

Decentralization was included in Mexico's 1989–1994 National Development Plan and 1990–1994 Health Program, but a majority of researchers agree that there was little support for health decentralization during the administration of President Carlos Salinas de Gortari. The Salinas government largely disregarded the decentralization process initiated by the preceding administration (Flamand Gómez 1997: 27). In fact, the discretionary funds available to decentralized states under Chapter 4000 of the budget were decreased even as an improving economy was supporting an increase in the related categories of the federal budget and as the federal government was designing and implementing new vertical health programs such as a program to improve maternal and child care (Birn 1996).

The hallmark program of the Salinas administration was the National Solidarity Program (Pronasol), which had three objectives: to improve the living conditions of marginalized groups, to promote balanced regional development, and to support and strengthen the participation of social organizations and local authorities. Pronasol was designed to combat poverty, and it covered activities such as improving nutrition, legalizing land titles and housing, improving health and education, providing potable water and electricity, and building agricultural infrastructure.

During the Salinas years, multilateral banks were financing programs similar to Pronasol in many countries under the rubric of Social Investment Funds (SIFs); these programs were aimed at softening the impacts of structural adjustment and cuts in social spending on the poor. Following the SIF process, a community group would submit a proposal, and program officials would evaluate it and negotiate the project design with the community group. Once a project was approved, funding was channeled to the community group. In the case of Pronasol projects, however, evaluation and funding took place with little or no involvement of local and state authorities or participation by the relevant government ministries. Communities favored the SIF approach because of its streamlined process and the speed of the government's response.

SIF projects, including those of Pronasol, did, however, have three important weaknesses: (1) the sustainability of projects, especially infrastructure projects, was jeopardized by the failure to involve the ministries; (2) the ministries' prestige and authority were often undermined because significantly more funds were channeled through the SIFs than were allocated to the ministries; and (3) the allocation of funds tended to be very arbitrary, often responding to political rather than technical priorities.

During its first two years, Pronasol was run directly (and discretionarily) out of the Office of the President, which allocated funds directly to community groups, bypassing governors, municipal presidents, and relevant ministries. At the end of 1991, Salinas created the Ministry of Social Development (SEDESOL) to run the program, which, because of its large budget (US$500 million in 1989 and rising to US$2.2 billion in 1993), soon became the most visible ministry of this administration (Rodríguez 1997: 77–79). To underline the program's importance, Salinas appointed Luis Donaldo Colosio, president of the PRI and future presidential candidate, to head SEDESOL.

The Office of the President still determined who would receive funds. Although the administration claimed that the direct transfer of funds to community groups reflected Salinas's interest in decentralizing, it was in fact a mechanism of political centralization to strengthen his political power and control of the country. This assertion is supported by the fact that at least sixteen constitutionally elected governors stepped down during Salinas's term, some because they opposed how National Solidarity Program funds were being allocated (Rodríguez 1997: 25). Traditionally, Mexico's president decided how to distribute the budget, but governors enjoyed substantial discretionary power to make allocations within their states. By bypassing governors and state secretariats, Pronasol weakened their visibility and prestige—in effect, undermining the political base of elected state political leaders, the traditional holders of regional power. It is not clear whether World Bank staff became aware of Salinas's political machinations, but the Bank remained willing to support him because he had embraced its neoliberal economic principles and had privatized hundreds of state-owned industries and the *ejidos*.[12]

---

[12] The *ejidos* were created after the 1910 Revolution to satisfy the peasantry's demand for land. Land was expropriated from haciendas and distributed to landless peasants who had usufruct of the land and could pass this right to their descendants. Ownership of the land remained with the central state. When a hacienda was expropriated and its land distributed to peasants, the latter were organized as an *ejido*. Each *ejido* had its own elected council with

The World Bank's position regarding parallel administrative structures is interesting. On the one hand, the Bank was highly critical of programs that responded to the political ambitions of new administrations, because such programs could become "disruptive when changes in administration or economic circumstances occur. The most glaring example in Mexico was the collapse of COPLAMAR, administered out of the President's office during the Lopez Portillo administration" (World Bank 1991: 10). The Bank was critical of COPLAMAR despite its success in the health sector. On the other hand, the Bank was fully supportive of Pronasol and lent it millions. Even though this program was run directly out of the Office of the President, the Bank affirmed that it was fully integrated with the regional planning system and that it was the basis for a second decentralization effort (World Bank 1994).

It is very possible that Salinas outsmarted World Bank officials, who were unaware how the Pronasol loan was used to centralize power and paralyze the decentralization begun by López Portillo, or perhaps the Bank did not care about how its loans were used. At the end of the Salinas presidency, Pronasol suffered the same fate as the programs that the World Bank had criticized: it was terminated. In the health sector, no Pronasol-related intervention could even remotely compare to the success achieved by IMSS-COPLAMAR.

In the late 1980s, health districts (*jurisdicciones sanitarias*) became the cornerstone of an effort led by the Pan American Health Organization to develop local health systems (SILOS) (Birn 1996; Flamand Gómez 1997: 37). Health districts are administrative subdivisions of the state health services that were created in the early 1980s to facilitate the supervision and management of the health centers, but which did not have any other administrative authority and did not manage any resources. The health districts are not legal entities. Geographically, their boundaries do not coincide with any other administrative subdivision, and most districts serve several municipalities (except large urban areas such as Monterrey, where one municipality is divided into several districts). Tabasco is the only state where health districts and municipalities overlap.

---

authority regarding water distribution, access to credit, and other communal decisions.

The SILOS initiative responded to the widely accepted principle that health has to be achieved through multisector interventions that include services such as public health, medical care, education, nutrition, sanitation, recreation, and adequate housing and employment. Theoretically, the SILOS would coordinate resources received from all sectors and assume responsibility for improving the health of a population in a given geographical area; in Mexico, these areas were made to coincide with the health districts. While the principle behind the local health systems was sound, their implementation was seldom successful; ministries were unwilling to transfer their resources to the health sector because this meant a loss of control. It is not surprising that in Mexico the SILOS had very small budgets and their health impact was negligible. Nevertheless, to emphasize his commitment to communities, Salinas endorsed the SILOS program, a decision that many interpreted as support for the health districts. A few years later, the Pan American Health Organization replaced SILOS with the Healthy Municipalities program, premised on the same principle but based in the municipalities rather than the health districts. It, too, has had very small budgets, and its future is uncertain.

RETAKING THE DECENTRALIZATION LEAD: A RENEWED EFFORT, 1994–2000

Ernesto Zedillo (1994–2000) assumed the Mexican presidency in the midst of a deep economic crisis that had grave political implications for the PRI. To emerge from the crisis, Zedillo had to open the country's political system to true competition. The key element of his government was New Federalism, a far-reaching program that embraced several areas: reform of the judiciary and of the revenue-sharing system, a reduction in the powers of the presidency, institutional strengthening of state and municipal governments, decentralization, and electoral reform.

Plans for the health sector were described in Zedillo's Health Reform Program (1995–2000), which identified decentralization as a key component. Decentralization would help achieve the following objectives: (1) improve efficiency by allowing the state health secretariats to allocate resources to cost-effective interventions tailored to the population's specific needs; to that effect, states were encouraged to complement the nationally defined basic health-care package with interventions of particular interest to the state; (2) shift responsibility for provision of services to the states and render state officials more accountable to their communities; (3) eliminate some of the bureaucratic procedures that slow decision making; and (4) establish a more equitable system for distributing federal resources to the states.

As was the case during the de la Madrid administration, Zedillo's decentralization was actively promoted only within the Health Ministry and did not affect services provided by the social insurance networks. Because Zedillo had learned a lesson from the first decentralization, he did not attempt to include IMSS-COPLAMAR this time around. Zedillo's reform aimed to increase the equity, quality, and efficiency of the health delivery system by optimizing the use of existing infrastructure through better integration of existing health care delivery networks (mainly SSA, IMSS, and ISSSTE) and through expanded health-care coverage.

To this end, IMSS offered a new insurance plan for informal workers, such as small business owners, the self-employed, and peasants. However, the new insurance plan enrolled only a few thousand families. A variety of factors explain its failure to recruit potential beneficiaries, such as a lack of health insurance culture among low-income workers, administrative hurdles, and the limited interest of some IMSS officials. It had been expected that, as potential beneficiaries enrolled, the number of users of Health Ministry services would decrease and the quality of the Ministry's services would improve. To increase equity and expand coverage, the Ministry of Health defined a package of twelve basic services that all state health secretariats had to offer free of charge to the uninsured.

As in other countries, the basic package responded to a World Bank initiative, and its definition was partly financed by a World Bank loan. The included services were: (1) basic sanitation (at the household level); (2) family planning; (3) prenatal, delivery, and postpartum care; (4) nutrition and child growth monitoring; (5) immunizations; (6) home management of diarrhea; (7) family deparasitation treatment; (8) management of acute respiratory infections; (9) prevention and treatment of tuberculosis; (10) prevention and control of hypertension and diabetes mellitus; (11) accident prevention and management of lesions; and (12) community health education. State health secretariats could complement this basic mandatory package with other programs of their choice, to be paid for with state funds. The implementation of this package was not entirely successful; the execution of some interventions—community health education, for example—was difficult to monitor and evaluate, and the quality of the implementation of others programs was questioned. For example, according to an official of the U.S. Agency for International Development (USAID), several states failed to procure medicines for the treatment of tuberculosis.[13]

By the end of the 1990s, the Pan American Health Organization had certified that 100 percent of the Mexican population had access to services, but, as documented in some of the case studies included in this volume, people complained that the basic package of services was very limited and could not even be labeled as simplified primary care. To increase access, some states organized mobile clinics that traveled periodically to remote areas. Politicians representing remote communities claimed that the mobile units were not always there when people needed them, and they disagreed with the official version that all Mexicans had access to health services.

The Decentralization Agreements

On August 20, 1996, the federal government, the thirty-one state governments, the Federal District, and the National Union of Health Ministry Employees signed the National Agreement for the Decentralization of Health Services (Acuerdo Nacional para la Descentralización de Servicios de Salud). According to this agreement, the states were to be responsible for facilitating access to health services for all uninsured. The next step was for each state to sign a Coordination Agreement for the Decentralization of Health Services (Acuerdo de Coordinación para la Descentralización Integral de los Servicios de Salud) with the federal government and to negotiate specific conditions for decentralization in each state (López Bárcena and Real Mata 2001).

Coordination between the states and the federal government would continue to occur through the National Health Council, created in 1986 during the first decentralization wave and whose structure and role remained ill defined. During the second decentralization, it was agreed that the National Health Council would include the health minister, four under-

---

[13] Personal communication with a USAID employee, El Paso, Texas, January 20, 2003.

secretaries, legal advisers to the Health Ministry, and the directors of all the state health secretariats. The Council's mission was: (1) to consolidate the national health system and assist state health systems, (2) to consolidate the decentralization of services for the uninsured, (3) to determine standards to evaluate service provision, (4) to facilitate the exchange of experiences among states, and (5) to seek innovative health financing mechanisms. However, in reality, the Council's main functions were to transmit information and instructions from the Health Ministry to the states and to support an exchange of experiences among states. The Council was, and continues to be, a useful communication instrument, but it cannot be characterized as a forum in which states can influence Health Ministry decisions.

To facilitate the decentralization process, the Health Ministry defined 184 functions to be transferred to the states, produced operational manuals, and trained the state personnel who would be responsible for implementing each function. The documents produced by the Health Ministry and the National Health Council to guide the decentralization process were compiled in a manual (*Manual de lineamientos generales para la descentralización*) which included eighteen appendices (López Bárcena and Real Mata 2001). The decentralization of health services required modifying federal and state laws and regulations, especially those referring to health and public administration. A temporary three-person state decentralization unit (UDE) was created within each state health secretariat to facilitate the decentralization of all resources and to provide information on the progress of the decentralization effort to those advising the Ministry of Health and the National Health Council.[14] The next five subsections analyze the complexity of the implementation process: organizational structure, physical infrastructure, and decentralization of financial resources, human resources, and programs.

Decentralizing organizational structure. The National Decentralization Agreement of 1996 required the creation of state health boards. In most states (twenty-six of thirty-two), these were presided over by the governor;

---

[14] The UDEs have facilitated transfers of human and financial resources, infrastructure, and equipment; the development of by-laws and organizational and procedural manuals; and the development of the State Health Programs.

in three cases (the Federal District, Veracruz, and Oaxaca) by the state secretary of health; and in another three (México State, Morelos, and Tlaxcala) by the secretary of administration, secretary of welfare, and a coordinator general, respectively (López Bárcena and Reyes Nájera 2001). Each state determined the composition of its state health board, but all had to include one representative from the federal government and one from the SNTSSA.

As the case studies in this volume illustrate, the State Health Boards are still relatively recent creations, and their mostly symbolic role is often limited to approving plans and suggestions made by the state secretaries of health. Similarly, state legislatures have little input in the health sector; with a few exceptions, their activities are restricted to solving the individual health problems of their constituents.

Following the World Bank's neoliberal health model, the National Decentralization Agreement stipulated that the core function of the state health secretariats was to regulate state health systems and ensure that those without insurance had access to services. This agreement created a decentralized public agency (OPD) in each state, which was responsible for operating the state's health services. As an autonomous agency, the OPD would have its own chief operating officer, who reported to the state secretary of health. The state health secretariat had the flexibility to purchase services for the uninsured through contracts with any public or private health care provider, including IMSS, the other social security programs, and the OPD. This modality of medical care delivery anticipated that sectoral efficiency would be enhanced through competition among providers. However, the model was never implemented, and the organizational structure of the state health secretariats remained virtually unchanged. The health secretariats continued to favor activities related to service delivery over regulation—partly because this is what they knew how to do, but also because the regulatory responsibilities and procedures were ill defined, and, consequently, financial resources and personnel could not be easily obtained.

During the second decentralization, several state health secretariats elevated their revenues by increasing the number and value of contracts for providing medical care to municipal government employees, social security beneficiaries who for reasons of distance could not easily access IMSS clinics and hospitals, and groups of uninsured. There is no information about how well these contracts have been operating and how they might be improved.

Decentralizing physical infrastructure. The transfer of federal resources to the states was formalized via a Certificate of Conveyance (Acta Complementaria de Entrega y Recepción). Lengthy negotiations typically preceded the signing of this document, and it was not until early 1999 that *actas* for the transfer of buildings and equipment had been signed with all states (see table 2.6). The actual transfer of approximately 7,370 buildings and 1,372,497 pieces of equipment took even longer (Real Mata 2003: 227). A key obstacle was the absence of documentation that established federal ownership of the properties. In some cases, the federal government had been using municipal or communal buildings for years, and locating the owners and arranging for the properties' transfer to the states was no easy task. Equipment transfers required a time-consuming updating of inventories, but state health officials saw these efforts rewarded because they could now dispose of obsolete equipment within the state instead of having to return it to the Federal District. Even so, many governors were reluctant to accept the newly transferred resources, fearing that, as had happened in the 1980s, they would be inheriting problems, such as old buildings in need of repair, without gaining the resources to address them.

Financial decentralization. After a Coordination Agreement for the Decentralization of Health Services had been signed with each state, the federal government began to transfer health funds from the federal budget directly to the state treasuries instead of routing them through the Health Ministry. To enable this procedural change, in 1997 Congress amended the Fiscal Coordination Law (Ley de Coordinación Fiscal) and created the special Health Care Savings Fund (FASSA) under Section 33 of the federal budget. FASSA funds remained earmarked for specific purposes for the first year, but beginning in 1998 the state health secretariats (in theory, the state health boards) could decide how to spend all FASSA funds except for personnel funds (which continued to be earmarked), and they were allowed to move funds within and between the other budget categories appearing in table 2.4. The state health secretariats could also use unspent personnel funds (left because of unfilled positions or absenteeism) to cover the costs of the newly contracted obligations that resulted from bringing state employees' benefits in line with those of federal employees. Examples include the vacation stipend and end-of-year bonuses given to federal employees but not previously enjoyed by state workers. State treasuries were also given responsibility for issuing payroll checks, something previously done by the federal government.

Table 2.6. Dates on Which States Signed Conveyance Certificates for All Federal Resources

State	Date
Campeche, Durango	January 31, 1997
Nayarit	February 3, 1997
Colima, San Luis Potosí	February 6, 1997
Baja California Sur, México State, Quintana Roo	February 14, 1997
Tlaxcala	March 10, 1997
Sinaloa	April 10, 1997
Nuevo León	May 23, 1997
Coahuila	May 30, 1997
Michoacán	June 2, 1997
Tabasco	June 9, 1997
Sonora	June 17, 1997
Oaxaca	July 15, 1997
Morelos	July 22, 1997
Guerrero	July 23, 1997
Guanajuato	August 5, 1997
Tamaulipas	August 19, 1997
Federal District	August 29, 1997
Aguascalientes	September 4, 1997
Puebla	September 23, 1997
Querétaro	September 24, 1997
Yucatán	October 24, 1997
Veracruz	November 4, 1997
Jalisco	March 9, 1998
Zacatecas	May 13, 1998
Hidalgo	June 30, 1998
Baja California	August 4, 1998
Chiapas	December 2, 1998
Chihuahua	February 1, 1999

Source: López Barcena and Real Mata 2001: 27.

Funds were transferred as soon as the state health boards approved the budgets presented by their respective state health secretariats. The health secretariats were accountable only to the state legislatures for how they used these funds; they had to adhere only to state law and were audited by state comptrollers. In 1998 the states directly received 66.4 percent of the federal budget (including funds for special programs such as Progresa and PAC that were supported by international agencies); by 1999 the states' share was 70.1 percent of a total budget of 33.78 billion pesos (Ares de Parga 2001).[15] All procurement functions were transferred to the states and had to be conducted in accordance with state procedures. In some states the procurement of health goods was carried out by the state comptroller's office, while in other states the health secretariats handled purchasing.

The basis for the allocation of federal funds to the health sector did not change significantly and continued to rest primarily on historical budgets that were highly inequitable (see table 2.7). The state with the highest federal per capita allocation received nine times more than the state with the lowest per capita allocation, and, according to González Pier (2003), those states with the greatest need received the smallest federal contributions. The only modification to the allocation formula was that each state was guaranteed its historical budget, adjusted for inflation. All remaining funds were allocated according to a formula that favored the states that received the lowest proportional share. The equity impact of this effort has been minimal because health budget allocations did not grow as expected and barely sufficed to cover the historical state commitments.

The states' contributions to their health budgets varied widely and contributed further to health inequities. The state with the highest per capita allocation contributed 156 times more than the state with the lowest per capita allocation (González Pier 2003). State contributions, including monies collected through user fees, represented on average about a fourth of total state health expenditures. Some states increased contributions to their health budgets following decentralization, but these increases were, and continue to be, constrained by the states' inability to raise funds. In the absence of a fiscal reform, state budgets will continue to be highly dependent on federal transfers (Merino 2003).

---

[15] This represents a significant change; in 1995, decentralized states were managing 23.4 percent of their budget, and nondecentralized states, 20.4 percent.

Table 2.7. Per Capita Federal Allocations to State Health Budgets, 1996–2000 (in pesos)

State	1996	1997	1998	1999	2000
Aguascalientes	263.6	411.5	552.3	608.9	891.5
Baja California	268.4	433.6	551.1	604.7	830.9
Baja California Sur	271.7	440.5	700.2	591.0	785.3
Campeche	469.7	721.2	930.7	1052.5	1442.1
Coahuila	230.3	371.1	490.9	527.6	732.2
Colima	237.1	372.4	558.3	531.6	796.7
Chiapas	322.1	475.3	612.0	658.3	911.2
Chihuahua	212.8	387.3	547.8	623.1	859.6
Durango	237.7	388.1	510.2	564.3	772.9
Guanajuato	162.9	277.1	367.8	409.1	573.0
Guerrero	204.4	301.5	393.8	438.7	608.8
Hidalgo	217.6	302.1	404.7	456.6	616.1
Jalisco	150.3	279.6	369.3	421.6	623.5
México State	165.7	256.5	325.4	421.2	556.2
Michoacán	239.6	378.3	467.1	536.5	732.2
Morelos	167.3	300.8	387.6	417.6	570.4
Nayarit	295.2	385.9	512.6	566.0	776.0
Nuevo León	153.0	226.1	276.4	298.6	399.8
Oaxaca	353.3	432.8	553.6	617.1	836.2
Puebla	196.5	261.9	352.1	400.5	553.9
Querétaro	196.6	329.9	422.2	474.5	673.2
Quintana Roo	285.3	512.2	602.8	716.1	1035.8
San Luis Potosí	265.9	355.7	489.5	549.3	769.5
Sinaloa	268.0	424.9	528.1	579.1	801.5
Sonora	275.5	476.8	622.5	675.7	914.5
Tabasco	110.9	203.1	267.6	287.4	410.8
Tamaulipas	262.6	491.7	661.9	736.0	1025.2
Tlaxcala	225.6	360.2	450.7	507.9	750.0
Veracruz	185.4	322.6	432.5	507.3	706.3
Yucatán	362.6	577.4	753.0	823.1	1150.0
Zacatecas	238.8	346.7	449.7	486.5	668.9
Federal District	130.5	198.5	230.2	233.6	326.3
National Average	238	375	493	541	753
Standard deviation	74	111	148	160	222
Minimum	111	198	230	234	326
Maximum	470	721	931	1052	1442

Source: Moreno Jaimes 2001.

Some state health secretariats were able to broaden their revenue base through contracts with municipalities and social security funds. The monies collected through such contracts were lumped together with those generated through user fees in an improperly labeled "user fees" category. As had happened in the first decentralization, state-generated funds were used at the discretion of the state health secretariats. In general, a large share (about 85 percent) was returned to the health facilities to reward the productivity of their workers, to improve the facilities, to purchase drugs and sundries, and to be held in reserve as petty cash. Another fraction (about 10 percent) remained with the state secretariats, and a small share (5 percent) was sent to the Federal Welfare Agency. State officials suggested that if they lost control over user fees, they would have difficulty retaining essential personnel, maintaining a stock of medicines and supplies, and preserving the amount and quality of services.

User fees were supposed to be set by each state health board according to a fee schedule developed by the Ministry of Health. However, the state health boards ignored the fee schedule and set fees based on their perception of the population's ability to pay. Health districts and hospitals followed suit and decided, without board approval, how much they would charge, and neither the state health secretariats nor the state health boards have challenged this practice.

Decentralizing human resources. The personnel problems that emerged in the second decentralization paralleled those that had appeared previously. The salaries, benefits, and working conditions of state personnel had to be upgraded to the level of federal workers. The National Decentralization Agreement specified that the federal government would shoulder the costs of the state employees' salary differential and new benefits, which totaled about 358 million pesos per year (López Bárcena and Real Mata 2001). All state workers were offered the ISSSTE social security benefits. Establishing uniformity in fringe benefits and working conditions was more difficult.

Following decentralization, there were four kinds of health workers: (1) some 138,328 who had always been federal workers; (2) about 25,202 state workers who were brought up to federal levels in terms of salary, benefits, and so on; (3) state workers who chose not to be homologized with federal

workers because they would lose certain benefits; and (4) temporary contract workers paid with state funds.

The management of federally funded positions was mixed. Only the
federal government could create new federally funded positions, promote
workers, or modify the job descriptions of the federal positions assigned to
each state. States could not exchange a federally funded position for another, even when such a change might produce savings, as in replacing a
physician with a nurse. However, location assignments within the state
became easier after decentralization because state health secretariats could
negotiate transfers with the local chapter of the SNTSSA. Salary increases
and workloads were negotiated at the federal level between the Health
Ministry and its union; the states did not participate in these negotiations.

Programmatic decentralization. States that complemented the federally
mandated package of basic services were required to implement the additional programs in accordance with Health Ministry protocols (Nigenda et
al. 2002: 79). Moreover, delivery of all vertical programs continued to be
supervised directly from the federal level, generating some unnecessary
expenditures and duplication in lines of command.

The main innovation in sanitary regulation was that the state health
secretariats could fine anyone who violated state or municipal sanitary
regulations, whereas before they could only carry out inspections and
report infractions to the Health Ministry, which would then levy the fines.
Several states attempted to decentralize responsibility for local sanitation
to the municipalities, but they had limited success. Municipal governments, especially in rural communities, did not want this responsibility
because they did not want to confront their constituents and risk losing
their friendship and/or political support.

Some states experimented with transferring limited decision-making
authority to health districts and municipalities. Although municipal decentralization was viewed as desirable, it was not found to be feasible, primarily because it would have required amending the General Health Law
(Article 4) to include municipal governments among those with regulatory
authority in health matters; as it now stands, the law only recognizes municipalities as providers of services (De Steffano 2001).

The majority of municipalities in Mexico implemented the Healthy Municipalities program, which represented an effort by the municipality (in coordination with other institutions, agencies, and citizens representing a broad array of interests) to improve the health conditions of the area through either environmental improvements or health promotion activities. Directors of the health districts were generally invited to participate in this initiative. In some cases, employees of the state health secretariat offered technical assistance, but only at the request of the municipality.

Achievements of the Zedillo Administration

It is undeniable that President Zedillo made an earnest effort to decentralize health services. FASSA was a major accomplishment in this direction. However, decentralization had little impact on improving equity, and Mexican policymakers have claimed that decentralization actually increased inequalities between the states (Frenk, Knaul, et al. 2004), in part because economic conditions did not permit establishing a sizable solidarity fund in the federal budget. The states were unable to increase their contributions to their health budgets because of limits on their ability to collect taxes, and they had to rely on user fees to raise funds. Wealthy states could contribute more to the health budget and could extract more in user fees than could poor states, contributing further to inequities among the states. The case studies in this volume also reveal that there were no efficiency gains and that the productivity of physicians and other health workers did not improve significantly despite the financial incentives these workers received from the states.

Progress in the transfer of physical infrastructure is indicative of the desire to move ahead with decentralization. Some states were concerned about receiving hospitals that required major rehabilitation without accompanying resources to cover the repairs. And decentralization to the health districts and municipalities did not move forward. Most health districts lacked the training to function effectively as autonomous entities, and the state health secretariats had neither the supervisory controls to ensure that the delegated decision-making authority would be used appropriately nor the auditing tools to curtail potential corruption. Like the states, the municipalities lacked the legal authority to levy the taxes needed to pay for local services, including health services. In addition, if decentralization to the municipalities were to be fully implemented, the health districts would become redundant. In this case, a major reorganization of health services would be required, creating new and difficult-to-resolve personnel problems.

The failure to implement the decentralized public agencies (OPDs) and to provide the state health secretariats with choices in contracting for medical services for the uninsured was indicative of the tendency of decision makers to design policies without considering the prerequisite conditions needed to ensure their successful implementation.

In sum, much was accomplished in the process of decentralizing the health sector, but much remained to be done by the incoming administration.

THE PRESIDENCY OF VICENTE FOX, 2000–2006

Vicente Fox was the first Mexican president elected from a party other than the PRI in seventy years, a testament to Zedillo's success in making the Mexican political system more democratic and pluralistic. President Fox named Julio Frenk, a former World Bank consultant and executive director of Evidence and Information for Policy at the World Health Organization, as his minister of health. Dr. Frenk had also worked previously at the Mexican Health Foundation (Fundación Mexicana para la Salud), a think tank founded in the 1980s by former Minister of Health Guillermo Soberón and funded by Mexican corporations. José Luis Bobadilla, a Mexican doctor working at the World Bank, identified the Foundation as the perfect partner for advancing the World Bank's health reforms in Mexico. The Foundation and the Bank soon identified their common interests and established a relationship of mutual benefit—to the point that in 1995 the World Bank requested its Latin American health officers to channel all consultancies for HIV programs in Latin America through the Mexican Health Foundation. The World Bank officers objected to this unprecedented request, and the idea was shelved.

In the 1990s the Mexican Health Foundation financed a large Health and Economy project headed by Frenk (Fundación 1994), which outlined a health system based on World Bank health policies. Several international advisers to the project were closely connected with the World Bank, including Bobadilla and Juan Luis Londoño, the Colombian health minister and advocate of Colombia's health reform.[16] Frenk hoped that President Zedillo would implement the ideas promoted in the project, but this did not happen. Frenk would have to wait until he was selected as Mexico's health minister in the Fox administration.

In 1997 Londoño and Frenk published a paper that outlined the principles of a health system model that reflected Londoño's experience in Colombia and the recommendations of the Health and Economy project. The basic principles of this model, labeled structured pluralism, would guide health policies during the Fox administration (Frenk, Knaul, et al. 2004).[17]

Under the health system envisioned by structured pluralism, the public sector would become a regulatory agency and would finance services for the uninsured through a new health insurance plan. This plan, the People's Health Insurance Program (SP), would cover the indigent and charge a sliding-scale premium (based on income) to the self-employed and other workers not covered by social security programs. According to the model, services for those covered by the various social security plans and the SP would be made available through an integrated network of existing public and private providers. Users could choose their own provider, opening service provision up to competition, which, according to the World Bank, increases efficiency and productivity. The Health Ministry would be the ultimate authority in the health system; IMSS and the other social security funds would cede control over the organization of medical care delivery for their affiliates; and the state health secretariats would be responsible for carrying out the Health Ministry's mandates.

After being named head of the Health Ministry, Frenk discovered that the IMSS was unwilling to sign on to a project that would take away its decision-making power and bring negative consequences for IMSS employees. In the face of IMSS opposition and a Congress controlled by an opposition alliance of left and center-left parties, the Health Ministry had to find new avenues for implementing a version of structured pluralism.

---

[16] Others closely related to the World Bank were Richard Feachem, Dean Jamison, and Christopher Murray.

[17] The Colombian reform also followed the principles of structured pluralism, but there are differences between the two. The Mexican reform includes significant adaptations to the national context; for example, Mexico has not fostered private third-party administrators.

Fox's National Health Plan, entitled Cooperative Federalism, included several decentralization objectives, including completing the decentralization of the Health Ministry. Achieving this objective, it was thought, depended on decentralizing service provision to the municipal level and distributing federal resources to the states more equitably (goals that previous administrations had failed to achieve). Yet by 2005 no attempt had been made to decentralize to the municipal level, and, as will be seen, decentralization to the state level was stalled. The National Health Plan also called for a deconcentration of the IMSS; the contrary occurred as the IMSS concentrated eight regions into three.

To set the stage for a more equitable distribution of federal resources and to find common ground with the opposition, the Fox administration offered the following: (1) the SP program, to be financed by a federal contribution to the states, with the amount based on the number of affiliated families; (2) a catastrophic insurance program for SP affiliates, also financed by the federal government; and (3) a solidarity fund that would balance existing inequities in the distribution of federal resources by favoring states with the highest mortality rates, highest state health-financing effort, and best health-sector performance (World Bank 2004).

After two years of piloting the SP, the Health Ministry prepared a bill to reform the General Health Law to include the innovations listed above. Congress passed the bill overwhelmingly (92 percent support in the Senate and 73 percent in the Chamber of Deputies) on April 20, 2003. The SP was officially initiated in January 2004, making any assessment of its success or viability as yet premature. The SP is free to families in the lowest two income deciles; families with higher incomes can join by paying a premium based on their income (table 2.8). The federal contribution per family should equal the per capita federal subsidy to social security programs, which in 2004 was at least 50 percent higher than the per capita allocation for the uninsured (Frenk, Gómez-Dantés, and Knaul 2004).[18] The state health secretariats also contribute to the SP, but the amount each state

---

[18] Official Health Ministry information about the SP program is not always clear, and figures are sometimes inconsistent. For example, Frenk, Gómez-Dantés, and Knaul (2004: 38) report that the SP family subsidy should be US$225, but the amounts vary by state on government Web pages, and none reaches the US$225 level (Comisión Nacional de Protección en Salud 2004a).

should contribute and the bases on which to assess the amount are not yet clearly determined.

Table 2.8. Yearly Health Insurance Premiums per Family by Income Deciles and Percentage of Families Enrolled in the People's Health Insurance Program as of June 30, 2004

Income Decile	Health Premium (in pesos)	Enrolled Families
I	0	65.3%
II	0	27.8%
III	640	5.7%
IV	1,140	0.9%
V	1,900	0.1%
VI	2,400	0.1%
VII	3,160	0.1%
VIII	3,780	0.0%
IX	5,040	0.0%
X	6,300	0.0%
Total		100%
Number of enrolled families (n)		799,902

Sources: column 2, Comisión Nacional de Protección en Salud 2004a; column 3, Comisión Nacional de Protección en Salud 2004b: table 6.1

The SP provides free coverage for 56 primary-care conditions, 35 hospitalization interventions, and 168 medicines (Comisión Nacional de Protección en Salud 2004b). It is expected that the package of services will be expanded periodically until it covers nearly all services and treatments except for "catastrophic" conditions (Rodríguez Pulido 2003: 244). Families who opt not to join the SP continue to receive health care through the state health secretariats, paying a user fee and purchasing their medicines.

Persons insured under the SP are to have catastrophic coverage through the federal Fund for Protection against Catastrophic Expenditures. As of early 2005, this fund had not yet been defined with sufficient specificity, and it was not known when it would become operational. However, as resources become available, it is expected that the list of catastrophic conditions will grow.

The plan for the SP is to enroll a maximum of 14.3 percent of the eligible population (or almost seven million people) each year starting in 2004.

By the end of 2004, over 1.5 million families had joined, with only 7 percent of them paying any premium.[19] By 2010, when the SP is to have been fully implemented and the entire population will be covered by one or another health insurance plan, Mexicans will be free to choose their health care provider from among any of the available public or private health networks.

The changes introduced in 2003 required that the Health Ministry separate the funds for medical services provision from those for regulatory activities and public health. FASSA monies are to be divided into two funds: FASSC (for community services) and FASSP (for personal services). However, the states should not receive less in total resources (FASSP plus FASSC) than the total amount received from FASSA in 2003.

The viability of the People's Health Insurance Program and its concomitant changes is yet to be tested. Federal government funding has not been secured to cover all of the newly acquired commitments, and the states have no legal authority to levy additional taxes to pay their still-undefined share. Leaving aside logistic problems, it is relatively easy to enroll users who do not have to pay a premium. Whether others who have to pay for services will enroll will depend on the state health secretariats' success in delivering the promised services, including medicines. It remains to be seen whether the SP will be able to instill an insurance culture among the low-income population; the absence of such a culture was partly responsible for the low IMSS enrollment rates among the self-employed in the 1990s. Families with very limited resources may not be willing to prepay for services that they are not sure they will need.

The federal per-family contribution available during 2004 was only about US$110, considerably less than the anticipated US$225, with the solidarity fund transfers to all the states totaling US$12.5 million.[20] This is

---

[19] This suggests that these people fall within the lowest two population deciles in terms of income. However, unconfirmed reports from the field have suggested that municipalities paid the premiums of some in higher income deciles in exchange for their votes during the elections.

[20] Some of the transferred funds were used to hire physicians to provide services in remote rural areas. These areas were previously served by new medical school graduates doing their required year of social service, but a decrease in the number of graduates had left some rural clinics without care.

too little to produce a significant impact. To date, little has changed, and there are questions about the program's success. For example, many rural areas lack support services such as labs and ambulances, and the logistics of a timely distribution of medicines and adequate storage are complex and costly. It could well be that the 2003 changes to the health system were accomplished with an eye to the 2006 elections, and the Fox administration is well aware that, unless the SP is well established before 2006, the chances that the program will survive beyond the end of the administration are small. It is a vicious circle: time pressure spurs improvisations, improvisations produce implementation constraints and failures, and these diminish the chances for continuity.

The SP and the other initiatives of the amended Health Law were prepared by a relatively small circle of persons in the Health Ministry, and these initiatives are being implemented as vertical programs. The state health secretariats have minimal authority to change the federal mandate. They can choose to join the SP or not, but once they join they have to offer the services dictated by the Ministry of Health. The states contract the needed physicians, but they are not allowed to incorporate these doctors as regular state employees; their contracts are temporary and must be renewed periodically. SP beneficiaries do not pay user fees, and as the number of beneficiaries increases, such fees—a resource that state health authorities view as a very important source of discretionary funds—will decrease. The loss of these funds will severely constrain state health authorities' ability to design and implement their own policies. Simply put, if the SP were fully implemented, state health secretariats would lose the little decision-making authority they have gained over the last twenty years.

Our analysis suggests that the Health Ministry introduced the 2003 reforms to align the Mexican health system with World Bank policies. In 2004 the Health Ministry began to contract with private medical providers for the SP, and the goal is eventually to contract in the same way with IMSS and ISSSTE. Once this is achieved, it will be easier to mandate that the social security programs allow their beneficiaries to choose providers from the private or public sector.

A 2004 World Bank document reflects the Fox administration's close proximity to the Bank's position. In order to reduce federal government expenditures, the Bank recommended that the federal government decrease its contributions to IMSS and ISSSTE, advice that the Fox administration followed. As occurred in Colombia, this policy weakened the social security programs that, according to neoliberal ideology, constrain free market competition and the development of the private sector.

There are more signs that Mexico's Health Ministry and the World Bank coincide in their views of Mexico's health sector. These two institutions are aware that the limited decision-making power the states achieved over the past twenty years of decentralization may now become an obstacle to the success of the SP program. For this reason, the Bank has shifted its position and now thinks that decentralization may not be useful:

> There are no doubts about the importance of decentralization to the state level in a country of the size and complexity of Mexico. However, the absence of a well functioning compact between the federal level and the state level can greatly contribute to fragmentation of health policy, increased inequality, and may reduce the accountability of states regarding the effective use of resources of the federation on services for the poor (World Bank 2004: 150).

Mexico's Health Ministry has echoed these sentiments:

> The decentralization of the delivery and financing of health services for the uninsured was extended to all states in the third generation of reforms [those introduced in 2003]. While this allowed the Ministry of Health to concentrate more on its stewardship role, the decentralization process continues to imply challenges in terms of capacity-building at the state level. Further, the decentralization has also exacerbated the financial inequalities between states, an issue that is being addressed in the 2003 reform (Frenk, Knaul, et al. 2004: 20).

Mexico's twenty-year history of decentralization supports the view of researchers (see chapter 1) that the World Bank promoted decentralization to reduce federal/central government expenditures and as a vehicle to privatize the delivery of health services. When privatization can be achieved

by other policies, as is the case in Mexico following the 2003 reform, the
need to decentralize is less compelling. The case to terminate decentralization is even more compelling if the authority that was transferred to the
states could become a barrier to the implementation of the 2003 reform. It
is in this light that we should understand the policy change regarding
decentralization in Mexico.

The story of decentralization in Mexico reached its end with the 2003
reform. After twenty years and billions of pesos in expenditures, decentralization has accomplished little. It has not increased efficiency, it has not
improved the quality of care in any measurable way, it has increased inequity, and health policymaking has not become more participatory. Decentralization could be a useful policy in some countries if policymakers have
a clear understanding from the very beginning of the functions they want
to decentralize, have the legal requisites and resources to implement it, and
design policies to compensate for the inequity that decentralization causes.
These conditions were not present in Mexico.

References

Ares de Parga, Rodrigo. 2001. "La descentralización financiera." In *Federalismo
    y salud en México: primeros alcances de la reforma de 1995*, ed. Juan Ramón de
    la Fuente and Joaquín López Bárcena. México, D.F.: Diana.
Barraca, Stephen. 2001. "Reforming Mexico's Municipal Reform: The Politics of
    Devolution in Chihuahua and Yucatán," *Journal of Law and Border Studies* 1,
    no. 1: 31–74.
Birn, Anne-Emanuelle. 1996. "Case Study of Mexican Health Care for the Unin-
    sured, 1985–1996." Report submitted to the Inter-American Development
    Bank, October.
Cardozo Brum, Myriam. 1993a. "La descentralización de los servicios de salud
    en México: hacia la amnesia total o hacia la recuperación de la política," *Ges-
    tión y política pública* 2: 365–91.
———. 1993b. *Análisis de la política descentralizadora del sector salud*. México,
    D.F.: Centro de Investigación y Docencia Económicas.
———. 1995. "La política de descentralización de servicios de salud: análisis de
    su proceso y evaluación de resultados." Unpublished report, June.
Comisión Nacional de Protección en Salud. 2004a. "Cierre presupuestal. Recur-
    sos transferibles del SPS al cierre 2004." México, D.F.: Secretaría de Salud.
    Accessed January 18, 2005.

————. 2004b. "Salud Seguro Popular. Catálogo de servicios esenciales de salud." México, D.F.: Dirección General de Gestión de Servicios de Salud, Secretaría de Salud.

Cornelius, Wayne A., and Ann L. Craig. 1984. *Politics in Mexico: An Introduction and Overview.* La Jolla: Center for U.S.-Mexican Studies, University of California, San Diego.

de la Madrid, Miguel. 1986. "Descentralización de la vida nacional." In *La descentralización de los servicios de salud: el caso de México.* México, D.F.: Miguel Ángel Porrúa.

De Steffano, Marco A. 2001. "Operación y competencia de las autoridades sanitarias." In *Federalismo y salud en México: primeros alcances de la reforma de 1995,* ed. Juan Ramón de la Fuente and Joaquín López Bárcena. México, D.F.: Diana.

Fajardo Ortiz, Guillermo. 2002. "Historia de la descentralización de los servicios de salud en México." Unpublished.

Flamand Gómez, Laura. 1997. "Las perspectivas del nuevo federalismo: el sector salud. Las experiencias en Aguascalientes, Guanajuato y San Luis Potosí." México, D.F.: Centro de Investigación y Docencia Económicas.

Frenk, Julio, Octavio Gómez-Dantés, and Felicia Knaul. "Salud: un diagnóstico," *Nexos* 317: 71–78.

Frenk, Julio, Felicia Knaul, et al. 2004. *Fair Financing and Universal Social Protection: The Structural Reform of the Mexican Health System.* México, D.F.: Secretaría de Salud.

Fundación Mexicana para la Salud. 1994. "Economía y salud: propuestas para el avance del sistema de salud en México." Final report. México, D.F.: Fundación Mexicana para la Salud.

Gershberg, Alec I. 1998. "Decentralization and Recentralization: Lessons from the Social Sectors in Mexico and Nicaragua." Final report. RE2/S02. Washington, D.C.: Inter-American Development Bank.

González Pier, Eduardo. 2003. "Federalismo en salud y reforma financiera en México." In *Federalismo y políticas de salud: descentralización y relaciones intergubernamentales desde una perspectiva comparada.* Ottawa and México, D.F.: Forum of Federations and Instituto Nacional para el Federalismo y Desarrollo Municipal.

Griffin, Charles. 1999. "Empowering Mayors, Hospital Directors or Patients? The Decentralization of Health Care." In *Beyond the Center: Decentralizing the State,* ed. S. J. Burki, G. Perry, and W. Dillinger. Washington, D.C.: World Bank.

Gutiérrez Arriola, Angelina. 2002. *México dentro de las reformas a los sistemas de salud y de seguridad social de América Latina*. México, D.F. Siglo Veintiuno.

Homedes, Núria, and Antonio Ugalde. 2005. "Why Neoliberal Reforms Have Failed in Latin America," *Health Policy* 71: 83–96.

Kern, R., ed. 1973. *The Caciques: Oligarchical Politics and the System of Caciquismo in the Luso-Hispanic World*. Albuquerque: University of New Mexico Press.

Krauze, Enrique. 1997. *Mexico: Biography of Power: A History of Modern Mexico, 1810–1996*. New York: HarperCollins.

Kumate, Jesús. 1989. "Descentralización de los servicios de salud a población abierta: situación actual." México, D.F. Mimeo.

Laurell, Asa Cristina. 1997. *La reforma contra la salud y la seguridad social*. México, D.F.: Ediciones Era.

Linz, Juan, and Alfred Stepan. 1996. *Problems of Democratic Transition and Consolidation: Southern Europe, South America, and Post-Communist Europe*. Baltimore, Md.: Johns Hopkins University Press.

Londoño, Juan Luis, and Julio Frenk. 1997. "Structured Pluralism: Towards an Innovative Model for Health System Reform in Latin America," *Health Policy* 41: 1–35.

López Bárcena, Joaquín, and Tlatoaní Real Mata. 2001. "Avances de la descentralización de los servicios de salud en México, 1995–1999." In *Federalismo y salud en México: primeros alcances de la reforma de 1995*, ed. Juan Ramón de la Fuente and Joaquín López Bárcena. México, D.F.: Diana.

López Barcena, Joaquín, and Rembrant Reyes Nájera. 2001. "Operación de los organismos públicos descentralizados." In *Federalismo y salud en México: primeros alcances de la reforma de 1995*, ed. Juan Ramón de la Fuente and Joaquín López Bárcena. México, D.F.: Diana.

Martuscelli Quintana, Jaime, and Sergio Sandoval Hernández. 1986. "Avances de la descentralización en material de regulación, y fomento sanitario." In *La descentralización de los servicios de salud: el caso de México*. México, D.F.: Miguel Ángel Porrúa.

Merino, Gustavo. 2003. "Descentralización del sistema de salud en el contexto del federalismo." In *Caleidoscopio*, ed. Felicia Knaul and Gustavo Nigenda. México, D.F.: Funsalud.

Moreno Jaimes, Carlos. 2001. "La descentralización del gasto en salud en México: una revisión de sus criterios de asignación." DAP 95. México, D.F.: Centro de Investigación y Docencia Económicas.

Nigenda, Gustavo, Rosario Valdez, Leticia Ávila, and José Arturo Ruiz. 2002. *Descentralización y programas de salud reproductiva*. México, D.F.: Casa Salud, Fundación Mexicana para la Salud, Instituto Nacional de Salud Pública.

Real Mata, Tlatoaní. 2003. "Balance de la descentralización de la política de salud en México: el Consejo Nacional de Salud." In *Federalismo y políticas de salud: descentralización y relaciones intergubernamentales desde una perspectiva comparada.* Ottawa and México, D.F.: Forum of Federations and Instituto Nacional para el Federalismo y Desarrollo Municipal.

Rodríguez, Victoria. 1997. *Decentralization in Mexico: From Reforma Municipal to Solidaridad to Nuevo Federalismo.* Boulder, Colo.: Westview.

Rodríguez Pulido, Raúl E. 2003. "Políticas de salud y federalismo." In *Federalismo y políticas de salud: descentralización y relaciones intergubernamentales desde una perspectiva comparada.* Ottawa and México, D.F.: Forum of Federations and Instituto Nacional para el Federalismo y Desarrollo Municipal.

Ross, Stanley R. 1955. *Francisco E. Madero: Apostle of Mexican Democracy.* New York: Columbia University Press.

Ruiz Massieu, José Francisco. 1986. "La descentralización de los servicios de salud: obstáculos y soluciones." In *La descentralización de los servicios de salud: el caso de México.* México, D.F.: Miguel Ángel Porrúa.

Soberón Acevedo, Guillermo, and Gregorio Martínez Narváez. 1996. "La descentralización de los servicios de salud en México en la década de los ochenta," *Salud Pública de México* 38: 371–78.

SSA (Secretaría de Salud y Asistencia). 1995. *Descentralización de los servicios de salud.* México, D.F.: Subsecretaría de Planeación.

World Bank. 1991. "Mexico: Decentralization and Regional Development Project for the Disadvantaged States." Report No. 8786-ME. Washington, D.C.: World Bank, March 4.

———. 1994. "Mexico: Second Decentralization and Regional Development Project." Report No. 13032-ME. Washington, D.C.: World Bank, August 19.

———. 2004. *Poverty in Mexico: An Assessment of Conditions, Trends, and Government Strategy.* Washington, D.C.: World Bank.

PART II

The First Attempt, 1983–1988

3

Decentralizing Health Services in Mexico: Formulation, Implementation, and Results

MIGUEL GONZÁLEZ-BLOCK, RENÉ LEYVA, ÓSCAR ZAPATA,
RICARDO LOEWE, AND JAVIER ALAGÓN

Decentralization involves the transfer of authority from a central administration to parastatal organizations, local governments, and/or nongovernmental organizations (Rondinelli and Cheema 1983). Various governments and agencies in developing countries have promoted decentralization as part of administrative reforms to increase equity and efficiency, in the belief that excessive centralization increases economic and social costs and can spur political unrest (World Bank 1987). The World Health Organization (WHO) thus sees decentralization as a way to enhance coordination and increase responsiveness to local needs through delegation of responsibility, authority, and resources to intermediate and community levels (WHO 1980). Further, decentralization has been praised as a way to attract community participation and promote local responsibility for health (Mills et al. 1987).

But decentralization is not a clear-cut concept. What at one level may be seen as administrative decentralization may, at another level, imply greater power to the central political authorities. This is the case with the form of decentralization called delegation, where a new parastatal entity is created at the margins of the central bureaucracy. By circumventing central bureaucratic interests and social and political pressures, delegation may enhance the central authority's power to target and deliver key social ser-

A somewhat different version of this chapter appeared previously in *Health Policy and Planning* (volume 4); this chapter is presented with the journal's permission.

vices. This power often implies highly centralized decision making, isolated from sectoral integration mechanisms or social participation.

Decentralization has usually been pursued for its supposed economic and political benefits, with less thought given to its putative advantages for health care. This is the case because administrative reform is a response to the prevailing economic and political context, and not a means of extending health coverage and improving equity, though these are the rationales that are usually given (Frenk and González-Block 1992). In effect, then, decentralization is a way to transfer some responsibilities for development from the center to the periphery and, consequently, to spread the blame for a failure to meet rural needs. This argument is particularly relevant in times of economic and fiscal crisis, when increasing social needs and dwindling central resources force the government to seek new forms of legitimation (Friedland, Fox Piven, and Alford 1978). Decentralization must be examined then as a strategy for shifting the costs for social services, protecting key political interests, and fashioning an image of democratic government.

This chapter explores the technical and political incentives for health services decentralization in Mexico and assesses its implications in the areas of finance, planning, and health services delivery and equity. The focus is on decentralization's short-term results in southern Mexico, the country's least developed area, a region comparable to the world's least developed nations.

CENTRALIZATION AND FRAGMENTATION OF THE HEALTH SECTOR

The centralization of health services delivery systems in Mexico was closely tied to the country's period of import substitution, which began with World War II. Health policy supported economic growth through abstract, technical approaches far removed from peasant organizations and more in line with the vertical, corporatist industrial leadership. Mexico's Ministry of Health (SSA) and Social Security Institute (IMSS) were created to implement these policies through greater federal financing and control. Indeed, the Health Ministry built hospitals across the country that were entirely dependent on federal funding and decision making, bringing state governments' share in health costs down from 50 percent to less than 10 percent. Although the IMSS was formally decentralized as a parastatal entity, the federation retained firm political control and used the IMSS as a powerful negotiating tool to control capital and labor.

In the early 1970s, Mexico's stagnating economy, growing social inequities, and widespread discontent with government prompted the central authorities to pressure the business sector to go along with a policy of "social solidarity," through which IMSS would collaborate with the federal government to provide preventive care and medical treatment to the organized peasantry. IMSS was to implement the program through its own administrative structure, with no controls from the Health Ministry or participation from local communities. Not surprisingly, once the political pressure on the central government eased, the program was all but terminated, with financing cut from 1.3 percent of the IMSS budget in 1976 to 0.3 percent in 1979 (Spalding 1980).

By the late 1970s Mexico's ruling Institutional Revolutionary Party (PRI) began to view centralization as a political liability. However, escalating poverty, together with the oil boom, led to a new wave of centralization, this time combined with mild efforts toward some coordination with regional organizations. On the one hand, institutions that were the recipients of delegated authority were strengthened and coordinated at the presidential level through an umbrella organization called the National Planning Group for Depressed Zones and Marginalized Groups (COPLAMAR). On the other hand, federal planning was deconcentrated through state-level Development Planning Committees (COPLADEs) and the linking of financial resources to state-level consolidated development agreements (CUDs).

In a drive to increase the coverage of health services delivery to the rural poor, the central government selected the IMSS, participating through COPLAMAR, to plan and institute more than three thousand clinics in Mexico's more remote areas within a two-year time frame. The program was to be financed with federal funds and would not be linked with the existing IMSS health program for urban workers. Although the rural clinics program had no legal or financial responsibilities for redistributive social solidarity, it was mounted on the same tracks and with the same social solidarity image as the previous program, which boosted the IMSS's welfare role.

The new wave of centralization meant that health issues and planning were not addressed by regional actors, furthering fragmentation in the health sector and preserving a redundancy in the services offered by IMSS and the Health Ministry. On the other hand, most Health Ministry representatives were unable to participate in complex state-level coordinating processes and thus were not able to profit from the monies distributed through the COPLADEs. Only the most developed states were able to benefit, turning the instruments of integral rural development into a regressive mechanism.

HEALTH SERVICES DECENTRALIZATION IN THE 1980s

Miguel de la Madrid assumed the presidency of Mexico in 1982, at the beginning of the deepest recession in the country's modern history. His administration was forced to cut the per capita health budget by 48 percent between 1982 and 1988, with the cuts falling heaviest on insured (formal-sector) workers and their families, a group that rose from 44.6 percent of the national population in 1982 to 52.1 percent in 1987. The insured population saw its per capita health expenditures reduced by 15.7 percent per annum between 1983 and 1987, at the same time that the uninsured population's per capita health budget remained nearly constant. Overall, the per capita health budget differential between the insured and uninsured populations fell from 3.62 to 1, to 1.39 to 1. This trend would constitute a major obstacle to the Health Ministry's pursuit of policies of sectorization and decentralization.

De la Madrid used Mexican constitutional federalism as a ready-made charter for deep political reform, positing devolution, deconcentration, and fiscal reform as his main strategies for strengthening the basic units of government (Beltrán and Portilla 1986). These strategies were to be coordinated by the head of the Ministry of Planning and Budgeting (SPP), who was also supposed to devolve to state governors the authority to coordinate the state-level field offices created during the preceding administration of José López Portillo (1976–1982). Thus, for the first time, the state governments' development plans were incorporated into an overall scheme, which allowed for a massing of financial resources to meet the economic crisis.

Before assuming the presidency, de la Madrid had served as minister of planning and budgeting. In that post, he had been concerned about the government's inability to provide high-quality health services within a well-coordinated structure, and he recognized that a root cause of the problem was the aggregation of multiple institutions into an unmanageable health sector. As president, therefore, he created the President's Health Services Coordinating Group to study options for achieving a national health system with universal coverage by incorporating the fourteen million people then estimated to be without any health services. The Coordinating Group's key recommendation was to combine sectorization and decentralization to achieve a strong health authority capable of resolving the problems that had accumulated over decades of centralized authority over a fragmented health sector (Soberón 1987).

However, groups that saw sectorization as a threat worked to thwart all attempts toward integration. For example, the leader of the Confederation of Mexican Workers (CTM) forced the administration to soften its definition of "integration," basing it on a formula of programmatic coordination that would guarantee the autonomy of the IMSS. And the IMSS proposed limiting fragmentation via a fusion of all federally funded rural health services around IMSS's own more efficient and qualitatively superior social solidarity infrastructure. The Health Services Coordinating Group questioned the validity of this suggestion, arguing that such an approach would only deepen the urban-rural dichotomy.

Recognizing that formidable obstacles stood in the way of implementing reform at the central level, the Coordinating Group, acting through the COPLADEs, established planning agreements with twenty state governors. Through these agreements, analysts were able to obtain information, ideas, and support for sectoral integration at the source of the problems and beyond the reach of the centralist power of national institutions, in effect combating fragmentation at the center with decentralization at the periphery.

While still president elect, de la Madrid adopted the Coordinating Group's proposal and prepared a national health law and a constitutional amendment to establish health as a universal right. The new charters were a means to legitimate the role of the Health Ministry as head of the health sector and to pave the way for a national health system.

De la Madrid's initiatives posed a threat to the IMSS, which would lose control over its prestigious Solidarity Program, thereby opening the door to redistributive demands like those than had surfaced in the early 1970s.

To avoid such an outcome, IMSS acted quickly to comply with the de la Madrid administration's philosophy of sectorization and decentralization, but on its own terms. IMSS implemented its own deconcentration plans by including the Health Ministry and other federal agencies in its state-level Social Solidarity Councils. This move channeled decentralization's momentum away from fusion and devolution and brought the federal government into a technical, paternalistic, and advisory role within the IMSS Solidarity Program. IMSS also vehemently argued that the Health Ministry was not capable of managing the social solidarity infrastructure and that the final result of integrative decentralization was bound to be negative.

Facing strong opposition to sectorization and decentralization, the Health Ministry set about formulating pilot projects for devolution and streamlining itself in preparation for its role as normative head of the health sector. As a preliminary step to fully fledged decentralization, the Ministry deconcentrated its field offices, giving them greater managerial responsibilities in areas such as planning and budgeting.

By 1984 the Health Ministry and IMSS had formulated a number of rival approaches to decentralization, and they appeared headed toward deadlock. To avert stalemate, de la Madrid decreed that the functions of the IMSS Solidarity Program would be fused with Health Ministry services in new entities that would fall under the authority of the state governments and the normative control of the Ministry (*Diario Oficial*, March 8, 1984). By the end of de la Madrid's term, only fourteen states had reached this stage in the decentralization process.[1] Together they accounted for about 40 percent of the uninsured population outside the Federal District (which did not decentralize) and 45 percent of health resources (Dirección General de Evaluación 1987).

Some factors that played into the decision to decentralize followed the dynamics of inter-institutional rivalry. Notably, most of the states to which authority was devolved were those with the least developed IMSS Solidarity infrastructure. This meant that IMSS was able to retain its health facilities and users in the remaining states, or 72 percent of its health centers and a serviced population of 6.5 million people. Decentralization was also fa-

---

[1] They were Aguascalientes, Baja California Sur, Colima, Guanajuato, Guerrero, Jalisco, México State, Morelos, Nuevo León, Quintana Roo, Querétaro, Sonora, Tabasco, and Tlaxcala.

vored by states that, for diverse historical reasons, had already achieved greater financial decentralization. Thus, prior to implementation, the selected states had contributed, on average, 17.43 percent of health expenditures, while those that would remain centralized contributed an average of only 5.58 percent. Basically, the Health Ministry aimed to decentralize those states where it encountered the least resistance from the IMSS and from state governors.

The implementation of decentralization also had a direct relationship to centralist political control and an inverse relationship to the pull of local or regional opposition forces. This is clearly demonstrated by the cases of Oaxaca and Guerrero. Oaxaca was the first state scheduled for decentralization, in the hope that decentralization might co-opt a statewide autonomist movement that was spinning out of control (Rubin 1987). Decentralizing health services seemed to offer the governor both the flexibility to manage resources to meet his political needs and the image of autonomy he needed to co-opt the groups that were questioning centralist dominance. However, the conflict continued to escalate, and the federal government applied its time-tested centralist muscle to quell it. The Health Ministry began to see decentralization more as a risk than an asset, and the decentralization plan for Oaxaca was aborted.

The IMSS, meanwhile, welcomed this outcome, given that Oaxaca contained that agency's largest concentration of Solidarity clinics. People in the Health Ministry also gave a sigh of relief, because they realized the huge complexities involved in decentralizing services that catered to a highly dispersed ethnic population which, moreover, had not been consulted about planned changes. In sum, it was determined that decentralization was not well suited for Oaxaca, a very underdeveloped state.

Although Guerrero and Oaxaca had comparable socioeconomic indicators and a similar number of Solidarity units, the central government felt that decentralization would work in Guerrero. Significantly, both the minister of health and his undersecretary for planning were Guerrero natives and strong candidates to its governorship (a post that the undersecretary assumed shortly after the decentralization plan was implemented). The decision to move forward in Guerrero confirms the highly centralist nature of decentralization policy despite official references to the governors' "political will" as the force driving policy implementation.

The suspension of the decentralization effort, which denied full decentralization to the fourteen states that had begun the process, can be explained in part by two key factors. The first was pressure from the IMSS to retain the Solidarity Program under its control; the second was a deepening of the 1985 economic crisis, which curtailed the federal government's ability to provide incentives to the states. The decision to suspend the decentralization process followed IMSS complaints about the deterioration in health services in rural areas of Guerrero, the state in which the IMSS had lost the most Solidarity clinics. IMSS took its complaints directly to President de la Madrid, who ordered an immediate evaluation of the decentralization effort. IMSS was able to convince the authorities that the changes in service indicators were the direct result of the new state health authority's inability to cope with decentralization, a view confirmed by a rather localized popular protest. De la Madrid ordered that decentralization be suspended pending a joint evaluation by the Ministry of Health and IMSS to suggest ways to remedy the problems. In the meantime, services in the decentralized states would be consolidated while the states pursued programmatic coordination to avoid a similar deterioration in service provision following decentralization.

DECENTRALIZATION'S RESULTS

The following discussion focuses on specific variables that can serve as indicators of the structural and process changes attributable to decentralization. The methodology allowed for a comparison of a decentralized and a centralized state within the same region, a possibility that emerged thanks to the break in decentralization's implementation, as discussed above. Through such a comparison, we can separate the effects of the economic crisis from those that were attributable to decentralization.

The study region includes the decentralized state of Guerrero and the centralized state of Oaxaca.[2] This region tests the adequacy of and obstacles

---

[2] This region contrasts with others in Mexico, which have fewer indigenous people, better communications, more urban populations, greater per capita income, and more industrialization, all of which make Mexico a middle-income country. The southern region, by contrast, shares traits with the poorest countries in Latin America, especially those in Central America.

to decentralized health planning and management in a particularly poor and underdeveloped area. Rondinelli, Nellis, and Cheema (1984) argue that decentralization is especially important in such regions in order to guarantee that health services are congruent with specific cultural and material realities. It has also been noted, however, that, given these conditions, local services are more likely to fall prey to traditionalist and authoritarian local interests and that the requisite administrative expertise may be lacking (Rondinelli and Cheema 1983).

Health institutions and programs in Guerrero and Oaxaca were polarized along the axes of political and administrative decentralization. Not only did Oaxaca's Solidarity Program remain under central administrative command, but it became even more centralized as officials grew weary of the early decentralization efforts in the state and ultimately reversed policy. Yet despite this policy reversal, the state legislature passed a local health law that enabled the governor to name a health secretary; he appointed the federal delegate to this post, thereby gaining some power over the federal health service machinery that could be used to implement his own health policy. The situation in Oaxaca, which resulted in only a limited administrative deconcentration of authority from the Health Ministry, yielded a more clearly defined charter for political decentralization.

For its part, Guerrero had strong centralist political muscle behind decentralizing health services to the state, a situation that facilitated the establishment of the Guerrero Health Secretariat. Decentralization even reached down to the municipal level, and Guerrero became the only Mexican state to sign decentralization agreements with most of its municipalities.

POLITICAL DEVOLUTION

Devolution is decentralization that confers or returns political authority to a lower governing unit (Rondinelli and Cheema 1983). Decentralization in Mexico was posited as this type of transfer, going beyond previous attempts at deconcentration and promoting a new, albeit limited, relationship between state health services, state governments, and the Ministry of Health.

State-level health services took a number of different forms, most of them designed at the center to comply with general norms and requirements. The options on offer included state health secretariats under the executive branch, health departments dependent on a ministry of wider scope, or parastatal organizations such as health institutes. Governors and state legislators could choose from among these options, selecting whichever best suited their policies and styles of government.

The state of Guerrero first adopted the model of a state-level health secretariat, which closely parallels the federal model. However, following the inauguration of a new governor, the state opted for a more decentralized parastatal agency, the Health Services Directorate, with its own semiautonomous governing council. This body aimed to circumvent the state-level bureaucracy and establish a tighter relationship with the center, given that none of its employees fell under the state's charters governing civil servants.

The states' freedom to institute changes created problems for the Health Ministry, which sensed that it was losing control over those in authority at the state level and that the human resources the Ministry had trained were going to waste. Furthermore, all administrative and technical posts were now open to state-level political negotiation, a situation that led to the existence of two rival factions in Guerrero, one controlling the governing council and the other, the leadership position at the Health Services Directorate. The resulting confusion limited mid-level functionaries' ability to develop plans and address problems. Furthermore, these functionaries had no ties with local-level politics, but they had also become alienated from the federal context in which they had previously moved freely. With time this situation led to increased control from the center, particularly following the center's appointment of the head of the Health Services Directorate.

The dichotomy between state and federal politics was present in Oaxaca as well, but the powers were more evenly balanced there than in Guerrero. The Oaxacan governor's appointment of the federal delegate as state secretary of health led to visible tensions between the demands of state authorities and those coming from the central government. As in Guerrero, mid-level employees identified more closely with the federal government, and none had strong local political ties. They resented the governor's interference and saw the federal delegate's new role as a distraction from more important responsibilities. Nevertheless, there were some positive results, such as increased federal involvement in state politics and, therefore, better coordination on local problems.

DELEGATION OF FINANCIAL RESOURCES

Two constants define the pattern shared by decentralized and centralized health service organizations: (1) the continued separation of federal and state sources of financing (with no state control over federal funds), and (2) the maintenance of the federal labor relationship with all "state" health workers across the entire state-level health structure. Thus, in terms of finance and control, all decentralized state health services became de facto parastatal agencies of both the state and federal governments.

Each state health service received direct funding from both the federal and state governments. The federal grant was allotted through monthly payments and distributed by state authorities according to a previously approved program budget. This gave state health services a degree of autonomy over expenditures, although a state government's power was clearly limited by the center's influence on programming and the state treasury's inability to access the federal funds.

Federal authorities justified the direct grants as a means of avoiding both the federal and the state governments' bureaucracies, thereby increasing the effectiveness of implementing national policies through local field offices. Through the direct grants, decentralization became more a measure to increase central control than a democratic principle or a response to political pressures from below. The center's retention of financial control thus offset the governors' newly strengthened power to appoint functionaries and the insertion of state health services within local politics.

State governments did not press for financial devolution because this would have carried more responsibility than they were equipped to handle. Despite fiscal and administrative reforms to strengthen local governments' revenue base, their share of federal appropriations was still meager and their own tax bases were weak. Assuming the financing of health services through such a fiscal transfer mechanism or through direct grants to the state was tantamount to accepting de facto most of the financial burden.

By retaining control of the financing mechanism, the federal government could allocate funds through channels isolated from other state-level legislative and executive politics at the same time that the federal government bestowed on the states the legal and political responsibility for their populations' health. Local governments—down to the level of the municipality—were also having to respond to demands from individuals, municipal authorities, workers' associations, and the federal government.

The state governments' new responsibilities began to transform their political relationship with the center. Formerly they had been passive recipients of (and experts at evading) demands for collaboration; now they began to demand resources from the center based on state-level health plans evaluated by the local legislator and submitted to the voters. On the other hand, wealthier states like Tabasco and Jalisco started to draw more monies from their own tax revenues, thus shouldering a greater share of health costs. The states' new political responsibilities were officially channeled through the National Health Council, where the decentralized state health authorities and federal minister of health exchanged views on finance and control.

Despite their increased political responsibilities, local governments in decentralized states did not have any more authority over financing than did those in states that remained centralized, even though all of them had to increase their financial contributions as the economic crisis progressed. The centralized states still showed a greater degree of financial decentralization, a situation congruent with the view that what occurred in the decentralized states was, in fact, federal financial delegation. It was noted above that decentralization policy gave preference to states whose governments contributed more toward health expenditures. Yet, as the economic crisis deepened, centralized states doubled their share of the financial burden, while decentralized states increased theirs by only 66 percent.

DECONCENTRATION OF PERSONNEL

All state health services employees, from janitors to the secretary of health, have remained on the federal payroll and within the federal labor relationship. This situation reflects the central authorities' unwillingness to challenge the corporatist trade union structure that defines labor's relationship with the federal government. The authorities felt that workers' rights should not suffer under decentralization. Further, no state governor was likely to accept new burdens on his or her state's payroll, and, more importantly, state governments could not offer the incentives required to deal with such a complex bureaucracy.

The federal government had to offer strong incentives to achieve the transfer of all Solidarity workers to the Health Ministry's payroll. These workers' salaries were adjusted to the IMSS pay scale, and many workers were tenured. The offer of better working conditions and ladder-ranked privileges brought about the transfer of 93 percent of the 3,969 Solidarity workers in the reformed states. Even so, labor conflicts did arise: because key Solidarity medical personnel were offered tenure within IMSS, there was a sudden drain on state personnel and a sharp decline in basic hospital services. The major labor conflict related to decentralization arose when the vertically structured anti-malaria campaign, in existence since 1956, was restructured horizontally.

The decentralization of personnel was limited to the deconcentration of authority for managing labor relationships. All high-level decisions, such as setting wage levels, were reserved for negotiation between federal government representatives and representatives of the National Union of Health Ministry Employees. However, the devolutionary context increased the scope and power of deconcentrated personnel decisions. The federal government "invited" state governors to be more concerned with "their" workers' problems and to consider these workers as part of their political constituency. In this way, high-ranking officials in state-level health services could receive economic incentives from the state government, over and above their federal salaries. Other forms of involvement were also encouraged, such as state oversight of workers' professional behavior and the curbing of corruption.

SECTORAL AND REGIONAL COORDINATION

A goal of the Ministry of Health was to strengthen the health sector's participation in the COPLADEs under the coordination of the state secretary of health or, in still-centralized states, the federal delegate. The COPLADEs were chosen as the most efficient way of matching resources to the states' identified priorities in a context that would include representatives of the health sector as well as authorities from the federal, state, and municipal levels (Soberón 1987).

An early concern of Health Ministry officials was the training of individuals who could operationalize the CUD funding agreements promoted by the Ministry of Planning and Budgeting through the COPLADEs. Ministry officials argued that a lack of training was fomenting a vicious circle of underdevelopment, in which only the best-trained functionaries in developed states were able to ask for and utilize federal monies channeled through the COPLADEs. Once properly trained, these new state secretaries of health would coordinate the development of state health plans by local authorities.

Despite efforts to achieve integration within the decentralized health sector, this goal proved elusive in both Guerrero and Oaxaca. Resistance to integration stemmed from these states' traditions of independent and centralized planning, which had been strengthened by the vertical and autonomous implementation of the Solidarity Program during the oil boom. Conflicts arose in the early stages of sector coordination in Oaxaca, as the IMSS claimed that it was covering the entire uninsured population through its Solidarity Program, thus threatening more than two hundred Health Ministry clinics with redundancy. When talks broke down between the two institutions, a planning officer delegated from the Ministry of Health simply wrote into the plan what he thought should be each institution's coverage. The state health plan thus complied with a blueprint supplied from the center. By contrast, in Guerrero, the health sector as a whole had a greater role in developing the state's health plan, even though the process was dominated by Ministry officials.

The establishment of the new, integrated, and decentralized health service administration in Guerrero led to an emphasis on sectoral planning and financial decentralization, but little attention was paid to regional coordination with other social policy agencies. The regional branches of COPLADE met only sporadically, and meetings were poorly attended. Negotiations with the population were structured vertically, and municipal presidents' petitions for new health centers were quickly denied, even though these officials offered to shoulder the costs of construction. On the other hand, the new decentralized administration made great efforts to establish decentralization agreements with most of the state's seventy municipal governments, exempting only the very poorest. These agreements sparked conflict when several municipalities called attention to the state authorities' failure to abide by past financial agreements and noted that local governments were being overburdened with responsibilities. By contrast, the economically important municipality of Acapulco had a financial agreement with the federal government and received its support directly from the same source, bypassing state-level negotiations. Thus, while the poor municipalities became truly decentralized financially, the wealthy ones effectively became further centralized.

The performance of the COPLADE in Oaxaca contrasts markedly with that of the Guerrero COPLADE. Once collaboration in the health sector became impossible because of the rift between IMSS and the Ministry of Health, the state government took over the Oaxaca COPLADE as a means of gaining control of the state's highly dispersed population. Oaxaca's eight regional planning subcommittees became very active beginning in 1984, and they involved Health Ministry delegates in discussions on a wide range of health-related topics, including epidemics control, nutrition, potable water, electricity, and drug supplies. In contrast, no delegates from the more important Solidarity Program were involved in these meetings.

DECENTRALIZATION'S IMPACTS ON EQUITY

Health officials and politicians frequently presented decentralization as a democratizing and redistributive policy, linked to the electoral promise of a more equitable society. Thus it was expected that, under decentralization, service distribution would respond more equitably to health needs.[3] To examine this proposition, we defined equity as the situation in which all population groups have equal probability of satisfying their health needs, as opposed to Musgrove's (1983) definition as simply the equal distribution of services. In the absence of reliable morbidity and mortality data, we chose an indirect approach to assess health needs. We used municipal-level census figures to identify risk factors for the prevalence of infectious diseases and infant mortality.[4] These variables were processed using principal

---

[3] Only public federally funded institutions catering to the uninsured population were analyzed; the social security institutions were not a target of decentralization. It is assumed that there was correspondence between the institutions and the populations they served, a situation that is generally true.

[4] The census indicators used for the stratification were illiteracy rate, rate of a language other than Spanish, rate of nonattendance of primary school among children from 6 to 12 years of age, overcrowding in sleeping areas, availability of sewerage, agricultural activities, degree of urbanization, and relative size of the 0–4 age group.

Table 3.1. The Noninsured Population and Some Per Capita Health Service Indicators by Socioeconomic Strata in Guerrero before and after Decentralization, and in Oaxaca, 1985 and 1986–87.

Strata	Noninsured, 1985	%	General First-time Consultations[a]			Total General Consultations[a]			First-time Pregnancy Consultations[b]			Complete DPT Vaccinations[c]		
			Before[d]	After[e]	%	Before[d]	After[e]	%	Before[d]	After[e]	%	Before[d]	After[e]	%
OAXACA														
1	157,644	7	0.49	.32	-34.9	0.12	0.07	-42.2	0.78	1.22	57.6	0.10	0.06	-38.6
2	596,499	26	0.29	0.30	1.6	0.12	0.11	-12.4	0.73	1.07	46.2	0.15	0.10	-30.6
3	1,315,969	56	0.31	0.29	-5.0	0.49	0.37	-24.5	0.88	0.90	2.6	0.17	0.14	-19.8
4	227,421	10	0.30	0.25	-16.6	0.77	0.50	-35.6	0.61	0.58	-6.0	0.26	0.19	-27.6
5	40,986	2	0.48	0.38	-21.0	0.59	0.56	-4.4	0.58	0.84	45.3	0.18	0.13	-28.4
Total	2,338,519	100	0.32	0.29	-9.2	0.40	0.29	-27.3	0.80	0.94	17.5	0.17	0.13	-23.2
GUERRERO														
1	289,909	18	0.29	0.46	58	0.19	0.69	257	0.38	1.26	230	0.19	0.22	18.6
2	123,809	8	0.15	0.26	77	0.11	0.39	259	0.29	0.95	220	0.19	0.20	5.2
3	1,056,031	66	0.25	0.22	-12.0	0.30	0.32	7.4	0.63	0.76	20.7	0.20	0.17	-16.5
4	109,232	7	0.35	0.25	-29.4	0.44	0.34	-20.9	0.44	0.38	-14.0	0.17	0.08	-52.9
5	17,034	1	0.22	0.11	-50.0	0.25	0.14	-46.5	0.21	0.12	-43.5	0.14	0.00	-97.9
Total	1,596,015	100	0.26	0.27	4.7	0.28	0.40	44.3	0.72	1.15	59.7	0.20	0.17	-15.0

Sources: Secretaría de Salud, Servicios Estatales del Estado de Guerrero; IMSS, Programa IMSS-COPLAMAR.
[a] denominator: all of the noninsured population; [b] denominator: pregnant women between 12 and 50 years of age; [c] denominator: children under 5 years of age; [d] 1985; [e] average of 1986 and 1987.

component analysis to stratify the municipalities or districts in Guerrero and Oaxaca into five groups (see table 3.1).

Official statistics on health services provided to the uninsured were used to measure satisfaction of health needs.[5] The selected indicators were: (1) general consultations; (2) extension of service coverage, measured through first-time consultations; (3) protection against pertussis, tetanus, and diphtheria, measured through the application of the third dose of the DPT vaccine; and (4) enrollment in prenatal care, measured through first-time prenatal consultations.[6] The analysis assessed the per capita distribution of each variable among the uninsured at the municipal level. For the DPT vaccination variable, we looked only at children under 4 years of age, and for the prenatal-care variable, we considered only pregnant women between the ages of 12 and 50.[7]

Variables were measured for the period 1985–1987, with 1985 providing the baseline against which to evaluate the impact of decentralization in

---

[5] Health variables were collected daily at the health-center level, and the data were aggregated by the researchers. It is assumed that all health service data correspond to people living within the municipality (or district, in the case of Oaxaca), and thus sharing similar socioeconomic status. This assumption seems warranted for the states chosen, given the significant homogeneity within municipalities and the marked dispersion of population, which makes geography an effective barrier to accessing the first level of care. Acapulco presents the only major exception; even though this municipality harbors a large and heterogeneous population, most of its residents are relatively better off (stratum 1 in Guerrero).

[6] Variables were selected using three criteria: they had to be important for the satisfaction of health needs; they had to be reliable over the periods considered; and their equity had to be susceptible to improvement through decentralization. Only first-level-clinic statistics were used because hospital care, though important, was difficult to differentiate by socioeconomic group with available data.

[7] The number of uninsured pregnant women was estimated using state-level data from the national health survey. The top socioeconomic strata in Guerrero and Oaxaca yielded a number above 1 for first-time prenatal care in the first trimester (the numerator). Because it is unlikely that, on average, pregnant women were enrolling for prenatal care more than once per pregnancy, this anomaly can be explained by the utilization of prenatal care by insured pregnant women not included in the denominator.

Guerrero.[8] The subsequent years—1986 and 1987—showed changes in the variables in Guerrero following decentralization, with Oaxaca serving to control for historical trends and the effects of the economic crisis. To measure overall impact, the two-year trend was averaged.

In Guerrero as a whole, three variables increased following decentralization, and only one decreased (table 3.1). In stark contrast, all variables except one fell during the same time period in still-centralized Oaxaca. Significantly, prenatal consultations in Guerrero increased by 59.7 percent and total consultations by 44.3 percent, though initial consultations increased only at the rate of population growth. This means that the services rendered went to the same population that had been covered in 1985; they increased their consumption of services, but there was little or no extension of coverage to new users. The one variable that showed a decrease in Guerrero was DPT vaccinations, which dropped 15 percent, reaffirming shortcomings in service outreach. Those variables that showed improvements in Guerrero can be explained by the central government's policy of favoring decentralizing states through additional resources offered as incentives.

Enrollment in prenatal care was the only indicator that showed an increase (17.5 percent) in Oaxaca during the study period. Decreases were especially notable in the number of total consultations and DPT vaccinations, which fell 27.3 and 23.2 percent, respectively. First-time general consultations dropped by 9.2 percent. These outcomes can be accounted for by the effects of the economic crisis, which produced shortages in health resources—such as DPT vaccine—and raised the economic barriers that kept the population from accessing services.

Prior to decentralization, the distribution of health services across the various strata of the uninsured population in Guerrero and Oaxaca showed a notable equitable pattern (table 3.1, figures 3.1 and 3.2). Preventive services such as prenatal care and DPT vaccinations showed a similar distribution across socioeconomic groups, confirming that services were being delivered following a principle of equality. General and first-time consulta-

---

[8] It would have been ideal to collect information for at least five years prior to 1985 in order to assess past trends. However, such information was not available due to a change in the system of official data collection and the discarding of old municipal-level registers.

tions showed the tendency toward equity, given that the most needy received significantly more consultations per capita, although in some cases the more affluent also received more care than did the middle strata. It can also be seen that most of the indicators are higher per capita in Oaxaca than in Guerrero.

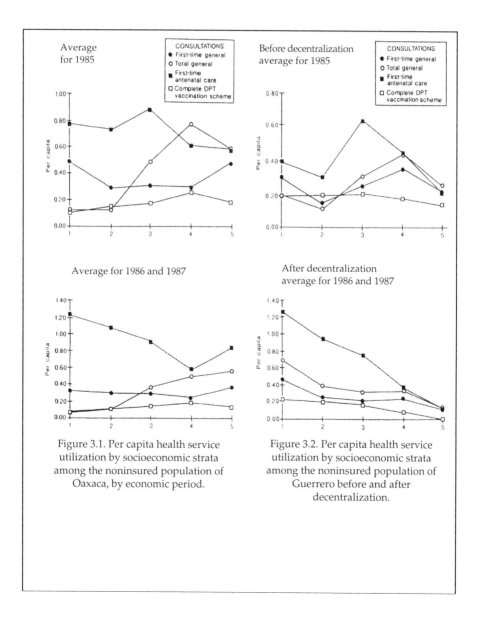

Figure 3.1. Per capita health service utilization by socioeconomic strata among the noninsured population of Oaxaca, by economic period.

Figure 3.2. Per capita health service utilization by socioeconomic strata among the noninsured population of Guerrero before and after decentralization.

The similar pattern in the distribution of service indicators between the two states demonstrates the fact that they had identical administrative systems and similar socioeconomic conditions before decentralization. How did the pattern change once Guerrero became decentralized? How did the economic crisis affect both states? And to what extent was decentralization a policy to protect against cuts in resources and purchasing power among health services and the population?

Oaxaca continued to distribute health services in 1986 and 1987 following a similar pattern as before, albeit with an important decrease in volume across all indicators (table 3.1, figures 3.1 and 3.3). General consultations, which had previously been delivered based on a pattern of equity, began to follow a pattern of inequity as reductions in health services were more marked for the top economic stratum. Thus issues of equity determined how the negative impacts of the economic crisis were assimilated across the five socioeconomic strata in the state that remained centralized.

In Guerrero after decentralization, a significant change occurred in the pattern of services distribution across socioeconomic strata (table 3.1, figures 3.2 and 3.3). The two highest strata were the only ones that benefited from increases in services, while the middle stratum, which comprised 66 percent of the population, experienced little change. The two lowest strata endured important decreases in all services. The most drastic changes were the increments in initial prenatal and total consultations—on the order of 220 to 260 percent—for the highest income group and the interruption of DPT vaccinations for the very poor.

Decentralization thus implied a 180° shift in the policy of health services distribution, from a pattern of equity to one of inequity. It is remarkable that, despite the economic crisis, Guerrero as a whole received more services, but all of the increases went to benefit the state's most important cities. Approximately 8 percent of the population—those in the lowest two socioeconomic strata, most of whom were Indians and peasants living a subsistence economy in small and dispersed settlements—suffered a significant reduction in services.

The shift to an inequitable pattern in health services distribution can be explained by policies that were followed in planning and resource allocation. Through municipal decentralization, Guerrero's tourist resorts received additional resources directly from the federal government, bypassing

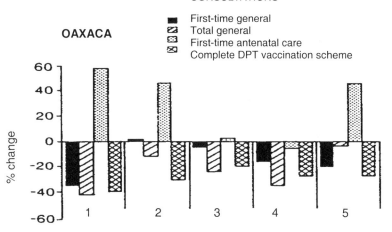

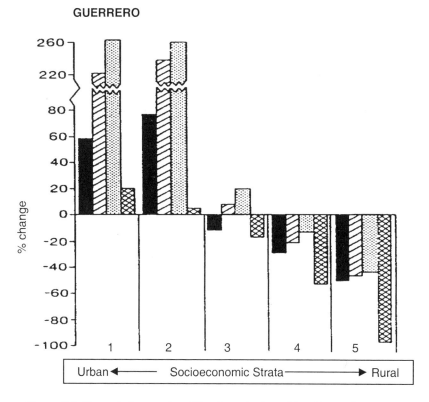

Figure 3.3. Percent changes in utilization of selected health service indicators by socioeconomic strata among the noninsured populations of Oaxaca and Guerrero, 1985 and average of 1986-87.

state-level negotiations. Municipalities in stratum 3, on the contrary, were saddled with added financial burdens and left to negotiate bilaterally with the state-level authorities. Municipalities in the lowest socioeconomic strata did not sign decentralization agreements and continued in a centralized relationship now more focused on state-level authorities.

Oaxaca's ability to preserve an equitable or egalitarian pattern of services distribution throughout the economic crisis can be explained by the fact that it did not prioritize resource assignments to key regions of the state. It seems that the politically motivated perpetuation of the dual health services infrastructure and the resistance to decentralization led to an emphasis on the status quo. A comparison of the two states shows that the incentives that central authorities offered to decentralize were better assimilated by the richer and economically more strategic municipalities, thereby turning decentralization into a distributive policy capable of stimulating further growth.

Decentralization was clearly associated with important increases in service utilization in urban areas. However, its association with reductions in services is more problematic, given the parallel effects of the economic crisis. Declines in the indicators of health services utilization among the two lowest socioeconomic strata were significantly greater in Guerrero than in Oaxaca (figure 3.3). Here it would seem that the inter-institutional conflicts around the implementation process were responsible for the excessive downturn, which was greater than what the economic crisis alone would have caused. We emphasize the negative consequences of conflicts at the central level rather than the benefits of decentralization itself. Indeed, given the utter poverty present in most of the municipalities ranked in the lowest two socioeconomic strata, no decentralization agreements were signed. It can be said that decentralization had more of a "rebound" effect in these municipalities rather than a direct impact on planning, finance, and operations.

In contrast to these outcomes in the lowest two strata, Guerrero did better for stratum 3 than did Oaxaca, with only a small drop in two indicators and an increase in two others (figure 3.3). This is significant because stratum 3 is where 66 percent of Guerrero's population and 56 percent of Oaxaca's were concentrated. The decentralization agreements signed in the (mostly rural) stratum 3 municipalities of Guerrero seem to have accorded some protection to services utilization against the effects of the economic crisis, perhaps by making health services accountable at the local level. This was in spite of the conflicts observed between state authorities and some municipalities. Given the importance of socioeconomic stratum 3, we can say that decentralization as a policy structure showed a net positive effect in the more prosperous rural areas of Guerrero, in contrast to the net negative effect due to the implementation process in the state's poorest rural areas.

CONCLUSIONS

We have analyzed decentralization as a complex and multifaceted policy, whose benefits were determined by the affected centralist, institutional, and political interests. We have also questioned the policy's capacity to generate and integrate services in specific development areas. Analysis at the central level revealed that, after decades of centralization and fragmentation in health services delivery in Mexico, the IMSS was skeptical of decentralization policy because it threatened IMSS hegemony over Mexican health policy. The rivalry for leadership, resources, and legitimization at the center—quite apart from the real problems encountered during implementation—undermined decentralization's anticipated benefits and led to the program's suspension.

This state-level study revealed that there was only a partial devolution in the center-local relationship regarding health care for the uninsured. State and municipal governments acquired greater political responsibility for health care, but service administration—particularly control over financing and personnel—was actually reconcentrated at the federal level along more integrated and less bureaucratized lines of command. This allowed for the channeling of local and especially federal resources to key economic enclaves in Mexico's most underdeveloped region. In contrast, the majority of the population in poor rural areas continued to bear the brunt of the economic crisis, receiving few benefits from decentralization. The very poorest, most dispersed, and most remote populations (often indigenous) actually lost services as a result of the centralist conflicts that hindered coordination during implementation, a situation probably exacerbated by the economic crisis.

The political and public health results of decentralization in Guerrero point to the widening of the health differentials between rural and urban areas, between economic sectors engaged in regional and national produce markets and those generating foreign exchange through tourism services. Decentralization became a distributive policy closely allied to the industrial modernization and export-promotion policies that were being followed in the Mexican economy. The policy thus pointed toward an alternative to the much-criticized corporatist arrangements of which IMSS is a vital part. Therein may lie an explanation for the IMSS's staunch defense of its centralist Solidarity Program.

Despite the vigor of the new decentralization policy, centralism actually prevailed in that IMSS was able to preserve and retain most of the Solidarity Program by pressing for the suspension and even reversal of decentralization. Under the administration of Carlos Salinas de Gortari (1988–1994), IMSS received renewed support to channel the benefits of promised economic growth to rural areas by revamping the Solidarity Program and placing the Health Ministry's entire rural infrastructure under it while keeping the successful urban areas decentralized.

The proposal was justified by blaming the negative outcomes in Guerrero's rural areas on the failure of decentralized institutions, rather than on the implementation process or, more importantly, the economic crisis. Once we factor in these two latter processes, we can see that, in the absence of economic recovery, this policy alternative would lead toward greater regional polarization. Indeed, the rural areas would continue to suffer the downward trend observed in Oaxaca, while urban areas would likely continue to improve their standards, as occurred in Guerrero. This would be even more notable once the two health infrastructures were formally separated between state- and federal-level authorities, diminishing the rural population's ability to access urban-based hospitals.

In the case of economic recovery, of course, integration of all rural services under IMSS presents an interesting prospect despite its initial divisive effects. It represents a route toward building a national health service, and perhaps a rapid route given that it would create a highly polarized and unstable situation. Indeed, IMSS would be responsible for caring for the two extremes of Mexico's working class: impoverished peasants and highly privileged urban and industrial workers. What would remain is responsibility for the urban unemployed and underemployed, a population that would not warrant the ample hospital infrastructure that the Ministry of Health has built over the years. The chances of fusing all federally funded health services under IMSS would thus be enhanced.

Recentralization of all health services for the rural uninsured would in itself exert pressure for greater access to the mainstream services enjoyed by the insured as the Solidarity Program would become the object of close public attention and Health Ministry control. However, it is unlikely that IMSS would favor this path. On the contrary, we argue that IMSS has accepted increasing responsibility for the uninsured as a contractor for the federal government only insofar as this gives industrial, corporate interests more negotiating power in society.

The Health Ministry's preferred policy alternative was to carry on with decentralization, to encourage regional integration and efficiency in services for the uninsured, together with the promotion of state-level health systems to coordinate the social security institutions and private medicine. As urban services improve as a result of decentralization, the potential for redistribution of benefits to the rural areas should rise. However, decentralization does not seem to foster redistribution, given that the benefits observed in urban areas were obtained largely thanks to the more autonomous negotiations at the municipal level. Furthermore, state-level authorities have little capacity to press for regional redistribution, particularly through the integration of services for the insured and uninsured.

A third policy alternative is the integration of all federally funded services under IMSS while at the same time maintaining the decentralized health authorities to assume a clearly defined role in supervision of the quality and equity of services that IMSS provides to various sectors of the population. IMSS would thus become more of a service provider while other institutions assumed the role of financiers, whether through tripartite or bipartite arrangements or directly through tax and public debt funds. This alternative would give coherence to the responsibilities that IMSS is increasingly assuming and defending, and it would lead to greater equity and efficiency in the delivery of health services.

There is no doubt as to the crisis affecting Mexico's public health institutions. Decentralization played a role in efforts to resolve this crisis, but it was an ambiguous role because benefits for some in fact meant liabilities for others. Which path decentralization follows in the future will very likely depend on the economic policies pursued, the actions of centralist interests, and the capacity of state-level authorities to assume a role in the political economy of health.

References

Beltrán, U., and S. Portilla. 1986. "El proyecto de descentralización del gobiemo mexicano, 1983–1984." In *Descentralización y democracia en México*, ed. B. Torres N. México, D.F.: El Colegio de México.

Dirección General de Evaluación. 1987. "Evaluación del proceso de descentralización de los servicios de salud." Typescript. México. D.F.: Subsecretaría de Planeación, Secretaría de Salubridad y Asistencia.

Frenk, J., and M. A. González-Block. 1992. "Primary Care and the Reform of Health Systems: A Framework for the Analysis of Latin American Experiences," *Health Services Management Research* 5, no. 1: 32–43.

Friedland, R., F. Fox Piven, and R. Alford. 1970. "Political Conflict, Urban Structure and the Fiscal Crisis." In *Comparing Public Policies: New Concepts and Methods*, ed. D. Ashford. Beverly Hills, Calif.: Sage.

Mills, A., P. Vaughan, D. Smith, and I. Tabibzadeh. 1987. *Decentralization and Health for All Strategy*. Geneva: World Health Organization.

Musgrove, P. 1983. "La equidad del sistema de servicios de salud: conceptos, indicadores e interpretación," *Boletín de la Oficina Sanitaria Panamericana* 95: 525–45.

Rondinelli, D. A., and S. G. Cheema. 1983. "Implementing Decentralization Policies: An Introduction." In *Decentralization and Development: Policy Implementation in Developing Countries*, ed. S. G. Cheema and D. A. Rondinelli. Beverly Hills, Calif.: Sage.

Rondinelli D. A., J. R. Nellis, and S. G. Cheema. 1984. "Decentralization in Developing Countries: A Review of Recent Experience." Staff Working Papers, no. 581. Washington, D.C.: World Bank.

Rubin, J. W. 1987. "State Policies, Leftist Opposition, and Municipal Elections: The Case of the COCEI in Juchitán." In *Electoral Patterns and Perspectives in Mexico*, ed. A. Alvarado. La Jolla, Calif.: Center for U.S.-Mexican Studies, University of California, San Diego.

Soberón, G. 1987. "El cambio estructural en la salud," *Salud Pública de México* 29: 1–177.

Spalding, R. 1980. "Welfare Policymaking: Theoretical Implications of a Mexican Case Study," *Comparative Politics* 13: 419–38.

WHO (World Health Organization). 1980. *Formulating Strategies for Health for All by the Year 2000.* Geneva: World Health Organization.

World Bank. 1987. *Financing Health Services in Developing Countries: An Agenda for Reform.* Washington, D.C.: World Bank.

4

Federalist Flirtations: The Politics and Execution of Health Services Decentralization for the Uninsured Population in Mexico, 1985–1995

ANNE-EMANUELLE BIRN

In numerous countries around the world, health services delivery systems and government social sectors generally are undergoing some form of "decentralization," usually proffered as an attempt to increase equity, efficiency, participation, intersectoral collaboration, and responsiveness, thereby improving health outcomes (World Bank 1993; Mills 1994). These claims are attractive but remain difficult to measure and generalize (Araujo 1997). Nevertheless, over the past two decades, multiple constituencies for decentralization have sprouted, from democracy advocates to bureaucrats, local activists, and international financiers (Willis, Garman, and Haggard 1999; Abrantes Pêgo 1997). In 1980s Mexico, a similarly diverse array of actors initially favored decentralization, but many subsequently soured on the reform. This essay examines the decentralization of health services for the uninsured population in Mexico in an effort to discern: (1) the motivations for the reform, the context for its implementation, and the politics of its suspension at a national level; and (2) the impacts, both intended and unin-

This study was adapted from my participation in Alec Gershberg's project for the Inter-American Development Bank entitled "Decentralization and Recentralization: Lessons from the Social Sectors in Mexico and Central America." The opinions expressed do not reflect those of the IDB or its board of directors. I am grateful to Alex Schwartz, Pat Wilson, and Sarah Zimmerman for their comments on earlier drafts of this essay, which was presented at a conference of the Association of Collegiate Schools of Planning in Ft. Lauderdale, Florida, in 1997. This work also appeared, in slightly modified form, in the *Journal of Public Health Policy* (vol. 20, no. 1) in 1999.

tended, of the reform effort at subnational levels of government. In the end, under the existing political regime the reform could not overcome political obstacles to decentralizing fiscal power, redistributing resources in an equitable fashion, and eliminating the inefficiencies of separate but unequal health systems for social security recipients and the uninsured.

Decentralization has been variously defined as fiscal federalism; an increase in administrative responsibilities at subnational levels of authority; the granting of political and managerial autonomy to subnational tiers of government; the creation of semiautonomous, publicly accountable agencies; and the privatization of public services (Mills et al. 1990; Rondinelli, McCullough, and Johnson 1989). In order to address some of these inconsistencies, decentralization is conceptualized here as the transfer of authority to the state or local level in four realms: (1) financing (federal transfers and subnational revenues and spending authority); (2) personnel management; (3) norms, regulations, and policy development; and (4) local participation in governance (Gershberg 1998).

This chapter tracks the rise and fall of the efforts to decentralize health services for the uninsured population in Mexico in the 1980s and early 1990s. Sparked by demands from below for greater democracy and better-quality health services, by a national economic crisis and pressure from the International Monetary Fund and other creditors for fiscal austerity, and by technocratic impulses to rationalize health services delivery, the decentralization reform was a major political initiative. Yet by the late 1980s, a confluence of forces had disabled the reform on several fronts. First, the reform effort was halted in 1988 after only fourteen of Mexico's thirty-one states had signed decentralization agreements. Then, in the states that underwent the reform, the limited financing and management authority that was transferred to subnational levels was gradually recentralized.

How did this promising idea stagnate? The reform took place in the midst of debt crisis–driven government spending cuts (Vázquez and Meyer 1985: 195–96; Laurell and Ortega 1992; Asthana 1994; Terris 1998; Rubio and Gil-Díaz 1987) which reduced per capita health spending on the uninsured by over 60 percent between 1982 and 1990 (Laurell 1997). By reducing tax transfers to the states, the budget cuts also impeded state contributions to decentralized health coffers. Fiscal constraints were exacerbated by the difficulties in overcoming the authoritarian centralism of

Mexico's long-ruling Institutional Revolutionary Party (PRI) and its corporatist clients (González Casanova 1970), who feared the potential loss of power and employment security implied by fiscal, policy, and participatory decentralization (Frenk 1998). Federal reluctance to cede fiscal power to the states escalated in the late 1980s as the opposition National Action Party (PAN) began to capture state governorships in the north of the country. Finally, the decentralization reform never addressed the underlying source of health services inequity and inefficiency in Mexico: the segregation of social security systems and the other systems for the uninsured on the basis of financing, coverage, and eligibility. The aspect of the reform that was carried out, the fusion of two programs for the uninsured population in approximately half the states, backfired due to popular uproar at the deterioration of services within the system for the uninsured.

An analysis of the aborted decentralization process at the aggregate level tells only part of the story. I next turn to case studies of three Mexican states to assess the subnational experiences of decentralization. The effects of the reform are examined in the areas of state and local-level financing, policymaking, personnel management, and local participation. Despite only minimal increases in discretionary authority, decentralized states were required to take drastic measures over which they had limited control. Notwithstanding a few innovations and the sparking of cautionary interest in decentralization, even the most technically capable states were squeezed.

This study is based primarily upon interviews with actors in the health decentralization reforms, from the federal level in Mexico City and from state and local government levels in the states of Jalisco, Morelos, and Hidalgo. Officials interviewed were responsible for budgeting, planning and programming, policy development, accounting, purchasing, supervision, evaluation and research, human resources, program administration, norms and regulation, delivery of health services, and overall management and leadership. At the local level, municipal presidents, health personnel (doctors, nurses, health promoters, and midwives), health committee members, and clinic users were interviewed as important stakeholders in the reform. An observation component of the study included attendance at community meetings and visits to health units, hospitals, and other health facilities. Finally, I interviewed academic analysts of decentralization from major national and regional research institutions.

BACKGROUND

Mexico's population of over 90 million people lives in some 2,400 municipalities in 31 states and the Federal District (Mexico City). Almost a third
lives in the four leading cities, which offer advanced technological facilities
to a privileged elite. But another third, including most of the indigenous
population of 8 to 10 million people, lives in remote rural enclaves.

Mexico's distribution of wealth is among the most extreme in the
world. In 1990, 63.2 percent of the economically active population (EAP)
did not earn enough to satisfy their basic needs (CONAPO 1994). In 1992
the richest 10 percent of the population received 38.2 percent of the national income, while the poorest decile received only 1.5 percent (Anexo
Estadístico 1994). From 1984 to 1992 these trends became ever more skewed
through periods of both economic recession and rapid growth.[1]

Like wealth inequities, health inequities have centuries-old roots in
Mexico. The European invasion introduced smallpox, measles, and other
infectious diseases to the Americas, killing millions of indigenous people in
the sixteenth century (McNeill 1976; Crosby 1972; Alchon 1991; Cook and
Lovell 1998). Soon thereafter, the colonial Spanish administration and the
Catholic Church carried Western medicine to the territories of New Spain,
building over one hundred hospitals for colonists and native populations.
A fragmented and overlapping set of public health authorities emerged in
colonial Mexico, with the viceroy and religious agencies overshadowing
the regulatory role of the Protomedicato (medical board) during epidemic
times (Cooper 1965). Between Mexican independence in 1821 and the
Mexican Revolution almost a century later, national public health authority
resided in the weak High Council of Public Health. Outside of Mexico City,
the Council was empowered to act only during epidemics or in response to
state requests for assistance, although in later years its purview grew under the leadership of Eduardo Liceaga (de Romo 1992). While state and
municipal governments held public health powers, actions were highly
circumscribed except when port towns were empowered to respond to
international epidemics (Menéndez 1984).

During the first century of Mexican independence, the government's
role in the provision and regulation of public health and medical services

---

[1] Personal communication with José Luis Rangel Díaz, Instituto de Economía,
Universidad Nacional Autónoma de México, March 1998.

was minimal. The private model of medical care delivery consisted of allopathic physicians serving urban elites, Catholic hospitals providing charity care, and traditional healers and midwives attending the majority of the population. Since the 1917 Constitution and subsequent legislation's expansion of government authority under a federal system that highly centralizes political power, there has been increased access to Western medicine and public health services (Hernández Llamas 1982). From the 1930s to the 1980s there were steady, though unevenly distributed, improvements in access to care, but since the economic crisis of the 1980s, the goal of integrating a national health system has been interrupted, and inequities in funding, delivery, and quality of care have worsened (Laurell 1991).

As in many countries of the region, contemporary Mexico's health sector comprises a hierarchy of public and private institutions. The three main divisions—social security, public health services for the uninsured population, and private services—roughly correspond to employment sector and ability to pay. Formal-sector workers and their dependents, slightly more than half the population (47.8 million people according to 1994 figures; Sistema Nacional de Salud 1994), are eligible for one of several social security insurance systems funded by payroll contributions by employers and employees. The Mexican Social Security Institute (IMSS), founded in 1943, provides health coverage, pensions, and other benefits to private-sector workers, approximately 36.6 million people in 1994. Although all workers in the formal sector are legally required to join the IMSS, there is considerable evasion, particularly by smaller firms and individuals wishing to avoid payroll taxes (IMSS Diagnóstico 1995). Federal and some state and municipal civil servants—9.1 million people—are covered by the Social Security Institute for State Employees (ISSSTE). Formed in 1959 through consolidation and expansion of existing civil servant benefits, ISSSTE provides extensive health, income, and life insurance benefits, and includes sports, housing, day care, and educational benefits. Several smaller social security systems exist for the armed forces (founded in 1926), railroad workers (1936–38), petroleum workers (1935), and others (Mesa-Lago 1978: 220–21). Together, these institutes covered 2.1 million persons in 1994. The financing and organization of social security benefits have come under attack, as they did in 1995 when modifications to the Social Security Law substituted private pension accounts for the collective retirement fund (Laurell 1997).

Informal-sector workers and their dependents, slightly less than half the population at 42.4 million, are not covered by social security and are served by several safety-net public health systems for uninsured populations. The Health Ministry (SSA) is responsible for the largest portion of the uninsured, or about 28.7 million people. Founded in 1943 at the ministerial level to replace the revolutionary era's Department of Public Health, the SSA runs primary, secondary, and tertiary facilities across the country. In Mexico City the SSA's program for the uninsured is under a separate administration (Federal District Department, or DDF). A third program for the uninsured is the IMSS system's special Solidarity Program for the Uninsured. This program was established in the 1970s (under the name IMSS-COPLAMAR, renamed IMSS-Solidaridad in 1989) to extend coverage to marginalized populations who had no geographic access to the SSA network. By expanding access through IMSS rather than through the Health Ministry, the federal government was responding to pressure in the early 1970s to share the social security surplus with nonindustrial workers. The decision to have the expanded coverage administered by the IMSS rather than the SSA also served as an implicit criticism of the Ministry's incapacity to effectively deliver health services to Mexico's uninsured population.[2] Since the late 1970s, the Solidarity Program has been funded by general revenues rather than by the IMSS, but it enjoys in-kind administrative and material subsidies from the IMSS. Finally, there are several smaller health and social services programs for indigenous and other vulnerable populations.

Eligibility does not translate automatically into enrollment or utilization of services; the wealthiest 2.4 percent of the population, who are usually eligible for IMSS, seek services in the private sector (increasingly through third-party payers, including managed care arrangements). Several studies suggest that the official figure of 47.8 million insured by social security may be inflated by more than 10 million people (Sistema Nacional de Salud 1994; Estudios de Regionalización 1994) due to company evasion of social security taxes, overestimates of the size of the formal sector, and individual

---

[2] Interview with a former IMSS director, Congressman Ricardo García Sainz, June 1996. See also Zapata and Cruz 1996.

decisions to opt out of social security coverage. In addition, approximately 12 percent of the population—almost 10 million uninsured people—do not have access to health services at all in terms of geographic proximity to the SSA or Solidarity units (Bloom 1995; Cruz et al. 1994). They and others may attend private physicians or traditional healers and midwives; there is little information about utilization of traditional providers and associated health expenditures (Lozoya Legorreta, Velásquez, and Flores Alvarado 1988). While the wealthiest quintile are most likely to use private health services, both insured and uninsured persons at lower income levels have an approximately one-third probability of using private health services if they are in poor health status (Secretaría de Salud 1994).

In sum, benefits, services, spending, and quality of attention vary widely by health delivery sector due to historical factors and the differing political power of corporatist and union forces. A 1994 survey suggests that the public views quality and service to be highest in the private sector, followed by IMSS, ISSSTE, and, in last place, the SSA (cited in Ruelas and Querol 1994). In the social security system there are 1.36 doctors, 1.96 nurses, and 1.22 beds per thousand compared to 0.93 doctors, 1.45 nurses, and 1.64 beds per thousand in the public safety-net system (Sistema Nacional de Salud 1993). The higher bed ratio in the safety-net system stems from the Health Ministry's large hospital network and the growth of maternity beds in Solidarity and SSA clinics. Because salaries tend to be lower in the safety-net system, total health spending by sector reveals even greater inequities. The social security sector covers 53 percent of the population with only 44.3 percent of spending; the uninsured sector (including those without geographic access to public facilities) is responsible for 44 percent of the population, with only 13 percent of total health spending; and approximately 2.4 percent of the population officially uses private health services while total private-sector spending constitutes 42.7 percent of health expenditures (Cruz et al. 1994).

These inequities are exacerbated by the overlapping of services. Not only are the three sectors (private, social security, and safety net) duplicative, but each institution within each of the sectors has its own administrative infrastructure, health personnel, hospitals, clinics, and other services. Though highly fragmented, this arrangement is not accidental: health services coverage mirrors current and historical regional, class, and labor force segmentation (González-Block 1990; Birn 2006; Navarro 1976; Roemer 1964). From a technocratic efficiency perspective, there is little doubt that the Mexican health sector warrants reform, if only to eliminate duplicate missions and infrastructure. There remains a parallel pressing need to address extreme inequities in spending, coverage, and quality of care. The next section will discuss how these ongoing dictates for system rationalization and equity were translated into a narrowly circumscribed health decentralization reform in the 1980s that ultimately resolved neither the efficiency concern nor the equity and quality concerns.

THE SEQUENCE OF EVENTS

In the midst of Mexico's early 1980s debt crisis, President Miguel de la Madrid (1982–1988) championed the "decentralization of national life" to support Mexico's commitment to federalism, to "achieve unity in the national development of a geographic, ethnic, and cultural mosaic" (de la Madrid 1986; Ward 1986), to respond to growing pressures for democratization and deflect anti–ruling party sentiment (Rodríguez 1997), and to demonstrate to international creditors that Mexico was serious about fiscal reform (Willis, Garman, and Haggard 1999).

Decentralization to the state level of health services for the uninsured population was devised largely by federal stakeholders, who at once promised autonomy to the north of the country, equity to the south, and greater overall efficiency. This entailed transfer of responsibility to the states for primary and secondary health services, including health clinics and general-care hospitals, but not specialty (tertiary-care) hospitals, which remained under federal control in most locales. Most existing state-level tertiary hospitals were transferred to the federal government.

It is important to emphasize that the health decentralization reform was targeted only at the programs serving the uninsured population (the SSA and Solidarity programs) and *not* at the social security systems for industrial workers and functionaries. Thus elimination of the quality, spending, and infrastructure inequities and duplication between social security and safety-net services was not even contemplated by the decentralization reform.

Fiscal decentralization was enabled by new legislation through which the federal government gave the states responsibility for organizing, delivering, supervising, and evaluating health services. First, the 1917 Constitution's general commitment to public health was expanded in February 1983 to guarantee the right to health. The following year the General Health Law established the basis for new state health laws and the decentralization of both responsibilities and expenditures for health services for the uninsured population. In March 1984 the president decreed that SSA and Solidarity health services for the uninsured be integrated into a single system. Given that decentralization was purported to increase democratic decision making, there was surprisingly little public debate over this matter beyond the institutional stakeholders (López Arellano and Blanco Gil 1993).

Starting in 1985, individual states began to sign decentralization agreements with the federal government that created unified state-level systems of health services delivery for the uninsured population, encompassing clinic care, health brigades, and nonspecialty hospital care. Unification entailed transfer of responsibility for uninsured populations from the Solidarity Program for the Uninsured to the state secretariats of the SSA. This meant that the Solidarity Program disappeared entirely in the fourteen states that signed agreements between 1985 and 1988, with infrastructure and most personnel transferred to the SSA. In exchange for budgetary transfers from the federal government and increased decision-making authority, these reform states promised to increase the state contribution to health spending for the uninsured population to 20 percent or more of the total budget and to take "responsibility" for the delivery of health services to this population. By the end of 1987, the Solidarity Program had turned over 23 hospitals and 911 rural medical units to state authorities in the 14 reform states, leaving it with 50 hospitals and 2,404 units for 9 million users in the remaining 17 states (IMSS-Solidaridad 1993).

The reform was interrupted in 1988, and no additional states signed decentralization agreements for almost a decade. Moreover, the fourteen decentralized states began a process of "recentralization" under the administration of President Carlos Salinas de Gortari (1988–1994), whereby general budgetary transfers were once more earmarked for specific programs and other powers that had been transferred to the fourteen reform states were gradually relocated to the federal level (Ornelas 1997). The government of President Ernesto Zedillo (1994–2000) returned to decentralization of health services for the uninsured with the signing of the National Agreement for the Decentralization of Health Services in August 1996, an initiative that is beyond the scope of this chapter.

The 1980s decentralization was thwarted for a number of reasons. First, the federal government's limited ability to decentralize the personnel budget meant that fiscal transfers to the decentralized states constituted less than one-fourth of spending for the uninsured. Because of their limited tax base (and limited ability to retain taxes at the state level), most states were unable to significantly increase their financing capacity even though they were assuming greater administrative costs. With little fiscal control, higher state accountability was illusory. Although one of the main objectives of decentralization was to localize programmatic decision making, the federal Health Ministry continued to exercise control of major program selection through the budgeting process. Finally, the fusion of Solidarity facilities with those of the SSA ultimately resulted in fewer resources and less equity in impoverished rural areas, leading to tremendous public outcry and suspension of the reform.

Throughout the country, the state-level fusion of Solidarity and the SSA was the most controversial aspect of the reform, even though overall budget cutting and decreases in quality occurred simultaneously. Real federal spending on health dropped by 47.1 percent from 1982 to 1986 (Soberón-Acevedo 1987), and real per capita health spending on the uninsured dropped by 61.1 percent from 1982 to 1990. Although per capita health spending increased in succeeding years, by 1993 it had reached only 54 percent of 1982 levels (Laurell 1997).

Spending cuts were exacerbated by the immediate loss of approximately 10 percent of personnel serving the uninsured population in decentralized states. Some Solidarity workers were IMSS employees and were relocated within the IMSS, while a small number resigned rather than join the SSA because of its inferior working conditions. A study comparing several decentralized and nondecentralized states in the 1980s found that, although human health resources grew more rapidly in the decentralized than in the nondecentralized states, coverage of the uninsured dropped in decentralized states by almost 30 percent while increasing by 20 percent in nondecentralized states from 1985 to 1989 (Cardozo Brum 1993).

The merger was also expensive, costing hundreds of millions of pesos for salary homologizing and severance pay; according to a 1989 report by the minister of health, the total cost of decentralization to the fourteen states was 140 billion pesos (Kumate 1989). Most important, because of the broad popular support that existed for the IMSS Solidarity Program—thanks to its more comprehensive and integrated services, better-staffed and equipped units, community work agreements instead of user fees, and superior outcomes—a merger with the lower-quality, less favored SSA was widely opposed by the public. The controversy over the unification of the two systems of care for the uninsured has been cited as the main reason for the reform's suspension in 1988 (Abrantes Pêgo 1997; González-Block et al., this volume; Leyva Flores 1993).

WHITHER DECENTRALIZATION?

De la Madrid's plan envisioned decentralizing all thirty-one states, but only fourteen states had signed decentralization agreements when the reform was aborted.[3] Formally, a state's enthusiasm for greater autonomy and its commitment to increase its contribution to health spending for the uninsured determined the pace of its inclusion in the decentralization process. Morelos, for example, promised to increase its contribution from 7 percent to 20 percent of the health budget, which it only came close to fulfilling in 1995. However, news of the impending collapse of the Solidarity Program into the SSA sparked large-scale protests in Oaxaca; and other states with large poor and indigenous populations, such as Hidalgo, held back their participation in the decentralization. As a result, with the exception of Guerrero—whose governor was the intellectual architect of decentralization—all of the decentralized states selected by the time the reform was halted had either a high level of socioeconomic development and/or a medium-to-low poverty rate. This has led analysts to conclude that state participation became based almost exclusively on relative wealth and lower resistance to change. Moreover, supporters of the Solidarity Program formed less opposition to the reform in wealthier states, where there tended to be fewer Solidarity health units and hospitals (González-Block et al., this volume; Cardozo Brum 1993; Leyva Flores 1993).

---

[3] They were Aguascalientes, Baja California Sur, Colima, Guanajuato, Guerrero, Jalisco, México State, Morelos, Nuevo León, Quintana Roo, Querétaro, Sonora, Tabasco, and Tlaxcala.

The suspension of the reform and the shared social and economic characteristics of the majority of the states that underwent reform created a natural experiment, enabling at least limited comparison of the fourteen reform to the seventeen nonreform states. Although the fourteen states were arguably more prepared for reform, a rapid evaluation of the conceptual categories used for measuring decentralization—financing role; personnel management; norms, regulation, and policy development; auditing and supervision; and local participation—suggests that the decentralization reform resulted in little transfer of control. On the eve of the reform in 1985, the states that would subsequently sign decentralization agreements contributed an average of 17.4 percent to health expenditures for the uninsured, compared to 5.6 percent in the other states (González-Block et al., this volume). By 1989, a study comparing four reform to four neighboring nonreform states found that the reform states contributed 22.6 percent of health care financing, compared to 7.8 percent for nonreform states, still a threefold difference (Secretaría de Salud 1989). Thus, through periods of economic growth and contraction, before and after decentralization, the three-to-one ratio between reform and nonreform states remained constant, suggesting that the decentralization reform did not stimulate significant growth in state contributions to health services.

The continued centralization of finances was also marked by the proportion of the health budget under state, as opposed to federal, control. In 1994, the only year for which data are available, reform states controlled 23.4 percent of their budgets versus 20.4 percent control in nonreform states (Secretaría de Salud 1995), a very small difference. State officials suggest that in the late 1980s, before the Salinas recentralization of several goods and nonpersonnel services, reform states had somewhat greater control over the goods and services portion of the budget than did the nonreform states. Nonetheless, in overall fiscal terms, on both the revenue side and the expenditure side, the decentralization reform did not result in significant new subnational powers. The inequitable system of historical budgeting also meant that, through 1995, wealthier and healthier states continued to receive disproportionately larger budgets.

The main impediment to reform states gaining more control over their health budgets has been the inability to transfer the personnel budget, which comprises almost 75 percent of overall health expenditures for the uninsured population. The personnel budget's continued centralization—which severely limits state-level personnel management and resource allocation—stems partly from federal reluctance to cede control to state governments and partly from resistance within the National Union of Health Ministry Employees to breaking up into thirty-one smaller units, a change that proved highly problematic in the education sector's decentralization in the early 1990s.

An exception to the general rule of fiscal centralization in Mexico has been the increasing reliance on user fees as a source of decentralized revenue over the last decade in both reform and nonreform states. User fees are collected for hospital care, dental services, and routine clinic visits, with exceptions for primary-care services for children, pregnant women, and the indigent. Case-by-case "socioeconomic" investigations are carried out in most states to determine the veracity of claims of inability to pay for health services. In 1994, user fees ranged from 2.3 to 16.1 percent of total state-level health spending. The employment of these funds differs by state. Until the mid-1980s, most user fees landed in federal coffers. In nonreform states, 85 percent of user fees now remain at the level of the health unit for the purchase of medicines and other supplies not covered by the regular budget, 10 percent go to state coffers, and 5 percent go to the Federal Welfare Agency. The exclusive state control of user fees in reform states was a small but significant element of the decentralization agreements of the 1980s; recent federal suggestions that the fees return to federal control have met with considerable opposition, especially as user fees have become an increasingly important revenue source, more than doubling as a proportion of total spending for the uninsured in reform states, from an average of 4 percent in 1985–1987 to 9.3 percent in 1994–1995. Nonreform states on average collected 6.9 percent of total spending in 1994–1995 (Secretaría de Salud/Funsalud 1996).

Although it generated greater subnational control over revenue, increasing reliance on user fees remains highly problematic. First, user fees may serve as barriers to care at the point of need, penalizing the sick and the poor. Second, they violate the principle of equitable financing of health services for marginal populations, leading to the poor paying a higher proportion of salary for health services than people in higher income groups. Third, they may cause people to delay or avoid care that may prevent more serious illness. Finally, as user fees become increasingly important revenue sources in the context of shrinking health budgets, these policies may end up further penalizing the poor (Russell and Gilson 1997). By giving health units or states purview over user fees, decentralization may induce greater inequities by penalizing the most vulnerable populations.

In sum, the 1980s decentralization reform led to little transfer to the states of power over fiscal and personnel management. This does not mean that it had no impact. In collapsing the SSA and Solidarity institutions in reform states, the reform at once eliminated one aspect of administrative duplication in fourteen states and changed the medical care arrangements for several million people, largely for the worse. Institutional opponents to decentralization (health unions and the IMSS program) joined with the uninsured themselves in opposing further decentralization. Decentralization policies were shaped by old and new political factors such as long-term political centralism, fiscal pressures, pork barrel politics, and institutional gamesmanship, but also by popular opposition to decentralization as an embodiment of health spending cuts and social-sector contraction during the 1980s. Thus, although the 1980s decentralization reform resulted in little decentralization, the reform's intent and rhetoric generated a new dynamic on the part of both institutional actors and health system users, even in nonreform states.

CASE STUDIES

This section examines the effects of the decentralization reform from the perspective of three states, two that underwent decentralization and one that did not decentralize in the 1980s but that has recently—and largely without approval—sought to expand its decision-making latitude. This subnational analysis suggests that some states may be capable of innovation and expanded administrative capacity, but health system rationalization and attempts at redressing inequities remain dependent on central distribution of fiscal and political power.

Jalisco

Jalisco is a large state (1996 population estimated at 6.3 million) with a strong industrial sector but also a large uninsured population (over 3 million) and pockets of extreme marginalization, particularly among the indigenous Huichol population.[4] The Jalisco experience shows expansion in the purview of the state health secretariat in a few areas: improvement in the collection of mortality data in rural areas; development of purchasing and acquisitions capacity for pharmaceuticals, office supplies, and uniforms; innovation in maternal and child health policies; encouragement of "healthy municipalities" projects; and streamlining of sanitary regulations. At the same time, Jalisco's health units remain understaffed, and state-level health spending is heavily biased in favor of three tertiary-care facilities in the capital city of Guadalajara.

Following its signing of the decentralization agreement in 1985, Jalisco faced the resistance of Solidarity personnel to join the State Health Secretariat at lower wages and benefits. However, because these contractual employees had few other options, over 90 percent of the 982 workers eventually joined the Secretariat. Although morale and productivity among these workers deteriorated, only a few Solidarity units were closed, and Jalisco did not suffer from virulent public protests over the reform, such as those that emerged in Guerrero. While Jalisco has overseen the building of dozens of federally funded health units since the mid-1980s, the state has had to fund over a thousand staff positions with user-fee revenues while awaiting federal approval for these positions.

Like other decentralized states, Jalisco is caught in the false freedom of managing its own user fees, which is a highly regressive form of funding basic medical personnel. Jalisco has sought to minimize regressivity by experimenting with a number of different user-fee designs. Following decentralization, the State Health Secretariat decreed in 1987 that there would be no user fees in rural areas, as a measure of support for poor, rural populations. By the early 1990s the principle of free services was reoriented to marginal areas after the State Health Secretariat responded to provider and popular arguments that marginalization was not an exclusively rural phenomenon. In addition, starting in 1989, federal guidelines stipulated that preventive services such as vaccines and routine visits

---

[4] The National Population Council (CONAPO) devised a methodology to determine the marginalization index of each of the country's 2,387 municipalities and 31 states plus the Federal District. Based on the 1990 census, the index is derived from data on housing, education, income, sanitation, crowding, and other variables.

should be offered free of charge. Jalisco expanded these services and offered further state incentives, including free childbirth if an expectant mother attends all of her prenatal visits. Another innovation was a maternal and child health booklet developed in the early 1990s and given to new mothers to track their own health status and keep records of their children's vaccines; it also included a growth chart, development scale for psycho-motor skills, and nutritional guidelines. These measures have proven popular and have been linked to improved infant mortality outcomes. At the core, however, there remains a system of subsidies by sick and near-marginalized populations to sick and even more marginalized populations, an extremely narrow band of redistribution. The State Health Secretariat is powerless to address the greater inequities of taxpayer-financed higher health spending in the private and social security sectors.

The Jalisco experience suggests the possibility of innovating new policies within a small maneuvering space. Yet state-level technical capacity cannot sufficiently mitigate against the larger inequities often created by decentralized policies, such as reductions in funding for basic health personnel.

Morelos

The second case, Morelos, is a small (1990 population of 1.2 million) central plateau state with approximately 550,000 uninsured and a level of marginalization similar to Jalisco's. In contrast with Jalisco, the transfer of Solidarity units in Morelos caused deterioration in quality and access to care, which was exacerbated by the state's inability to raise resources to offset spending cuts.

When the decentralization agreement was signed with Morelos in 1985, Solidarity turned over twenty-three rural medical care units and the regionally important sixty-bed Cuautla hospital to the Morelos Health Secretariat (SSM). In the first years there was a marked deterioration in quality of care (López Arellano and Blanco Gil 1993). As in other decentralized states, Solidarity personnel in Morelos were given the option of joining the SSA at SSA salaries, and 90 percent of these personnel did so. The regionally vital Cuautla hospital suffered from the departure of managerial personnel and attending physicians. Although new specialists and managers were hired, they were not accompanied by resources for maintenance, training, equipment, and other operating expenses, and the state did not contribute its own funds. Numerous state officials recounted that the Cuautla hospital deteriorated so much that a large number of patients stopped going there.

A further complication resulted from the replacement of the Solidarity Program's principle of community quid pro quo (a system whereby the community provides workdays supporting the units in lieu of paying for services) with a system of user fees by the Morelos Health Secretariat. The deterioration of quality, in combination with the institution of user fees, lowered demand for services. In response, the governor decided in 1986 to suspend user fees for all primary health care services, including lab tests and x-rays, but he did not replace these lost funds with financing from other sources. While demand initially increased in response to the provision of free primary care, the loss of revenue meant that medications could no longer be provided to persons attending the health units, once again resulting in a decrease in attendance. Unlike Jalisco, Morelos failed to reinstitute community service or to mobilize state subsidies to resolve these continuing problems.

Morelos offers a striking example of reform-related worsening of outcomes. Morelos saw a 27 percent increase in infant mortality from 1986 to 1990, compared to a 1.3 percent decline in Jalisco. Because of Morelos's small size and its experience with capturing underreported infant deaths, the 1980s increase does not appear to be an artifactual result but one that may relate to worsened social and economic conditions and, at least partially, to the deteriorated public health infrastructure and capacity following its decentralization. All states, including Morelos, saw declines in infant mortality in the early 1990s, which apparently resulted from national vaccination and maternal and child health efforts, as well as improved economic conditions.

Morelos had neither the administrative capacity nor the state responsiveness to carry out the 1980s reform. While other states lamented the fact that very few functions had been transferred, Morelos was unable to handle the responsibilities it did obtain. The merging of SSA with the Solidarity hospital and units caused a rapid decline in quality and access to services. The deterioration of health services resulted from insufficient training and management, but also from the failure of leadership and of civil society to demand improved performance. In part this may have stemmed from organizational structure; because state governance of health was shared first with social security and then with welfare services, health was a secondary priority.

While the suspension of newly imposed user fees marked state responsiveness to public demands, Morelos's inability to replace these funds with state contributions led to a downward spiral in quality and productivity at the unit level and became an important state accountability failure.

Hidalgo

Hidalgo, a state that did not undergo the 1980s decentralization reform, recently achieved significant control over resources and policymaking. One of the four most marginalized states in Mexico, with almost 70 percent of its 1.9 million residents uninsured, it has gained experience in state control over policy, purchasing, and supervision thanks to the boldness and capacity of its administrative team, which has challenged federal rules over personnel management and policy and programming. At the same time, Hidalgo retained a highly successful Solidarity Program, demonstrating the success of a well-administered, better-funded, integrated model of delivery that remains largely centralized.

Before addressing changes related to the operation of SSA-Hidalgo (Secretaría de Salud 1995), the state's Solidarity Program requires analysis. With 4 hospitals and 205 rural medical units covering 824 communities, Solidarity was responsible for over 730,000 people, spending US$26/capita in 1995 (IMSS-Solidaridad 1995). This compares to 368 units for the state's coordinated services (SSA-Hidalgo), covering over 890,000 people at US$13/capita (Secretaría de Salud 1995). Solidarity's operating principles and organizational structure enable it to operate without user fees, provide somewhat higher salaries, maintain units in better condition, operate seven days a week, guarantee a physician in each unit, ensure the availability of drugs, transport patients to rural hospitals, and fund community participation activities.

The Solidarity Program's popularity and steady increase in coverage are based on its health promotion approach to the community. For example, in the plot of land surrounding each unit there are true-size models of various types of latrines and ecological ovens, herbal medicine plots, and nutritional education centers, which are used for weekly instruction and demonstrations. Since 1984 the Solidarity Program has used a model of integrated health care and periodically monitors family medical files, taking advantage of each medical encounter to update vaccine regimens and carry out routine preventive services. A disadvantage of the Solidarity model is its heavy reliance on sixth-year medical students to staff its units. Although the nurses are permanent, the annual arrival and departure of medical students can cause disruptions.

With the exception of community participation on health committees, Solidarity's operations originate at the central level. The health committees, health promoters, and unit staff jointly devise community activities, usually funded by a combination of Solidarity and municipal donations. Over 98 percent of the units have health committees, which are responsible for maintenance of the unit's buildings and laundry services as well as health promotion activities such as latrine construction and monitoring children's vaccine schedules. Individuals are either nominated or volunteer to serve as promoters or health committee members as part of the community's legal requirement to maintain the unit and promote the public's health in return for services. This system is particularly successful in states like Hidalgo, with large indigenous populations. The traditional practice of *tequio,* or individual labor for the good of the community, persists in many indigenous communities. Thus, instead of charging user fees, Solidarity contractually obliges participation, which in turn generates a strong sense of community ownership of the units.

The Solidarity Program in Hidalgo (and around the country) has created a model that responds to local needs, not by bringing accountability for the financing of health services to the state or local level, but by providing comprehensive care through well-staffed, well-maintained, and well-equipped units. That regulations and budgeting are centralized does not impair the delivery of services. Instead, the quid pro quo of community participation in exchange for medical services and a preventive, health promotion orientation enable the program to be locally responsive without the implementation of strict management-accountability mechanisms. According to interviewees, the Hidalgo experience is not unique to the state but is fairly typical in this centralized Solidarity system. A final note is that Solidarity has been partially shielded from spending cuts and politi-

cal changes because the regular IMSS can furnish some backup maintenance and provision of supplies and, perhaps more important, because its
managers are professional functionaries, not subject to electoral turnover.

Within its State Health Secretariat, Hidalgo, a nonreform state, has
paradoxically achieved greater control than either Jalisco or Morelos, particularly around policy and programming. One of the most important elements of the Hidalgo experiment is the delivery of health services by
demographic group: children under five years, school-age children,
women of childbearing age, adults, senior citizens, and community health.
Based on health promotion rather than curative care, this arrangement
seeks to carry out a range of actions each time a person is in contact with
the health system (for example, during vaccination campaigns, clinic visits,
and school health days) and thus avoid "missed opportunities." In addition, local health teams can adapt the package to meet their own needs.
Originally designed for the fifteen most marginalized municipalities in the
state participating in a targeted World Bank project, it has now been extended statewide. The design stems from the philosophical convictions of
the SSA-Hidalgo team, some borrowing from Solidarity's integrated attention model and from experience at the local level, where both providers
and patients were frustrated by the traditional vertical program arrangement whereby care is organized on a disease-by-disease basis and responsibility for monitoring is diffuse and uncoordinated.

Hidalgo's local development of policy and health service delivery is not
consistent with national norms, however, and has generated complications
for the budgetary process, which retains a rigid structure of programs and
goals. As other states learned about the Hidalgo innovation, they sought to
learn more, despite the fact that Hidalgo never requested permission to
change the existing structure of program-based services.

Notwithstanding Hidalgo's defiance of policy norms, the budgeting
and programming process is less pliant. The organization of sanitary juris-
dictions in the early 1980s provided substate knowledge of and exposure to
budgeting but without commensurate increases in local decision making.
In the past several years, budget programming has been democratized by
allowing municipalities to set their own goals according to the local epidemiological profile. The profile is based on family "microdiagnostics"—
routinely collected information about family nutrition, hygiene, sanitation,

exercise, alcohol and drug use, transportation, local communication, education, recreation services, access to water and electricity, sewage disposal, crowding, housing, local environmental conditions, and individual health and socioeconomic status. Because the federal budget process continues to be based on programmatic goals, however, the state must carry out budgetary gymnastics to convert its demographically based goals into federally mandated programmatic goals.

The rigid centralization of the personnel budget has had further implications in Hidalgo, where new job categories have been implemented but not approved. The municipal coordinators, who previously served as directors of health units, have been trained to coordinate all health-related activities with the municipal president, health institutions, departments of education and water provision, and other sectors. Likewise, Hidalgo has designed regional supervisory teams with an integrated approach, to replace the expensive and inefficient individual supervisors who made separate trips around the state to monitor each disease program. Neither the municipal coordinator nor the supervisory team functions are recognized by the federal government; these new titles exist in a budgetary vacuum.

Hidalgo offers an interesting solution to the Catch-22 dilemma of decentralization: in order to gain management and administrative experience, states need independence from the federal government and local control over resources; the federal government, however, is reluctant to relinquish control to states that have no experience. The widespread interest that the basic packages of preventive health services have generated suggests that states can learn from each other and that demonstration projects, at least in well-defined areas, can potentially work. In a sense, SSA-Hidalgo has functioned as though it had received a federal waiver. SSA-Hidalgo was afforded the flexibility to learn from its mistakes in the execution of this program. New SSA-Hidalgo leadership devised fresh job categories with an innovative supervisory structure, a model of health promotion and preventive services based on the successful Solidarity integrated package, and community diagnostics as a foundation for needs-driven budgeting and policy development. Concerns quietly raised by members of the Hidalgo teams were the absence of a legal infrastructure for many of the changes they had instituted and whether their innovations might be dismantled by a new administration.

The basic package of health services that is the brainchild of the SSA-Hidalgo team was developed in spite of the federal constraints on budgeting and programming. The implementation of community diagnostics as a basis for programming has not succeeded in changing the annual federal budgeting process, and not all of the new job categories created in Hidalgo have been federally approved—even though they are already operational.

Ironically, and perhaps most significantly, the Hidalgo case also demonstrates that subnational control over resources and policy is not a prerequisite for improved performance. The experience of Solidarity's centralized financial management and supervision but flexible and responsive integrated model of preventive health care shows tremendous success and popularity in Hidalgo, suggesting that decentralized financing and administration are not essential for improved accountability. Instead, the contractual arrangement between Solidarity and the localities that establishes community responsibility for the maintenance of the unit and for health promotion activities in exchange for high-quality, accessible services illustrates an alternate path to improved service delivery.

SSA-Hidalgo is incorporating many of the successful elements of the Solidarity Program, such as an integrated model of preventive services, strong community relationships and participation mechanisms, improvements in drug supplies, medical staff increases, and community health diagnostics, all within a framework that also seeks to expand budgeting and policymaking accountability. Clearly the Solidarity model has influenced the efforts of the SSA-Hidalgo. On the surface it appears that the most relevant variable may not be the level of government that is responsible, but the design of the model and an assurance of redistributive funding. Due to the political context of the turnover of elected officials, funding, and priorities every three or six years, the greatest challenge for SSA-Hidalgo is to provide permanence to the changes it has pioneered through legal, bureaucratic, or other mechanisms.

DISCUSSION

The three states analyzed above had different experiences under the decentralization reform. In Jalisco, cumulative experience with user fees, maternal and child health policy, and other areas demonstrates growing state capacity within a narrow band of activities. When criteria for free services did not match need in rural areas, the criteria were changed. When free childbirth was offered in exchange for consistent prenatal attendance, the state lost a source of revenue but infant mortality improved, saving money over the long term. Still, persistent reliance on user fees to fund permanent health posts demonstrates the continued obstacles posed by underfunding and the hierarchical pluralism of Mexican health care policy. Morelos, on the other hand, had neither the state capacity to manage the transition nor the political flexibility to change unsuccessful policies. Although there was no formal decentralization in Hidalgo, innovations in supervision, the model of care, and intersectoral collaboration have begun to radically re-structure the delivery of health services in that state. Paradoxically, the centralized, well-funded, more equitable Solidarity model is being emu-lated by Hidalgo's own "decentralizing" policies.

Careful analysis of the decentralization reform process at the national and state levels reveals that the Mexican decentralization reform decentral-ized little. States did not gain significant control over health services deliv-ery, and most of the few new powers they did gain have slowly been taken away from them. Indeed, the 1980s decentralization was ultimately not designed for decentralization but rather as a vehicle to obfuscate drastic reductions for public health services on the order of 50 to 60 percent of spending. This was achieved by passing responsibility to states for health without financing this responsibility. If efficiency and equity had been serious goals, a fusion of Mexico's multiple systems of health coverage for both social security recipients and the uninsured should have been con-templated.

Fiscal decentralization was generally employed as a political instru-ment, one that waxed and waned with the country's economic prosper-ity—generally favoring greater decentralization when central government coffers were emptier and pressures from creditor agencies were greater. The heart of the decentralization effort—the state-level fusion of two sepa-rate safety-net systems that provide health care services for the unin-sured—proved highly controversial because the more popular, higher-quality system was eliminated in the states that underwent reform. At the beginning of the 1990s, with economic crisis and fiscal reform pressure reversed, the Mexican government resorted to two of its recurring twentieth-century projects: modernization and sovereignty, better stated as inequitable growth and the rhetoric of sovereignty wrapped in the robes of domestic and foreign capital alliances.

The failure of decentralization reform, then, is one story that emerges from this analysis. The ruling party's aversion to state-level power sharing thwarted decentralization. The reform was aborted by protests against large spending cuts in the public health sector and the replacement of the popular Solidarity Program with the lower-quality services of the SSA. Though the decentralization reform process did succeed in enhancing state and local knowledge and execution of the budget, the removal of social security subsidies for coverage for the uninsured, along with the retention of a highly inequitable financing system whereby historical budgeting and state lobbying capacity determine budgets, precluded fairer allocation.

Another story is also important. Unplanned policy decentralization resulted in the creation of pockets of local capacity and new relationships between the health system and the public. For example, municipalities now tend to rank their health priorities based on the local epidemiological and, to some extent, socioeconomic profile, rather than strictly following national programmatic priorities. This has led to greater awareness of local health problems and to attempts to increase health promotion and disease prevention activities. However, the budgeting process continues to be organized around federal programs, requiring state planning and budgeting personnel to carry out gymnastics—often rather adeptly—to justify state policies according to federal budget guidelines.

In the end, even failed policies can help lead to new policies and political forces (Hirschman 1984). Though the 1980s decentralization may well have strengthened PRI power (Rodríguez 1997), it also opened possibilities for local claims on the state, as demonstrated by the popular uprising that began in Chiapas in 1994 to oppose the North American Free Trade Agreement and to demand greater redistribution, social services, and democracy.

References

Abrantes Pêgo, R. 1997. "La reforma de los servicios de salud en México y la dinamización y la politización de los intereses: una aproximación," *História, Ciências Saúde Manguinhos* 4: 245–63.

Alchon, S. A. 1991. *Native Society and Disease in Colonial Ecuador.* Cambridge: Cambridge University Press.

Anexo Estadístico, Sexto Informe de Gobierno de 1994, Mexico D.F. and Instituto Nacional de Estadística, Geografía e Informática. 1995. "ENIGH-94 Encuesta Nacional de Ingresos y Gastos de los Hogares," Aguascalientes, Mexico.

Araujo, J. L., Jr. 1997. "Attempts to Decentralize in Recent Brazilian Health Policy: Issues and Problems, 1988–1994," *International Journal of Health Services* 27: 109–24.

Asthana, S. 1994. "Economic Crisis, Adjustment and the Impact on Health." In *Health and Development*, ed. David R. Phillips and Yola Verhasselt. New York: Routledge.

Birn, A. E. 2006. *Marriage of Convenience: Rockefeller International Health and Revolutionary Mexico.* Rochester, N.Y.: University of Rochester Press.

Bloom, E. A. 1995. "Health and Health Care in Mexico." México, D.F.: División de Economía, Centro de Investigación y Docencia Económicas.

Cardozo Brum, M. 1993. "Análisis de la política descentralizadora en el sector salud." México, D.F.: Centro de Investigación y Docencia Económicas.

CONAPO (Consejo Nacional de Población). 1994. "La marginación en los municipios de México, 1990." México, D.F.: Secretaría de Gobernación.

Cook, N. D., and W. G. Lovell. 1998. *Born to Die: Disease and New World Conquest, 1492–1650.* Cambridge: Cambridge University Press.

Cooper, D. B. 1965. *Epidemic Disease in Mexico City, 1716–1813: An Administrative, Social, and Medical Study.* Austin: Institute of Latin American Studies, University of Texas Press.

Crosby, A. W., Jr. 1972. *The Columbian Exchange: Biological and Cultural Consequences of 1492.* Westport, Conn.: Greenwood Press.

Cruz, C., F. Álvarez, J. Frenk, C. Valdés, and R. Ramírez. 1994. *Las cuentas nacionales de salud y el financiamiento de los servicios.* México, D.F.: Funsalud.

de la Madrid, M. 1986. "Descentralización de la vida nacional." In *La descentralización de los servicios de salud: el caso de México,* ed. M. de la Madrid et al. México, D.F.: Miguel Ángel Porrúa.

de Romo, A. C. 1992. "Revisión de la historia de la salud pública en México." México, D.F.: Department of History of Medicine, Universidad Nacional Autónoma de México.

Estudios de Regionalización Operativa de las Entidades Federativas. 1994.

Frenk, J. 1998. "20 años de salud en México," *Nexos* 21: 90.

Gershberg A. 1998. "Decentralization, Recentralization and Performance Accountability: Building an Operationally Useful Framework for Analysis," *Developmental Policy Review* 16: 405–31.

González-Block, M. 1990. "Génesis y articulación de los principios rectores de la salud pública de México," *Salud Pública de México* 32: 337–51.

González Casanova, P. 1970. *Democracy in Mexico*. Trans. Danielle Salti. New York: Oxford University Press.

Hernández Llamas, H. 1982. "Historia de la participación del Estado en las instituciones de atención médica en México, 1935–1980." In *Vida y muerte del mexicano*, ed. Federico Ortiz Quesada. México, D.F.: Folios Ediciones.

Hirschman, A. 1984. *Getting Ahead Collectively: Grassroots Experiences in Latin America*. Elmsford, N.Y.: Pergamon.

IMSS Diagnóstico. 1995. México, D.F.: Instituto Mexicano del Seguro Social.

IMSS-Solidaridad. 1993. *Diagnóstico de salud en las zonas marginadas rurales de México, 1986–1991*. México, D.F.: IMSS.

———. 1995. "Delegación estatal en Hidalgo, autoevaluación anual." Pachuca, Mexico: IMSS.

Kumate, J. 1989. "Descentralización de los servicios de salud a población abierta: situación actual." México, D.F. Mimeo.

Laurell, A. C. 1991. "Crisis, Neoliberal Health Policy, and Political Processes in Mexico," *International Journal of Health Services* 21: 457–70.

———. 1997. *La reforma contra la salud y la seguridad social*. México, D.F.: Ediciones Era.

Laurell, A. C., and M. E. Ortega. 1992. "The Free Trade Agreement and the Mexican Health Sector," *International Journal of Health Services* 22: 331–37.

Leyva Flores, R. 1993. "La descentralización municipal de los servicios de salud en México." Cuadernos de Divulgación. Guadalajara: Universidad de Guadalajara.

López Arellano, O., and J. Blanco Gil. 1993. *La modernización neoliberal en salud: México en los ochenta*. México, D.F.: Universidad Autónoma Metropolitana–Unidad Xochimilco.

Lozoya Legorreta, X., G. Velásquez, and A. Flores Alvarado. 1988. *La medicina tradicional en México: la experiencia del Programa IMSS-Coplamar*. México, D.F.: IMSS.

McNeill, W. 1976. *Plagues and Peoples*. New York: Anchor Books.

Menéndez, E. 1984. "Centralización o autonomía: la nueva política del sector salud en México," *Boletín de Antropología Americana* 10: 85–95.

Mesa-Lago, C. 1978. *Social Security in Latin America: Pressure Groups, Stratification, and Inequality*. Pittsburgh, Penn.: University of Pittsburgh Press.

Mills, A. 1994. "Decentralization and Accountability in the Health Sector from an International Perspective: What Are the Choices?" *Public Administration and Development* 14: 281–92.

Mills, A. J., P. Vaughan, D. L. Smith, and I. Tabibzadeh, eds. 1990. *Health Systems Decentralization: Concepts, Issues and Country Experience*. Geneva: World Health Organization.

Navarro, V. 1976. *Medicine under Capitalism*. New York: Prodist.

Ornelas, C. 1997. "El proceso de descentralización de los servicios de salud a la población abierta en México." Prepared for the Comisión Económica para América Latina y el Caribe, January. Mimeo.

Rodríguez, V. E. 1997. *Decentralization in Mexico: From Reforma Municipal to Solidaridad to Nuevo Federalismo*. Boulder, Colo.: Westview.

Roemer, M. 1964. "Medical Care and Social Class in Latin America," *Milbank Memorial Fund Quarterly* 42, part I: 54–64.

Rondinelli, D. A., J. S. McCullough, and R. W. Johnson. 1989. "Analyzing Decentralization Policies in Developing Countries: A Political Economy Framework," *Development and Change* 20: 57–87.

Rubio, F. L., and F. Gil-Díaz. 1987. "A Mexican Response." Twentieth Century Fund Paper. New York: Priority Press Publications.

Ruelas, E., and J. Querol. 1994. *Calidad y eficiencia en las organizaciones de atención a la salud*. México, D.F.: Funsalud.

Russell, S., and L. Gilson. 1997. "User Fee Policies to Promote Health Service Access for the Poor: A Wolf in Sheep's Clothing?" *International Journal of Health Services* 2, no. 7: 359–79.

Secretaría de Salud. 1989. "Evaluación de la descentralización de los servicios de salud a población abierta en cuatro entidades federativas." México, D.F. Mimeo.

———. 1994. Encuesta Nacional de Salud II. México, D.F.: Secretaría de Salud.

———. 1995. "Descentralización de los servicios de salud." México, D.F.: Subsecretaría de Planeación, Secretaría de Salud.

Secretaría de Salud/Funsalud. 1996. Unpublished data. Mimeo.

Sistema Nacional de Salud. 1993. *Boletín de Información Estadística: Recursos y Servicios*. México, D.F.: Secretaría de Salud.

———. 1994. *Boletín de Información Estadística* 14.

Soberón-Acevedo, G. 1987. "El cambio estructural en la salud. IV. El financiamiento de la salud para consolidar el cambio," *Salud Pública de México*: 29, no. 2: 169–77.

Terris, M. 1998. "Epidemiology and Health Policy in the Americas: Meeting the Neoliberal Challenge," *Journal of Public Health Policy* 19: 15–24.

Vázquez, J. Z., and L. Meyer. 1985. *The United States and Mexico*. Chicago: University of Chicago Press.

Ward, P. 1986. *Welfare Politics in Mexico: Papering over the Cracks*. London: Allen and Unwin.

Willis, E., C. Garman, and S. Haggard. 1999. "The Politics of Decentralization in Latin America," *Latin American Research Review* 34, no. 1: 7–56.

World Bank. 1993. *World Development Report 1993. Investing in Health*. New York: Oxford University Press.

Zapata, O., and C. Cruz. 1996. "La reforma del sistema de salud y la descentralización de los servicios de salud en México." México, D.F.: Dirección General de Estudios en Economía de la Salud, Subsecretaría de Planeación, Secretaría de Salud. Mimeo.

PART III

Trying Again, 1994–2004: Case Studies from Five States

5

"Decentralized" in Quotes: Baja California Sur, 1996–2000

LUCILA OLVERA SANTANA

This chapter analyzes the process of decentralizing the services of Mexico's Ministry of Health (SSA) in Baja California Sur (BCS). This is the first independent study of the decentralization process in the state; it presents the content and dynamics of the decentralization process and discusses how decentralization was conceptualized and implemented. The objective of this chapter is to assess the institutional capacity for implementing decentralization, the degree of success in achieving its formal objectives, and the degree of autonomy effectively acquired by the Baja California Sur Health Secretariat (SSBCS) to adapt health services to local needs.

The study was implemented in two phases. During the first phase, we collected information from secondary sources, including a review of the literature on health reform and health services decentralization; in Baja California Sur we collected statistical information, financial records, official documents, and other archival information, including a report, written in 1999 and based on information provided by SSBCS employees, that presents a synthesis of the decentralized functions (SSA 2001).

In the second phase, we conducted twenty-seven semi-structured interviews—with ten expert informants (including four union leaders), six policymakers, and eleven SSBCS employees involved in the decentralization process. To identify the interviewees, we used the guidelines of the Latin American and Caribbean Regional Health Sector Reform Initiative (LACHSR 2000). The semi-structured interview methodology allowed us to develop rapport with the interviewees and to seek clarification on points that could be misinterpreted. This methodology was appropriate for our study because we were trying to elicit information that is frequently characterized as confidential in nature, especially when those interviewed hold important public positions. This methodology also allowed us to probe for the underlying reasons that motivated politicians and government officials to take action, something that would have been impossible through quantitative research methods.

The semi-structured interviews, which included a common set of key questions for all interviewees, allowed us to add questions depending on an informant's experience and on information we had gained in previous conversations. In addition, at the suggestion of the interviewees, we broadened our sample to include informants not initially considered (Ratcliffe and González del Valle 2000; Mercado Martínez 2000; Castro 1996; Taylor and Bogdan 1987).

Two interview guides were designed: one for use with persons directly involved in the decentralization initiative (fifteen interviews), and another for policymakers and social agents (twelve interviews). The group of expert interviewees included key people involved directly or indirectly in the decentralization process and who had at least ten years of service with the SSBCS. They included the secretary of health; the directors of planning, health regulation, administration, and health services; those in charge of human resources; the decentralization team; health district and state hospital directors; and one representative of the SSBCS's labor union.

The group of social agents and policymakers included representatives of civil society organizations involved in health activities; leaders of political parties; the general secretaries of the labor unions of IMSS, ISSSTE, SSA, and the Education Ministry (SEP); the president of the Medical Association; a researcher in decentralization policies from the Universidad Autónoma del Estado de Baja California Sur; the director of the decentralized public agencies of the state government; and the manager of a private health insurance company.

The interviews were conducted during August and September 2001. All interviews were recorded, transcribed, and analyzed using the Atlas Ti program for qualitative analysis. In order to maintain the interviewees' anonymity, direct citations are referenced with the interview number only.

THE SETTING

Baja California Sur occupies the southern part of the Baja California Peninsula. Though it is Mexico's ninth-largest state (with 3.8 percent of the country's surface area), it is also the least populated, with 424,000 inhabitants, or 0.4 percent of the national population, and a population density of 5.09 inhabitants per km² (INEGI 2000).[1] It is divided into five municipalities: Mulegé, Comondú, Loreto, La Paz, and Los Cabos. Of the 2,743 localities (small towns) registered in 2000, 98 percent have fewer than 500 inhabitants, and they account for only 10 percent of the state population; 81 percent of the population is rural. Only 4.2 percent of the population is illiterate.

After the onset of a severe economic crisis in 1982, commercial activity in the state—primarily fishing, mining, and tourism—diminished notably. As in most Mexican states, the Institutional Revolutionary Party (PRI) had long dominated political life. But in 1999, due in part to the economic crisis and in part to corruption in state government, a coalition of the Party of the Democratic Revolution and the Labor Party (PRD-PT) swept into power, capturing the governorship, all of the state's seats in the federal Senate, seventeen of the state's eighteen seats in the federal Chamber of Deputies, and three of the five municipal presidencies.

The population's geographic dispersion has challenged the state's ability to offer universal health coverage. Forty percent of the population does not have health insurance. Infant mortality is 23.5 per thousand for males and 18.4 per thousand for females, and life expectancy is 74 years for males and 79 years for females (SSA 2002).

In 1999 there were 1.6 doctors and 2.1 nurses for every 10,000 people, and the public per capita health expenditure was 2,299.20 pesos (SSA 2002). The State Health Secretariat reports that the state has 133 primary care clinics, three general hospitals, two tertiary hospitals, and a total of 1,435 workers, including 336 doctors, 467 nurses, 166 technicians, 46 other professionals, and 420 administrative personnel. Administrative personnel form 29 percent of all health service employees.

---

[1] Because of its small population and lack of physical infrastructure, Baja California Sur remained a federal territory—an administrative political dependency of the federal executive—until 1974. The state's economy is based primarily on fishing, mining, and tourism.

THE DECENTRALIZATION OF MEDICAL CARE SERVICES

Baja California Sur began the decentralization process in July 1985 with the signing of its decentralization agreement. Only high-level state officials and members of the decentralization support unit (created to facilitate the decentralization process) "participated" in the first stage of the process. The individuals who occupied those positions have indicated that they had full access to all information and were consulted on decentralization strategies, but their input only prompted adjustments to the project as already defined by the Health Ministry. According to one interviewee:

> The decentralization process was a federal initiative. There were meetings, but only to inform us of the project;... they gave the states the opportunity to openly express opinions which were taken into account in [the preparation of] the National Agreement for the Decentralization of Health Services ... and finally produced the document that permitted the development of decentralization. [E:5]

Participation in the second phase of decentralization was also limited and generally restricted to consultation. When questioned, some high-level employees of the State Health Secretariat offered the following:

> There was a company that interviewed health-sector workers, but most of them were high-level executives; they didn't consult the program directors, those who are in touch with daily problems, shortcomings, and possible solutions. [E:3]

> There was a consultation in 1995, if I recall, consultation forums, retreats. Between 1993 and 1994, the head of the State Health Secretariat was in Tlaxcala proposing the reform of the local health systems. [E:8]

> My opinion [on local participation]? I don't know. I think that they consulted; there were national meetings of the heads of the state health secretariats. [E:9]

> They consulted by telling us how they were going to do this decentralization; that is how they consulted. [E:6]

A labor leader from the National Union of Health Ministry Employees (SNTSSA) indicated:

> There was a talk at the federal level, and the national union participated. It was through the union's leadership that we were informed; they told us: this is going to be done, and it will benefit you. [E:11]

In sum, the head of the State Health Secretariat and the individuals in charge of decentralization participated at the national level in informational lectures or talks where the upcoming changes were explained to them. But the policy of decentralization per se was defined at the federal level and imposed on those states that opted to accept it during the first stage of the process. Baja California Sur could only make cosmetic changes to adapt decentralization to the state's conditions.

According to official discourse, the meetings to which the states were invited were intended to inform participants about the expected benefits, offer them support, and facilitate a community needs assessment and evaluation of the health system for the uninsured, on the basis of which the state could present a proposal for strengthening the local infrastructure. In practice, the meetings' objective was to legitimize a decision that had already been made and guarantee its implementation. The result was that, instead of "adapting the implementation of decentralization to local conditions," as affirmed in the national meetings, the federal government conditioned its support to the states on their ability to respond to the federal mandates.

The strengthening of health resources in preparation for the second decentralization effort began in Baja California Sur in 1996, the purpose being to increase the probability of success. According to the interviewees:

> Baja California decided to ask for more and more resources.... Hospitals were strengthened. [E:8]

> In those days there were many resources in the state, and from that perspective, yes, they [the health services] benefited. [E:13]

However, these resources only functioned "to prepare the state for decentralization," as proposed by Guillermo Soberón (1986), the architect of health care decentralization in Mexico. The problem, according to the SSBCS employees interviewed for this study, was that, despite having received plentiful resources, these still were not sufficient, and the state remained ill prepared to face the decentralization challenge:

> They [Health Ministry officers] decentralized many respon-
> sibilities without allocating adequate human and financial
> resources, and one had to be creative with the limited budg-
> ets and with annual operational programs that we had to
> adapt to our geographic location and resources.... That was
> the disadvantage. They decentralized functions without giv-
> ing us enough resources [material, financial and human]....
> We assumed that they would not abandon us, that they
> would not cut the umbilical cord. The state of Baja California
> Sur was not ready to accept responsibility for the decentral-
> ized functions. [E:6]

At the beginning of the 1985 decentralization, Baja California Sur and many other decentralized states followed the recommendations of the federal government. Of the three organizational models presented in chapter 2 (see table 2.3), Baja California Sur adopted the model with two institutions: a state health secretariat and a decentralized public agency (OPD), which in Baja California Sur is called the Health Services Institute of Baja California Sur. The Health Secretariat is responsible for coordinating the state health system and is the state health authority. The OPD is responsible for providing medical and public health services, and it has a separate legal identity and separate assets. This division of functions was and continues to be theoretical. From the beginning, these two institutions have been under the management of the state secretary of health. One interviewee described the functional reality as follows:

> To date, the state is a good example of the failure to separate
> the Health Secretariat and its functions as a governing insti-
> tution from the health services delivery unit [OPD]. [E:3]

The promoters of decentralization envisioned the Ministry of Health coordinating and integrating all public medical services networks, including the OPD, the networks of IMSS and ISSSTE, and state and municipal health infrastructures. This vision has not materialized. Medical care in Mexico continues to be fragmented. One individual illustrated the situation that prevails in Baja California Sur in this way:

> There is much disengagement among the ISSSTE, the IMSS, and the SSA. I do not see any cohesion in the health sector. I see that each institute is dedicated to its own interests, and when we have tried to establish collaboration agreements, we have failed. They have not worked; I do not know why this is. In my opinion, it would be important for us to have an integrated health system, in which all the institutions were linked together. [E:18]

In 1996, eleven years after Baja California Sur had signed the first decentralization agreement, the governor signed a second one: the Coordination Agreement for the Integral Decentralization of Health Services. The agreements' aim was to grant some administrative autonomy to the state and to establish the commitments and responsibilities of the state and the federation with respect to the organization of state health services, including the transfer of human, material, and financial resources from the center to the states. The agreements also specified that the OPD would assume the transferred functions within sixty days after each agreement was signed.

Administrative Reorganization after Decentralization

In 1995 the Baja California Sur Health Secretariat had four divisions (Health Services, Sanitary Regulation, Planning, and Administration), five subdivisions, and twenty-two departments. By 2000, the five subdivisions had become fourteen, and the twenty-two departments were reduced to twenty-one (see tables 5.1 and 5.2). This increased bureaucracy did not translate into administrative improvements or increased productivity. The expanded bureaucracy did little to improve service provision, decision making, or coordination with the health districts, as will be seen later. The following comments are very explicit in this respect:

Table 5.1. Structure of the Baja California Sur Health Secretariat, 1995

Director	Divisions	Subdivisions	Departments
Secretary of Health			Legal affairs
			Internal audit
Subtotal			2
	Health services	Preventive services	Epidemiology
			Preventive medicine
			Health education and health promotion
			First care level
		Medical services	Second care level
			Training and research
Subtotal	1	2	6
	Sanitary regulation		Regulation and sanitary promotion
			Sanitary control
			Sanitary administration
Subtotal	1	0	3
	Planning		State programming
			Informatics
			Statistics
			Evaluation and administrative modernization
Subtotal	1	0	4
	Administration	Human resources	Payments and operations
			Labor relations
		Physical resources	Payments, warehouse purchases
			Conservation, maintenance, and general services
		Financial resources	Budget integration
			Budget control and accounting
Subtotal	1	3	7
Total	4	5	22

Table 5.2. Structure of the Baja California Sur Health Secretariat, 2000

Director	Divisions	Subdivisions	Departments
Secretary of Health		Private secretary	Public relations
			Social work
		Legal affairs	Internal audit
		Internal audit	
Subtotal		3	3
	Health services	Training and priority programs	Training
			Noncommunicable diseases
		Medical services	Reproductive services
			Surveillance
		Epidemiology	Health promotion
		Health promotion and disease prevention	
		Statistics	
Subtotal	1	5	5
	Sanitary regulation	Sanitary regulation and promotion	Goods and services
			Occupational and environmental health
			Supplies and regulation of health services
Subtotal	1	1	3
	Planning	Informatics	Evaluation and administrative modernization
Subtotal	1	1	1
	Administration	Human resources	Payments and operations
			Labor relations
			Payments
		Physical resources and general services	Warehouse and inventory
			Purchases
			Conservation, maintenance
			Budget analysis and integration
		Financial resources	Financial control
			Accounting
		Renovation and maintenance of infrastructure	
Subtotal	1	4	9
Total	4	14	21

> They [the Health Ministry] gave us new positions, and we
> were fattening the Secretariat bureaucracy through useless
> organizational charts, because many identical functions were
> assigned to two or even three people.... I feel that decentrali-
> zation had harmful consequences for our organizational sys-
> tem. As a practical example, the number of administrative
> positions at the SSBCS tripled. We have more staff than the
> Health Secretariat of Sinaloa, and our population is one-
> twentieth that of Sinaloa. [E:8]

It is important to note that the State Health Secretariat's Planning Office
lost its programming and statistics departments during the transformation,
even though one objective of decentralization was "to enable decision making at the site where problems must be resolved and to bring about har-
monious and equitable regional development in response to local needs"
(Consejo Nacional de Salud 1996). Planning is a basic ingredient in decision
making and in adapting services to local needs. The hope was that decentralization would strengthen the planning procedure, not weaken it by
removing crucial units.

One participant in the State Health Secretariat's organizational reform
explained that the reduction in planning capacity in Baja California Sur
reflected weak planning at the federal level. Because the federal budget
was allocated to priority programs, there was little room to make changes,
which meant that the role of local planners was diminished:

> There was nothing to plan because they [the Health Ministry]
> gave you exactly what they wanted, and they didn't respect
> the program managers. We could never estimate the cost of a
> vaccine or of distributing family planning methods, the cost
> of treating a diabetic patient.... And we didn't even attain
> their objectives; we spent the money but on things not in-
> cluded in the plan. This is the reason why the planning direc-
> torate was weakened, because there was nothing to plan,
> nothing to pursue. [E:8]

In addition to recognizing the administrative deficiencies that existed,
some respondents also acknowledged that decentralization brought disor-
ganization by opening the doors to local political influence:

> Political influence is the bad thing. In the final analysis, poli-
> tics win; decisions are basically political. I believe that there
> should be a balance between politics and technical needs.
> [E:25]

The lack of technical skills at the state level continues to be a problem, perhaps even more so since decentralization because more decisions are now made at the state level. One of the people interviewed indicated that:

> The people who are making decisions do not have the tech-
> nical knowledge. Not even the secretaries or undersecretaries
> have training in public health.… This is a major blunder that
> is hurting us. [E:19]

One respondent remarked that despite the organizational changes, in practice little has changed due to the control exerted by a group of physicians:

> It's incredible; they keep on using the same people who have
> always been there. The old-timers are like a cyst; they can't
> be removed but they control everything. [E:22]

Another person confirmed the minimal impact that the changes have had on the organizational chart of the State Health Secretariat:

> It continues to be a pyramidal … hierarchical structure. What
> purpose does decentralization serve if the system continues
> to function in the same manner? [E:23]

The leaders of the National Union of Health Ministry Employees felt that decentralization gave them more participation in the appointment of employees and that it expanded their decision-making power. In this sense, a representative of the union commented:

> An advantage we now have is that the state health secretary
> requests the union's opinion on political appointments (*pues-*
> *tos de confianza*); this did not happen before. The persons who
> were going to occupy such positions were appointed by

those at the top.... Now they seek input from the union so
that there is more harmony and a better work climate....
Those in authority make the final decision, but how nice that
we can now give our opinion!... We now have more influence over what happens in the state than we had before. Before, everything had to be resolved at the federal level; now
most of the conflicts are resolved here. There is a good relationship between the union and the authorities at the Health
Secretariat. [E:11]

Decentralization of Human Resources

The most complicated aspects of the decentralization process were the
negotiations on labor issues. There were 1,320 unionized health workers in
Baja California Sur. It was agreed that the health workers' union would
continue to represent workers at the federal level, where the issues of
working conditions, wages, and benefits would be negotiated, and that
state-level positions would be brought up to the level of federal workers.
This meant a wage increase for state workers; but even more important, it
meant that their contracts would be bound by the rights, prerogatives, and
benefits contained in the General Labor Law.

The process of workers' homologation and the introduction of new
practices for personnel management were slow, and the individuals responsible for those activities had to be trained in the new system. One of
the directors who oversaw the process said that many mistakes were made
because personnel did not know how to implement the changes:

They came and imposed a system, and later they trained the
personnel. In the meantime, those in charge of the system
learned through a process of trial and error and by working
very long hours.... That was how they learned the new system. [E:17]

Decentralization added flexibility to the management of human resources. The state's secretary of health can now place employees where
they are most needed and can transfer them to other centers as necessary.
But implementation of the new rules has been slow, and the new system
has its limitations. According to an SSBCS executive:

> We can fill the vacancies; we have the authority to change
> our organizational structure to respond to the needs of the
> state ... but it wasn't until this May [2001] that they gave us
> the authority to make changes such as staff changes.... Those
> had always been done in Mexico City. All of this just hap-
> pened in May, and supposedly the decentralization was
> completed in December 2000. [E:7]

Several respondents indicated that the decentralization of human resources is incomplete, because the states cannot increase the number of
personnel nor can they decide what personnel are needed to perform the
various functions:

> For example, hospital staffing needs continue to be decided
> at the federal level ... not here and not based on the hospi-
> tal's perception of need. [E:10]

According to another informant:

> I feel that decentralization has only proceeded halfway; the
> management of labor was transferred to the states, but the
> authority to create positions and the assignment of funds
> continue to be at the federal level. So in fact it is a sort of fed-
> eralism ... but halfway ... because they decentralized labor
> management but not the resources. Yes, those remain con-
> centrated in the Federal District. Well, that is how I see it; the
> negative side is that they have not transferred the decision-
> making authority to the states. [E:18]

Equally, the transfer of federal funds to the state does not mean that the
state has the freedom to use these monies for human resources. One SSBCS
employee noted:

> Although they send the funds to us, we have to use them in
> accordance with what the federal level dictates. And if there
> is a need for new positions, we have to create them and pay
> for them with state funds. [E:4]

This interviewee pointed out that while the federal government has authorized new positions requested by the Baja California Sur Health Secretariat, these have not been sufficient. Many more workers are needed, and the state is unable to contract them. In some cases, the state government contracts personnel on a temporary basis, paying them out of state funds, but the state can only offer these workers low wages.

The negative repercussions of this personnel policy need to be discussed. One problem is that states with more resources will be able to advance faster than states with fewer resources, increasing the gaps between states and exacerbating existing geographical inequities. Another problem is that contracting temporary employees at low wages generates labor stratification within the Health Secretariat. Baja California Sur presently employs more than two hundred people on temporary contracts. One interviewee saw the problems thus:

> I imagine that this is good for a state that has a lot of resources, but in a state like ours, with few resources … the time will come when there will be an imbalance. Workers in the states with fewer resources will earn less, but perhaps in the end this is how it must be: each state will develop its system according to the resources it has. This is one of the disadvantages I see and one of the risks. In the states with greater economic resources, workers will see their salaries rise over time, and the salaries of those working in poorer states will stagnate. [E:5]

Baja California Sur does not have a system for monitoring efficacy and transparency in the filling of temporary positions. There are no norms for defining job priorities, advertising positions, recruiting, setting compensation levels, and selecting and appointing personnel. The majority of temporary contracts are paid from user fees that are managed by the health districts, hospitals, or the central office of the State Health Secretariat.

Decentralization has not increased workers' productivity. Before the decentralization agreement was signed in 1995, physicians averaged a very low 4.2 consultations per day. This number was unchanged in 1999. And specialists had only one daily consultation. Physicians, and specialists in particular, work in several institutions as well as having their own private practices. As a result, they do not work at the SSBCS the number of hours per day or number of days per week that are set in the agreement's section on the general conditions of work. This is a problem that decentralization has not resolved.

As noted in chapter 2, the states have had to assume the costs of raising state workers' benefits to the level of federal workers, the most expensive being the generous end-of-year bonuses. For its part, the federal government assumed the costs of the salary differential. One interviewee described the financial hardship that the additional payments imposed:

> The famous annual bonus is given to all workers … and for the workers who were homologized … it has to be paid with state funds. If we were truly decentralized, we could allocate resources to what we decide are the real needs of the State Health Secretariat.… But in this case, the decision to pay the annual bonuses is made at the federal level, and the state has to find the funds to comply with this mandate.… The state has to look for surplus funds in different sections of the budget … and assess all the financial commitments because the money [for the bonuses] comes from there.
>
> There have been years when we had to request authorization from Mexico City because the state did not have sufficient funds; and the federation ended up sending us the resources we needed to meet this commitment. The federal government has done an analysis and knows that the resources of the state are … not enough to cover [all bonuses], and it has allocated an additional amount to the regular budget. Last year we were able to cover all personnel-related expenditures with state funds, but to do this we had to transfer resources from all other budget items. [E:7]

The Transfer of Physical Infrastructure and Equipment

The decentralization agreement specifies that the state will be responsible for: (1) all functions related to the acquisition, management, administration, and distribution of equipment, supplies, goods, and properties; (2) the provision of general services; and (3) the maintenance and construction of public infrastructure. The agreement established that the federation would remain responsible for all debts, overdue or pending at the moment of the transfer, that the government had incurred in constructing and maintaining medical and administrative facilities. As noted earlier, the federal government had requested an evaluation of the infrastructure and equipment of all SSA facilities and had promised the states that it would contribute resources to improve the infrastructure.

All formal aspects of the transfer of physical infrastructure were carried out without difficulty. However, some interviewees commented on the economic burden placed on the state when transferred buildings were in poor conditions or not yet fully constructed. For example,

> They handed over infrastructure that was in poor condition.... The transfer of buildings that were not finished represented a problem for us.... In Baja California Sur we have a very old hospital that needs major renovation or, to put it simply, needs to be rebuilt. [E:4]

This informant was referring to the State General Hospital and an adjacent building, known locally as "The Tower," which would provide additional space for outpatient services and house the state's blood bank and blood transfusion center. But when the fieldwork for this study was under way, the "Tower" was still under construction and it was not clear that it would be completed. The following is the opinion of one respondent:

> What we need is health, right? We do not need more hospitals; we need equipment. But an order comes from the federal level saying that, instead of equipment, we have to construct another hospital. The reality is that we need better equipment, more personnel, and more medicines; however, we have to comply with requests from the federal level because, if not, we do not get anything. And if you don't give me any other choice, what can I do? I have to accept your offer even if I have other priorities. This experience tells me that it is extremely important to fully decentralize all resources, all authority and decision making. [E:14]

Our respondents agreed that there was sufficient infrastructure, although at the time of the transfer it was in poor condition. The investments that the state needed did not come until several years later when, in 1999, the PRD-PT coalition was elected to the state government, replacing the PRI. Most of the people interviewed, from both the current and former administrations, mentioned that the government had recently invested substantial resources in renovation. For example:

> Yes, a lot of renovation has been done. This is very unusual; no money had been invested in the Health Secretariat for many years. But now the state government has supported the SSBCS and has allocated resources. [E:11]

Yet despite recent investments, some believed the results had been meager:

> We have nothing. Look at how things are. This is the government that has allocated substantial resources to health, and it is difficult to see what has been accomplished with those resources, in part because the allocations have been directed toward enhancing their political image by investing in hospitals. The problem is that the money does not get to the people.... The state of Baja California Sur has an enviable infrastructure, and nearly 98 percent of the uninsured population has access to the services provided by the SSBCS.
>
> Nevertheless, this year the main problem is the shortage of supplies and medicines. In the last two years the state government has invested a lot in equipment, but we are still behind; we have about 60 percent of the equipment that the standard indicates we should have in each unit. [E:8]

One of the most important problems that respondents perceived involved the provision of supplies and medicines:

> What produced the worst chaos for the State Health Secretariat was that we had to pay for all operational expenditures out of the budget allocated by the federal government. This included supplies and medicines that the Health Ministry always used to send us. They always sent us all the supplies for family planning, all contraceptives, all supplies for the dengue fever and malaria programs, all provisions for ma-

ternal and child care, and all surgical equipment. When we
were decentralized, we had to purchase all of these things
ourselves....

The truth is that the State Health Secretariat never had administrative capacity to offer tenders.... In my opinion we
were better off when we received quarterly shipments of all
those provisions.... The federal government purchased in
bulk for the entire nation, and our health centers were better
stocked then than they are now. When we were decentralized we did not know what to do, we did not know how to
ensure that all of the State Health Secretariat's facilities received adequate stocks, and we did not know how to manage the financial resources they sent us. [E:8]

With respect to contraceptives for the family planning program, which
the state considered a top priority, one interviewee noted:

Last year we were without supplies for eight months, and
now we have been without funds for six months; people are
not doing things well. [E:21]

Two quotes are indicative of how those inside and outside the State
Health Secretariat perceived the shortage of supplies that resulted from
decentralization:

I have not seen any great benefits. The last thing that got my
attention was that the health center was pretty, very well
painted, but empty. It continues to have the same problems,
and the people continue to complain about the lack of medicines, equipment, and staffing. And the personnel complain
that there is no equipment, that there are no medicines, that
there are many shortages. [E:14]

I don't know, but something must change because somehow
this is not working. We have seen that sometimes we have an
excess of supplies in the hospitals, and sometimes we do not
have the things we need in order to work. The medicines are
very expensive. It's not that people don't want to get better,

but they can't pay for the services and the treatment. We
need to do a good analysis of all of this. [E:21]

This much stands out from the preceding discussion: there is a lack of
resources as well as inefficiencies in managing them. According to the aims
of decentralization, both situations should have improved. It was expected
that state contributions would gradually increase and that alternative
funding sources would be found. In addition, according to the Health Sector Reform Program 1995–2000: "The orderly implementation of the decentralization process will result in the medium term in a more agile and efficient operation of services" (SSA 1995: 16–17). Unfortunately, none of this
occurred in Baja California Sur.

Financial Autonomy

Like those in other states, Baja California Sur's Health Secretariat has three
sources of financing: federal, state, and self-generated funds or user fees.
According to the decentralization agreement, the two organizations involved in the financing of health services in Baja California Sur are the
OPD and the State Welfare Agency (PBP), with the latter using a percentage of the resources collected by the state and the municipal governments
to finance welfare agencies and a handful of health programs.

The OPD was created in December 1985, but the funds to cover the
costs of health services were not transferred until the second decentralization agreement was signed. When the fiscal transfer occurred in 1996, it did
not bring a major shift in decision-making responsibilities. The state continued to have very little financial decision-making authority because most
of the federal funds transferred to the state's Health Secretariat were used
to pay salaries. The following comment expresses the state's lack of financial independence in this area and how this impacts its decision-making
autonomy:

> We depend on the federal government. Eighty-five percent of
> the total state budget comes from the federal government.
> [To become independent] one has to have entrepreneurial
> talent to look for additional resources. [E:2]

Table 5.3. Source of Funds for the Baja California Sur Health Secretariat (in millions of 1994 pesos)

Source of Funds	1996		1997		1998		1999		2000	
	$millions	Percent	$millions	Percent	$millions	Percent	$millions	Percent	$millions	Percent
Federal	42.5	85.9	43.8	86.6	61.8	89.0	59.3	88.4	74.6	88.5
State	2.0	4.0	1.6	3.2	2.7	3.9	2.9	4.3	3.9	4.6
Self-generated	5.0	10.1	5.2	10.3	4.9	7.1	4.9	7.3	5.8	6.9
Total	49.5	100.0	50.6	100.1	69.4	100.0	67.1	100.0	84.3	100.0

It was expected that the states would increase their contributions to the health sector following decentralization. However, that has not occurred in Baja California Sur (see table 5.3). Federal contributions increased from 1996 to 2000, providing an important overall increase in funds over the study period. But the amounts can be misleading because the increases followed significant cutbacks made during the 1980s recession. The end result is that Baja California Sur's Health Secretariat continues to be under-funded. According to an interviewee from the SSBCS:

> The Health Secretariat does not have sufficient funds to de-velop programs, and the debt keeps growing and growing. Today, the debt is no longer payable. [E:8]

In 1996, the State Health Secretariat's debt represented 2.6 percent of the state's total health budget; by 2000 it had risen to approximately 5.6 percent (about 16.5 million pesos), and this figure does not include the interest on the debt. This debt accumulated over both the PRD-PT and PRI administrations.

Moreover, there are questions regarding the allocation of resources. When additional funds were received, they were used to renovate build-ings instead of going to finance operational expenditures and purchase supplies. For example, in 2001 the state allocated 5.5 million pesos in ex-traordinary funding to equip the most advanced state hospital, Juan María de Salvatierra Hospital in La Paz (the state capital), and another 5 million pesos to purchase equipment for health centers.

Persons interviewed said that the functions that were decentralized to the state are now centralized at the state level. One interviewee affirmed:

> We decentralized from Mexico City and recentralized in the state capital. Our hands are tied [at the local level]. One of the objectives of the decentralization was to strengthen the much-heralded new federalism, a phrase that sounds like a lot but means very little. The aim is that the states should have a greater capacity to operate according to the assess-ments made by our own communities. [E:2]

The State Health Secretariat sets user fees and determines how the generated funds are to be used. Ten percent of the funds collected by the health districts and hospitals are sent to the Federal Welfare Agency (PBPF), 5 percent to the State Welfare Agency, and the remainder to the health units that generated the funds.[2]

A financial analysis of the Baja California Sur Health Secretariat suggests that: (1) the federal government is not contributing sufficient resources to operate what it considers high-priority national programs; (2) the state does not have sufficient resources to operate the system and has failed to find alternative financing sources; and (3) there are inefficiencies in the administration of resources. In sum, decentralization's financial objectives—to increase efficiency in resource management and to increase the number of financing sources and the states' contributions—have not been achieved.

A question that arises regarding financial decentralization is, how can the SSBCS justify renovating buildings and creating a transplant program when it has such a huge debt and suffers continuous shortages of essential medicines and other basic supplies? One possible answer is that local politics interferes with the objective allocation of resources. Other explanations include poor planning, unawareness of the users' needs, and managerial incompetence.

Autonomy in the Provision of Services

One objective of the health reform was to increase equity by guaranteeing universal access to a package of basic health services, with the states providing additional services at their own cost. The problem was that Baja California Sur did not have any extra resources:

> As [a decentralized] state, I have the freedom ... to add services that I want if I can afford them. If I want, I can decide that the basic package covers twenty-four interventions instead of the current twelve or thirteen. Fine; then there will twenty-four, but only if I can afford them. [E:2]

---

[2] Health units need authorization from the State Health Secretariat for purchases over 300 pesos.

Others made similar comments, such as the following:

> Decentralized in quotes, in theory, yes, but in practice, no, be-
> cause we continue to depend on resource availability. [E:10]

For some, the basic services package is only a charity program for the
very poor:

> To give something to the poorest of the poor, to the super
> poor, because it is ... that group to which the World Bank
> targets the funds. And what [the Ministry of Health] says is
> that the rest should fend for themselves. [E:22]

According to the respondents, one outcome of decentralization is less
supervision, which contributes to inefficiencies:

> But they [the Health Ministry] have neglected some adminis-
> trative dimensions. We worry because the benefits of super-
> vision are being overlooked due to the lack of money....
> Since services were decentralized, the federal level has rarely
> come to supervise. I believe that the state health units do not
> receive even minimal supervision due to the lack of money,
> and the services will undoubtedly deteriorate. [E:3]

Another respondent echoed this perspective:

> The National Agreement for the Decentralization of Health
> Services established that the federal level would be responsi-
> ble for all normative functions and for supervision and
> evaluation. They have continued to evaluate, but it appears
> that since the new [Fox] government took office, the federal
> level has not supervised with the same intensity as under
> previous administrations. Traditionally the federal evalua-
> tions were very comprehensive. They evaluated how we
> were implementing all the high-priority programs, they vis-
> ited a health district, assessed the performance of all the
> workers, and monitored whether we were complying with

national rules. They even ascertained whether we had enough supplies and personnel.

Since President Fox took office, the federal level has not supervised us. Supervision can be seen as federal-level interference in the affairs of the state, but it has the advantage that most supervisory visits included recommendations for improvement and on-the-job training. The end result was that they raised workers' skill levels, and this had a positive impact within the system. [E:5]

Observing how resources were allocated, some interviewees perceived a tendency to prioritize certain curative activities:

There is a little bit of this mentality, always looking to use technology.... The greater the use of technology, the better; and this means more earnings, right? [E:21]

Salvatierra Hospital ... had an excess of beds, and the hospital administrators insisted that all the beds should be filled.... Worse, they also wanted to abandon the old hospital and build another one in the same area, at a cost of 520 million pesos.... They paid one million pesos just to prepare the project. Can you believe this? It's not logical, and it's not a priority. What happened is that this was done by politicians who think they know everything—the type of today's politicians who are medical doctors, architects, lawyers, professors who know everything and have an opinion on everything. [E:8]

One interviewee summed up as follows:

With respect to the national programs, we can say that there has been no true decentralization. There continues to be little flexibility and not much room for innovation—in part because the scarcity of funds has prevented the state from adding programs to the basic health services package and because all state contributions are needed to cover operational costs. With respect to other stated objectives, universal coverage, at least in its broad sense, has not materialized. [E:13]

Community Participation

As discussed earlier in this volume, advocates of decentralization argue that it can encourage community participation in decision making, but the health officials of Baja California Sur's Health Secretariat have not promoted community participation as a part of decentralization. When asked their opinions regarding community participation in health policymaking and oversight of health care delivery, the interviewees agreed that it would be important. Nevertheless, they confirmed that no formal effective mechanism had been created to enable community participation. They see the community as a source of information about service needs and quality, but not as an actor in policy decisions:

> The opinion of the population is taken into account in some aspects, yes, because they help us understand the value and performance of our programs, but to include them in the planning and development of such [programs], no; that is something different. [E:1]

Health Secretariat personnel and some representatives of civil society organizations have doubts about how to ensure community participation:

> At the moment the [participation] program is barely being implemented. We're not certain how this will be established … how this democratization will happen. [E:3]

Some health officials tend to blame the poor for their poverty and believe that the poor have no interest in improving or participating in the health sector:

> Society is also very apathetic; I see it as very apathetic. In Baja California Sur, civil society doesn't have any input into the programs. Policymakers dictate, and the rest obey; there is no public discussion. There are areas where people live in very unhealthy conditions and they remain there; they have no interest in making a formal proposal [to improve their conditions]. [E:25]

Another interviewee expressed the same idea with the following words:

> We had a certain amount of participation in the consultation
> forums, but people are very apathetic; they resist participat-
> ing. Some associations participated—the medical school, the
> medical association—and some health workers presented
> proposals. [E:13]

On the other hand, interviewees from civil society organizations hold a
different opinion:

> Here in the state, the State Health Secretariat has invited us
> on just a few occasions. The [Health Ministry] sometimes in-
> vites our national representatives, but here, no. As an organi-
> zation, they do not take us into account. [E:21]

This viewpoint is shared by other members of civil society:

> Although there should be greater openness, I generally do
> not experience it. They are very reluctant to share informa-
> tion or include others.... We requested some indicators, and
> they never gave them to us.... The data are generated here,
> and they have a lot of information. They have a very com-
> plete information system ... but they do not share it with
> anyone.... There is no transparency....
>
> The health sector is always a problem.... We are supposed
> to be included in decision-making committees such as the
> State Development Planning Committee (COPLADE), the
> health committees, the safe motherhood taskforce;... all of
> them are inter-institutional groups, right? Well, they have
> never called us.... Maybe they have never met, we don't
> know, or they don't want to include us.
>
> Well, that's what I see from outside ... that, in fact, decen-
> tralization has not resulted in consultations and has not in-
> cluded other players and/or other sectors.... They have not
> consulted with community organizations to improve plan-
> ning. We have never been included, and to my knowledge
> the Red Cross has not been included either. Unless some-

thing exceptional happens or the federal level puts pressure
... they [the State Health Secretariat] do not include anyone.
For this reason ... we need federal pressure to convene a
meeting. And in formal meetings [where community organizations are present] nothing is decided because ... the government makes the decisions.... This is ironic because the
neoliberal reform says that the central state should play a
lesser role. [E:22]

There is a general recognition that participation is, to a certain extent,
induced and controlled by the State Health Secretariat:

They [community organizations] participate in what the authorities want them to participate in—for example, in health
committees or school health committees. Yes, they participate, but that's because someone has prepared the meeting to
make sure that people express what the organizers want
them to say. [E:5]

A comment by another interviewee confirms the lack of participation:

Often the members of the health committees are appointed
by the State Health Secretariat, and in most cases the members accept what the secretary says, and that's that.... It's
protocol. People do not participate as expected, but I believe
that this is mostly our fault as health workers, rather than the
people's responsibility. We are not able to provide continuity
and to motivate them to participate actively. [E:8]

The preceding statements suggest that the State Health Secretariat
wants communities to legitimize the decisions already made by the institution. The following highlights another form of community participation:

When people pressure government officials to build a health
center or a clinic, or to bring a doctor, this is how they participate in decision making, increasing pressure on government officials when they want more health services. This is
how much of the health infrastructure was built in the area of

> Los Cabos. We have already constructed three health cen-
> ters;… the new settlements require a new health center with
> a physician, nurse, health promoter, and all of that. [E:5]

This respondent expressed concern about the new role that patients have
learned as consumers of health services:

> Now it seems that there is more intense pressure from users.
> People are more participative, more demanding, and it seems
> that they want to have more control over how services are
> delivered.… Now they question how services are rendered
> and they even sue. Before, even if somebody died, a mother
> or a child, nobody said much. Now there are more and more
> charges taken to the media. This is good; it helps us improve.
> [E:5]

A director of services commented:

> We are in a period of transition. We need to practice medi-
> cine in a context that has never been faced before. We have to
> practice "new medicine," the new medicine being whatever
> the client decides, what the client rates as desirable. The cli-
> ent judges the quality of the services. The client is no longer a
> passive recipient. This is the case even for our most impover-
> ished patients. Why? Because television bombards them with
> messages from the secretary of health: "you have the right to
> receive quality services" and "you should receive individual-
> ized attention." These messages have a tremendous impact.
> Now I hear demands, complaints.… This forces the doctor to
> adopt the attitudes he should have had all along, and to
> comply with all official Mexican standards, behave ethically,
> provide information, obtain informed consent from the peo-
> ple. That is the new medicine that did not exist before. [E:10]

When questioned about the formal mechanisms of participation that
have been implemented, our respondents mentioned surveys, health
committees, complaint/suggestion boxes, consultation forums, and the
public hearings at which people can express their needs and concerns di-

rectly to the governor. However, when making decisions, executives need only take into account the opinions expressed during consultation forums (on health regulation) and the requests made during audiences with the governor. Undoubtedly, responding to demands presented directly to the governor has a political dimension. One interviewee thought that the forums and surveys were not helpful:

> The so-called opinion surveys, the slips of paper at the health forums … I believe they are a complete waste. [E:10]

Further, the system of lodging complaints through suggestion boxes does not operate well at all health facilities:

> We need to improve the complaint system … because the complaints traditionally remain locked in a desk, and this should not be. We should pursue the complaints, be accountable to our citizens. But this is not something the director should do; it should be done by a special office.… Right now, here in this hospital, I know that the complaint and suggestion box is not working because … it has disappeared. [E:9]

There is also a lack of community participation at the municipal level. One of the persons interviewed explained:

> There is no community participation in the municipality. Suddenly we start seeing committees being formed in the neighborhoods, but they stop functioning when politicians begin meddling and try to control them. [E:5]

Some observers see the user fee system as a potential point of community participation. However, the federal government established the user fees, and communities do not participate in determining the amount of the fees or defining the fee-exemption policies. The funds generated through user fees have increased substantially in recent years, and Baja California Sur Health Secretariat officials see this as very positive; in their view it is an indication of an improvement in the performance of the health system. Yet a closer look reveals that although the amount of funds generated through user fees in 2000 was 16 percent higher than in 1996, the relative increase is not so striking; the contribution of the federal government increased by 75 percent over the same period.

The challenge for Baja California Sur is to reduce its dependence on user fees to finance the health sector. The patients of the Health Secretariat are the poorest in the state, and increases in user fees would negatively impact the equity of the system.

In sum, there is no agreement on what constitutes community participation, although it is considered to be important. Some interviewees from the State Health Secretariat suggest that the community does not want to participate, but civil society organizations have not been invited to participate, and the Health Secretariat has not created formal mechanisms to ensure effective community participation in decision making. It is important to recognize that the consultation forum and public proposals for changes to sanitary regulations were a step in the right direction.

CONCLUSIONS

The decentralization of health services is the core of Mexico's program to reform the health sector. Two rationales underlie decentralization. The first is political: to bring the government closer to the citizenry and to involve citizens in health decision making. This logic is presented as part of the ongoing efforts to democratize the Mexican political process. The second rationale is economic: to increase efficiency in the provision of health services. However, our findings in Baja California Sur suggest that the real purpose behind decentralization is to bring the health sector in line with the new imperatives of economic and political modernization inherent in the neoliberal model of capital accumulation that the country has embraced.

Decentralization is a complex process that has technical, social, and political dimensions. In Baja California Sur, the implementation process has been controlled from the federal level and was carried out as stipulated by the federal government. The central government determined how decentralization was to be executed, and there was no consultation with local policymakers and technocrats. State leaders were willing to accept this situation for a number of reasons: (1) the federal and the state governments belonged to the same political party; (2) the federal level promised that

state health services would be strengthened following a local needs assessment; and (3) state officials hoped to gain more autonomy in managing
resources.

The principal proponents of decentralization did not include transparency, equity, and community participation among the program's objectives. The Health Ministry retained centralized authority to issue rules; as a
result, the Baja California Sur Health Secretariat has not produced any
rules at the state level, only a few cosmetic adjustments to mesh with specific state needs.

The State Health Secretariat did, however, have the flexibility to reorganize the state's central administration and to appoint upper- and mid-
level administrators to strengthen the Health Secretariat's managerial capacity. The reorganization of services had the undesired outcome of duplicating functions, which presumably implied increased costs, though the
amount is not yet known. It is not clear that the administrative reorganization of the State Health Secretariat has improved communication between
state administrators and those at the operational level (in health districts
and hospitals). The new organizational structure of the Health Secretariat
resembles that of the Ministry of Health, centralizing its very limited
amount of delegated autonomy in the hands of a few executives.

The transfer of authority for human resources management has been
very limited. The state can only make minor adjustments in order to
achieve the objectives jointly agreed upon by the Ministry of Health and
the State Health Secretariat's labor union. The State Health Secretariat can
hire temporary workers, but it does not have a system of rules and controls
to ensure that the recruitment and management of the new personnel is
done in a transparent manner or that it responds appropriately to the
health needs of the population. The productivity of Health Secretariat personnel is very low, and there is a need for an in-depth analysis to determine the causes for this and to identify possible solutions.

One of the most important problems in the state's health system is the
shortage of supplies and medicines. The State Health Secretariat has little
or no decision-making capacity in managing financial resources because
most of the funds are federal. State contributions are equivalent to only
one-twentieth of the funds received from the Health Ministry, and other
stable sources of financing have not materialized. There has been no im-

provement in the administration of resources, and the Health Secretariat's indebtedness continues to rise.

The limited transfer of decision-making authority from the Health Ministry to the State Health Secretariat, coupled with the state's very small contribution to the health budget, has not permitted the development of programs to address the specific needs of the state's population. Baja California Sur's claim of universal health coverage exists more in theory than in reality. People do have geographical access to health facilities, which are abundant and well staffed, but this by itself does not guarantee that users of health services will receive quality care and the treatment they need to resolve their health problems.

Health authorities in Baja California Sur understand that community participation is important, but they do not view it as a goal of the decentralization strategy, and they have not established formal mechanisms to encourage it or to elicit public opinion. The users and providers of health services have no contact outside of the consultation room, and the residents of the state do not participate in the planning or evaluation of health services. Some providers suggest that the population is not interested in participating, but this opinion contrasts with the position of leaders of nongovernmental organizations and other interest groups, who say they are rarely invited to participate in meetings with health authorities. The only invitations they have received from the State Health Secretariat were to discussions about programs that the civil society groups themselves have volunteered to carry out.

According to the State Health Secretariat, communities participate when they pay fees to use health services. This is a cynical interpretation of community participation, particularly when users do not have a voice in determining the amount of the fees or the use to which they are put. The poor are the ones who use the facilities of the State Health Secretariat, and it is easy to understand that fee increases may also increase inequity.

Today, approximately twenty years after the launching of the decentralization of health services, the main characteristics of the health delivery model—shaped over decades of centralism—have not changed in any significant way.

References

Castro, R. 1996. "En busca del significado: supuestos alcances y limitaciones del análisis cualitativo." In *Para comprender la subjetividad: investigación cualitativa en salud reproductiva y sexualidad*, ed. I. Sasz and S. Lerner. México, D.F: El Colegio de México.

Consejo de Salud. 1996. *Hacia la federalización de la salud en México*. México, D.F.

INEGI (Instituto Nacional de Estadística, Geografía e Informática). 2000. *Anuario Estadístico Baja California Sur*.

LACHSR (Latin American and Caribbean Regional Health Sector Reform Initiative). 2000. "Lineamientos para la realización de análisis estratégicos de los actores de la reforma sectorial en salud." Venezuela, January.

Mercado Martínez, F. J. 2000. "El proceso de análisis de los datos en una investigación sociocultural en salud." In *Análisis cualitativo en salud: teoría, método y práctica*, ed. F. J. Mercado Martínez and T. M. Torres López. Mexico: Universidad de Guadalajara.

Ratcliffe, J. W., and A. González del Valle. 2000. "El rigor en la investigación de la salud: hacia un desarrollo conceptual." In *Por los rincones: antología de métodos cualitativos en investigación social*, ed. C. Denman and J. Haro. Mexico: El Colegio de Sonora.

Soberón, G. 1986. *Descentralización de la vida nacional. La descentralización de los servicios de salud: el caso de México*. México, D.F.: Miguel Ángel Porrúa.

SSA (Secretaría de Salud y Asistencia). 1995. "Programa de Reforma del Sector Salud, 1996–2000." México, D.F.: SSA.

———. 2001. "Descentralización de los servicios de salud a las entidades federativas: memorias 1995–2000." México, D.F.: SSA.

———. 2002. "Sistema de información en salud, SISPA." México, D.F.: SSA.

Taylor, S., and R. Bogdan. 1987. "La entrevista a profundidad." In *Introducción a los métodos cualitativos de investigación*. Barcelona: Paidos.

6

The Slow and Difficult Institutionalization of Health Care Reform in Sonora, 1982–2000

RAQUEL ABRANTES PÊGO

This chapter discusses the technical and institutional capacity of the State Health Secretariat of Sonora (SSS) to implement the decentralization of health services, as well as the political dimensions of decentralization— including the roles played by professional associations, health workers' unions, political leaders, and the private health sector.

The data were gathered in February 1999.[1] The fieldwork began with seven in-depth interviews with researchers knowledgeable about the state health system and the political and socioeconomic realities of Sonora. The researchers assisted in identifying pertinent documents and in preparing a list of key informants that included fourteen people: eight officials and former officials of the Sonora Health Secretariat, three medical school representatives, four political leaders, three members of health worker unions, two members of the State Health Council, four employees of social security

---

[1] This chapter is part of a study by the Mexican National Institute of Public Health in Oaxaca, Guanajuato, and Sonora, funded by the International Development Research Centre of Canada (Brachet-Márquez 2002). The study analyzed the relationship between macroeconomic policies and health-sector reform and the effects on the access, utilization, and quality of health services.

Fieldwork coincided with the Mexican Congress's approval of the controversial proposal to reform the Mexican Social Security Institute (IMSS), opening the door to private-sector provision of health services for IMSS beneficiaries. Labor unions and the Party of the Democratic Revolution (PRD) actively opposed the proposal, and the national debate that followed was widely reported in national and international media.

institutes, and two members of other health commissions (the total exceeds fourteen because some interviewees fall into more than one category).[2]

The guides for the semi-structured interviews covered the following: (1) identification of the most important problems related to the funding of and demand for health services; (2) the level of state autonomy, the nature of the relationship between state and federal authorities and among the different health institutions in the state; (3) existing channels of communication for informants to express their concerns to state and federal decision makers; (4) views on the health reform and its impact on the daily work and performance of health institutions; and (5) suggestions to improve the reform program. Finally, interviewees were presented with a series of hypothetical scenarios with different health problems to identify the problems' severity and possible solutions given available resources.

The aims of the research were explained preceding each interview, and each subject was given the option of answering anonymously. There were no refusals to participate in the study or objections to taping the interviews. None of the interviewees requested anonymity, although in some cases they asked that the information they provided be used only for academic, not political, purposes. Most interviews lasted between one and two hours. All were carried out, recorded, and transcribed by the author. The information obtained in the interviews was classified according to categories created during the project's design stage.

At the time of the research, I held a teaching appointment at the National Institute of Public Health. Some interviewees interpreted my position there in ways that may have affected their responses. For example, one interviewee viewed me as a representative of the federal Ministry of Health (SSA) and assumed that he could take advantage of the interview to transmit requests and demands. Another mentioned that he knew the director of the National Institute of Public Health very well and would report to him any problem caused by the research.

---

2 The researchers were Drs. Almada Bay and Catalina A. Denman of El Colegio de Sonora; Drs. Rosario Román Pérez and Mario Cambreros Castro (experts on social and economic problems in Sonora), and Ernesto Camou (an expert on Sonora's political process), from the Centro de Investigación en Alimentación y Desarrollo; and Drs. Manuel Santillana Macedo and Ramón Rascón, from the Research Unit of the Mexican Social Security Institute in Hermosillo.

SONORA: A SNAPSHOT OF HEALTH-SECTOR FEDERALISM

Sonora is one of the six Mexican states that borders the United States. It is the second-largest state in Mexico in terms of surface area (185,431 square miles), and in 2000 it had a population of 2.2 million, half of whom resided in the four major cities. The state's gross domestic product (GDP) per capita is above the national average (17,770 Mexican pesos in Sonora, versus 14,396 for the nation overall in 1999). Between 1993 and 1999, Sonora experienced an average growth rate of 16 percent (compared to 8.5 percent for Mexico as a whole), and the state's education levels are also above the national average.

About 56 percent of the population is covered by social security, and per capita health expenditures in 1999 were slightly above average (1,300 Mexican pesos versus 1,214 for the nation). Total fertility and infant mortality rates are below national averages, at 1.65 and 11.68, respectively, versus 1.74 and 12.5 in Mexico as a whole. The maternal mortality rate was the lowest among the country's northern states, at 2.66 per 10,000 live births.

Sonora was one of the few states that achieved a GDP increase (3.2 percent) in 1983 despite the economic crisis that had swept the country in the preceding four years (Presidencia de la República 1985: 327). This growth was attributed to market liberalization and to the increasing number of *maquiladoras* (in-bond manufacturing plants) along the U.S.-Sonora border (Jasís and Guendelman 1991: 469)—two strategies that probably benefited Mexico's northern border states more than those in the interior.

At the time when functions of the Health Ministry began to be decentralized, the Ministry provided health services for Sonora's uninsured population, and the various social security funds (IMSS and ISSSTE) provided services for employed workers. Alongside these services, there was also a small private health sector, which included a dynamic corps of traditional healers (Haro 1998). The state also sponsored the Social Security Institute for Employees of the State of Sonora (ISSSTESON), which provided health services to state employees. Also, in 1954, IMSS insured a number of *ejidos* that could afford the IMSS premiums (Hernández Llamas 1984: 29), and in 1971, 13,500 Yaqui Indians became beneficiaries of the IMSS (IMSS 1984: 356).

Ministry of Health services in Sonora were part of the Ministry's National Office of Coordinated Services and were administered by the State

Coordinated Public Health Services, headquartered in Hermosillo, the state capital. Other health agencies and hospitals in Sonora include the Health Commission on Sanitary Engineering (Delegación Estatal de la Comisión Constructora de Ingeniería Sanitaria), two hospitals (the Campestre Cruz del Norte and the Niño del Noroeste), the state office of the Undersecretariat for Environmental Improvement (Delegación Estatal de la Subsecretaría de Mejoramiento del Ambiente), and the National Commission for the Eradication of Malaria (Comisión Nacional para la Eradicación del Paludismo), which reported directly to other departments of the Health Ministry.

In the early 1980s, the State Coordinated Public Health Services in Sonora comprised 17 health districts (Pérez Duarte 1988: 98), 212 health clinics (*casas de salud*), and 92 rural health centers (*centros de salud rural*), the latter staffed by nurses and physicians doing their obligatory year of social service (SSA 1982: 747). The indigenous population could also receive health services in the 19 urban health centers that offered specialty services and in secondary-level hospitals in the cities of Hermosillo, Ciudad Obregón, Álamos, and Ures. Sonora received 16 percent of the federal resources allocated for health (Soberón 1987: 172) despite its small population and good health indicators.

Some students of Mexican health policy suggest that regional policymakers do not influence Health Ministry decisions and that the Ministry does not take state-level political dynamics and needs into account in its decision making. Cadena Pelarde (1989: 30) shares this view, asserting that, because of centralism, health services did not keep pace with Sonora's rapid population expansion in the 1970s. Other observers offer a slightly different analysis. Abrantes Pêgo (1998) argues that local political patronage influences the distribution of federal resources within the states, and Pineda Pablos (2000: 28) suggests that, before blaming centralism for the discrepancy between needs and resources at the local level, one should first examine the patronage relations between the Health Ministry and the various state organizations of the Institutional Revolutionary Party (PRI) and also look at the influence of local political bosses, political leaders, and peasant organizations. Without this information, it is difficult to determine whether local demands are best addressed through federal or state-level decisions. Local political patronage intervenes in the distribution of state resources (Abrantes Pêgo 1998).

DECENTRALIZATION IN THE 1980s: FROM THE CENTER FOR THE CENTER

In 1985 Sonora was the third state to sign a decentralization agreement with the federal government, initiating a slow and controlled process of power transfer from the federal to the state level. Officially, Sonora was included in the first phase of decentralization because it met all requirements and because of the strong interest of its governor, but, as discussed in chapter 2 in this volume, the criteria that determined which states should be decentralized were never completely clear.

Sonora established two administrative structures as part of the decentralization process. One, the Coordinated Public Health Services (later renamed the Sonora Health Secretariat, coordinated planning and the administration of programs and resources in the health sector (Pérez Duarte 1988: 97). The minister of health appointed its first director. The second structure was Sonora Medical Services (SEMESON), established to operate the state network of medical services and the IMSS-Solidarity Program. The governor appointed its first director, but the Ministry of Health closely managed its activities.

The interviews conducted as part of this research elicited a good deal of information about these early steps in the decentralization process in Sonora; in the interest of maintaining the respondents' anonymity, direct citations that appear below are referenced solely by the number of the interview.

> When decentralization was being negotiated, the states made commitments to provide resources for health services. The state government of Sonora pledged to contribute at least 30 percent of the state's health budget. [E:2]

> This contribution and the logistical support of local private industries for health campaigns were sustained during the two remaining years of the de la Madrid administration [1985–1987]. With these resources the State Health Secretariat carried out massive immunization campaigns, organized 350 health committees, and, in February 1987, created five health districts—in Hermosillo, with 70 health centers; in Caborca, with 26 centers; in Cananea, with 36; in Ciudad Obregón, with 46; and in Navojoa, with 110 health centers. [E:4]

Each district had a director and three divisions (preventive services, medical care, and health promotion) and an administrative unit (Pérez Duarte 1988: 98). The districts' directors were physicians who had recently graduated from schools of public health or were public health enthusiasts [E:1].

The interviewees reported that decentralization did not allow state health authorities to manage financial and human resources, nor were state authorities responsible for health planning. For example, after 1984 people had to pay a user fee to access health services. The Ministry of Health set the fee levels, and all funds collected through this mechanism had to be remitted to the Ministry. According to the first state secretary of health in Sonora, the state had to lobby long and hard before it was finally authorized in 1987 to retain user fees. According to one state administrator, decentralization had converted state bureaucrats into "endorsers of checks and nothing else" [E:8]. According to another health official:

> In its first phase, decentralization resulted in the transfer of nothing—nothing. Everything remained there [in the Health Ministry]: the people, the training…. [To satisfy our own local needs], Sonora had to make a major effort and recruit personnel, train them, and prepare its own leaders. [E:3]

For these reasons, the political support for and commitment to decentralization gradually waned in the state, and many health officials in Sonora opposed the implementation of decentralization as dictated by the Ministry of Health. Those who participated in the negotiations saw a lack of transparency in the process and did not share the vision of the then-minister of health, Dr. Guillermo Soberón. Some criticized Soberón and his colleagues for their lack of experience in public health institutions and lack of political experience (they were not PRI militants).

According to a former SEMESON executive, the decentralization that Soberón promoted had a generally solid framework, but "it was a decentralization process led by academics and technocrats" [E:3]. Another former executive noted:

> [Soberón] was a physician who specialized in biochemistry; he was a researcher. He kept experimenting with models, always generating ideas that were not very practical…. [His

staff] did not have their feet in the real world ... kids from Harvard with no social experience, out of touch with the people with needs. [E:4]

The result, as reported by those interviewed, was a limited decentralization managed by federal bureaucrats, a process full of improvisation and little participation from regional stakeholders who could have managed the decentralization process more appropriately. The decentralization that Soberón championed was accepted in principle, but there was a "generalized resistance from local and regional forces, and the measures were weakened" for lack of support, according to a researcher from Sonora [E:1]. Decentralization was perceived as a policy initiated by a federal-level elite of technocrats who produced "lots of paper" but provided little logistical support and retained too much control [E:4].

Though decentralization remained part of political rhetoric during the presidency of Carlos Salinas de Gortari (1988–1994), the process itself was virtually paralyzed. The major event of the Salinas administration in terms of its impact on Sonora's health sector was the implementation of the North American Free Trade Agreement in January 1994. NAFTA made it easier for U.S. and Canadian health insurance providers, managed care companies, and private hospital chains to invest in Mexico.

Mexico's doctors feared that their private practices could be threatened by the entry of U.S. and Canadian physicians and that their professional autonomy would decrease because they would have to comply with rules imposed by foreign health corporations. They also felt threatened by what was called the "transborder patient," raised in a culture that fostered malpractice litigation, something unknown in Mexico at that time.

The expansion of the private health sector and the lack of investment by the public sector led public institutions to subcontract some services to private providers. Previously, such subcontracting had been limited to ISSSTESON, but during Salinas's administration, the Health Ministry and IMSS began to subcontract services as well, particularly high-tech services. The public sector entered into a relationship of dependency with the private sector, pressured to use private-sector services even when they were not needed.

THE SECOND WAVE OF DECENTRALIZATION: INCREASING UNCERTAINTY
Decentralization as Seen by State Health Officials

The decentralization effort promoted during the administration of President Ernesto Zedillo (1994–2000) took place at a time of economic crisis and political uncertainty. Interviews with executives of the Sonora Health Secretariat revealed that the second phase of decentralization offered more scope for negotiating with the federal government about the utilization of financial and human resources and about program design. Despite this increased negotiating capacity, however, the interviewees still saw decentralization as directed from the federal level, with little room for state autonomy.

Most health funds continued to be transferred from the federal government to the states, but the states had no voice in the preparation of the federal budget. The Ministries of Health and Finance prepared the budget based on historical allocations. The present research found that state authorities lacked programmatic autonomy, even in priority programs such as immunizations, family planning, and reproductive health. An official in the Sonora Health Secretariat described these limitations as follows:

> The center [the Ministry] retains control over rules and regulations. It defines how funds are to be spent, when they are to be made available, and when they are to be used. Even more, they [the Ministry] define the profile for each person to be hired and the training to be given. When training is required, the center decides its scheduling and content. [E:3]

Other respondents expressed similar views. For them, the vertical hierarchical relationship continued despite the rhetoric of decentralization. Another interviewee complained that the National Health Council (which includes Health Ministry representatives and all state secretaries of health) only serves to rubberstamp decisions made by the Health Ministry. He suggested that other more democratic forms, such as forums, should have been organized. In his words:

> In forums, agreements could have been reached that would have been less biased than what comes out of the National Health Council meetings. At meetings of the National Health

Council, the issues brought up for discussion have already been decided, or there is already an outline to follow and they [Health Ministry executives] are only looking for the state to validate what has already been decided. [E:3]

Other respondents felt that the relationship between the federal and state governments had a paternalistic bias. As examples of federal paternalism, they mentioned the barriers that were raised when the state presented its own initiatives. The federal government also stopped local initiatives, citing the state officials' lack of technical capacity. A state executive summed up this perception as follows: "If you transfer everything to the states, they won't know what to do with the money and the wrong decisions will be made" [E:3].

Likewise, there were comments from respondents at the Sonora Health Secretariat indicating that the federal government was not transferring sufficient funds and that the financial problems of the state health sector had increased in recent years due to payroll shortfalls.[3] Lack of funds also made it difficult to maintain the physical infrastructure and to make timely payments to public hospitals and pharmaceutical suppliers [E:7]. Preventive care and health promotion programs—especially for AIDS, dengue, and cholera—suffered as well from the lack of resources. Furthermore, because resources were insufficient, the State Health Secretariat acknowledged a growing tendency to extract contributions from poor communities, either through user fees or through community labor in exchange for services.

In Sonora, such community contributions via user fees or labor have generated concern and controversy: "charging user fees limits access to health services, because families cannot afford to take all their children [to the clinics]" [E:4]. The state also utilizes other strategies to capture funds from the community. It organizes community groups to do housekeeping, repairs, and maintenance work at the health centers, and it creates trusts and health committees. The trusts are volunteer organizations that contribute toward specific activities, such as health campaigns, and cover medical care costs for the indigent; health committees maintain the physi-

---

[3] As indicated throughout this volume, following decentralization, states had to cover the costs of certain employee benefits, adding to overall labor costs.

cal plant or contribute to the financing and implementation of some activities, such as food preparation during immunization campaigns. According to officials of the Sonora Health Secretariat, this is a highly distorted understanding of what "community participation" should be.

However, State Secretary of Health Dr. Manuel Robles Linares Negrete held a view that differed from that of many technical officials in the State Health Secretariat. Robles Linares Negrete felt that all such forms of contributing were reasonable and appropriate.

> Everyone helps according to their means. It can be one peso or a thousand pesos. In Palma, a person can contribute one thousand pesos to the committee, and in other places they ask people for one peso because they have nothing. [E:5]

The Sonora Health Secretariat faces other financial challenges that cannot be resolved at the state level because they involve IMSS, a federal institution. When workers lose their jobs, as thousands have done during Mexico's recent economic downturns, they also lose their medical coverage through the Mexican Social Security Institute. If they cannot afford private medical services, their only remaining alternative is the State Health Secretariat's clinics and hospitals. Moreover, an estimated 30 percent of people receiving health services through the Sonora Health Secretariat are IMSS beneficiaries who prefer the State Health Secretariat because its wait times are shorter or its facilities are closer to the patient's home. A respondent commented:

> Thirty percent of the insured population demand that services be located nearby … and there is no mechanism to sign an agreement or collaborate with the IMSS.… The people seek services at the State Health Secretariat, and our budget is tight. [E:4]

The interviewees expressed little confidence that the Social Security Institute would reimburse the State Health Secretariat for services provided to IMSS beneficiaries. According to one interviewee, resource utilization cannot be maximized due to the lack of coordination between institutions. In a situation of scarcity, greater inter-institutional coordination could result in a more balanced use of resources. Other interviewees expressed similar ideas and even suggested that the health sector's fragmentation can be attributed to the attitudes of health executives:

> Each institution is concerned with its own survival and seeks to solve its problems to guarantee its own continuity.... Policies for intersectoral cooperation are moribund, because none of the institutions is willing to put a cent into them. [E:3]

Like the first phase of decentralization, the second phase in Sonora was incomplete, intended by design to be a halfway decentralization. Responsibility to implement programs defined by the federal Health Ministry was transferred to the state, but this occurred without the needed funds or the authority to manage personnel. In the words of an interviewee:

> They were virtual changes. Previously, the center [the Health Ministry] was in charge of the malaria program. Now the state is, but with the same people who were here before and who continue to be here now. [E:4]

The implication here is that the bureaucrats maintained their allegiance to the Health Ministry; this is easy to understand given that the Ministry continues to pay their salaries. The same official questioned the absence of any significant changes in the organizational chart of the Health Ministry:

> When the change happened and they said, "the rules and regulations stay here, and the operations go there," there should have been a change in the composition of human resources [at the Health Ministry]. If they are only going to regulate and they are not going to run operations, why do they need to keep so many people at the Health Ministry? [E:4]

According to the interviewees, something that illustrates the unfinished nature of the decentralization is that the rules and regulations for the majority of programs continue to be issued by the Health Ministry even though Sonora has trained people to carry out these functions. In the words of a director of health services:

> The Ministry defines the indicators we have to use in the programs and the information we have to collect. We include some problems that are local, such as epidemiological surveillance of the effect of pesticides on health ... and we develop indicators. But for the rest of the programs—for example, vaccine-preventable diseases—the information systems continue to be designed in Mexico City.... At times we have been able to modify them to fit our needs, taking into account the training of our personnel or the personnel available in each locale. The organization of training sessions has been one of our concerns. [E:8]

During the second decentralization, the Health Ministry gave the state more flexibility in managing financial resources. One official believes that there is a little more autonomy, the result in part of the scarcity of resources, and now it is possible to shift funds from one budget category to another. The state also has more autonomy in the purchase of medicines.

Another step forward took place in personnel management. In Mexico's health sector, job assignments, promotions, and layoffs are negotiated with labor unions. The National Union of Health Ministry Employees (SNTSSA) opposed decentralization, fearing it would break the union into independent state unions. This did not happen, and the union remains centralized. What has been achieved is that the Sonora Health Secretariat and state leaders of the federal union negotiate issues regarding federal jobs; prior to decentralization, such negotiations took place between the Health Ministry and the central leadership of the union.

At present the state hires for positions paid by the federal government. What the state cannot do is create new federal positions or change the categories of existing positions by, for example, replacing a physician with a nurse:

> Now, personnel can be hired, appointed, and laid off freely. Labor-related problems are solved here in the state. That is, the state becomes the workers' boss. [E:8]

By 1997 the Sonora Health Secretariat had generated a set of internal rules for the nine departments and their divisions. The State Health Council was created a year later and had its first assembly in 1999. The Council is chaired by the governor, with the state secretary of health as vice chair; the Council includes a technical secretary, representatives from public and private health organizations, and representatives from associations of health professionals. Its functions are to advise the state secretary of health and facilitate inter-institutional coordination.[4] One result of its first meeting was the creation of the State Medical Arbitration Commission. According to the Council's technical secretary, the purpose of the Arbitration Commission is:

> to solve medical claims, in a friendly way, in good faith, without getting into legal issues of any kind between providers and users, in both the public and private sector. [E:6]

Another positive result that emerged from the second decentralization was the creation of the Health and Welfare Commission in the state legislature. This Commission is important because, as decentralization advances, the state legislature can become an increasingly important forum for health policy discussion and design.

A FAILED ATTEMPT TO PRIVATIZE

As noted in chapter 1 in this volume, several authors have suggested that decentralization is a mechanism to privatize health service delivery. Differences between decentralized public and nonprofit private hospitals could

---

[4] Council members include eight representatives from the public health sector (the IMSS northeast regional director, the IMSS state delegate, the ISSSTE state delegate, the general director of ISSSTESON, the director of the National System for Integral Family Development [DIF] in Sonora, the directors of the Regional Military Hospital and the Naval Hospital, and the state delegate of the National Indigenous Institute [INI]); six representatives of nonprofit organizations (the Red Cross, the Medical Federation of Sonora, the Health and Welfare Commission); and two representatives of the private sector (the presidents of the Association of Private Hospitals and the Private Assistance Board).

be small, and to some extent public hospitals could contract out services to the private sector.

The health-sector changes introduced during the 1980s and 1990s created substantial confusion and uncertainty among public health workers. The IMSS Reform Law talked about increasing private-sector participation in health service provision.[5] NAFTA opened the door to foreign investors and possibly to workers from Canada and the United States. And decentralization of the Health Ministry offered a possible way to foster the private sector and allow state authorities to define the terms of public-private collaboration.

Our respondents echoed the uncertainties that these various changes raised. Questions about the future framework of the health sector, its financing, and the new delivery model confused even state health executives. State officials were totally unfamiliar with the content of the Health Ministry's "Health-Sector Reform Program, 1995–2000," published in March 1996. Executives at the Sonora Health Secretariat learned of the existence of this report only after this author sent them a copy, underscoring the isolation of regional stakeholders in the health reform process. One of them expressed these doubts:

> It is not clear what the reform includes, if decentralization is a part or a component of the health-sector reform that includes the IMSS.... But for me, the reform is blurred; it is not very clear where the government is going. And we in the health sector don't have a clear perception of where things are going. [E:8]

State officials had little trust in the federal government. According to them, the federal authorities had failed to formulate explicit policies, establish mechanisms to regulate service quality and price, regulate private health insurance companies, and guide health care investments to ensure that public and private investments would complement each other.

---

[5] The World Bank provided a loan of over US$800 million to finance some aspects of the IMSS health reform, along with other loans to finance recurrent expenditures of Progresa and PAC, two programs aimed at increasing access to basic health services among the indigent and dispersed rural populations.

The possibility of privatizing health services was one of the more controversial issues that surfaced in discussions. Some of the interviewees expressed their interest in keeping a system that is predominantly public. One of them commented:

> My work has always been at IMSS.... I am not a member of any political party, and when reporters ask me what party I belong to, I tell them the IMSS is my party.... All of my children were educated in the public sector, and this is why the public sector is so close to my heart. I am convinced that the public administration needs to be re-dimensioned and re-evaluated. [E:9]

Others acknowledged that Mexico's health system is a private-public mix, in which the two sectors are highly intertwined and most physicians work for both sectors. Thus:

> The private sector is part of the health provider system; in the morning we provide care in public health centers, and in the afternoon, in private clinics. We are the same people in both sectors, and this is the way it is across the country. [E:5]

The director of Sonora's General Hospital was of the opinion that the private sector should play a larger role in the provision of health services, and he offered several suggestions on how to broaden private-sector participation. One option was the mandatory purchase of complementary private insurance by all public-sector professionals. Such a policy would free up public health resources. A second option would allow beneficiaries of public health insurance funds to choose between the public security funds and various private health insurance plans. People who favored an increase in the private sector's involvement did not express any concerns about the potential conflicts of interest that could arise when public health officials, including health policy decision makers and regulators of the health sector, have business interests in the private sector, either as beneficiaries of subcontracts or as owners or shareholders of private institutions.

Some of the interviewees offered examples that raise doubts about the possibility of establishing relationships of trust between the public and private sectors. According to an IMSS official, the private sector seeks to maximize profit at any cost. Private providers tend to foment demand for unneeded services, even when subcontracted to provide services to IMSS beneficiaries. As stated by this official, the director of a private hospital in Sonora "considered that the IMSS represented a potential market [for subcontracting]," and our respondent added:

> IMSS had a contract with the CIMA hospital [a private hospital owned by a U.S. corporation] for treating kidney stones.... All of a sudden they [CIMA executives] tell me: "we are going to raise our fee.... The existing contract is not good anymore." I do the math and find out that I'm better off paying for a plane and sending patients to Tijuana [30 minutes away by air] or someplace else.... Three months later, CIMA lowered the fee and we renewed the contract. [E:9]

According to this same informant, because the private sector seeks to maximize profits, it is to its benefit to discredit public institutions: "[it] magnifies the quality problems of the [public sector] in order to attract clients." In such cases, IMSS invariably is the target institution because it offers services that can be very lucrative for the private sector. The informant feels that the private sector's excessive craving for profits results in unnecessary use of high-tech procedures and creates expectations among public-sector beneficiaries that exceed the capacity of the Mexican public sector. According to this informant, a country with increasing poverty, a country that still has much to do in the field of social medicine, should not allow that kind of demand to grow. This informant echoed the assertion of other interviewees that there is a lack of federal leadership to define a coherent health policy:

> We lack clear direction and determination from central political, technical, and legal institutions.... These institutions must agree on what an at-risk group is and which public health problems to fight ... and be able to lend each other a hand. [E:9]

Uncertainty about the future of the public health sector limits the capacity of regional officials to utilize existing resources creatively and to define a long-term development plan that takes advantage of the small amount of decision-making power they have acquired with decentralization. According to one respondent, if there were clear direction from the federal level, the states would respond. This informant cites as an example the medical brigades that were formed in Sonora with personnel from the State Health Secretariat and IMSS [E: 9]. Working together, these two institutions were able to bring services to underserved communities.

REACTIONS FROM MEDICAL ASSOCIATIONS

The lack of clarity about the future of the health sector also produced an impact on medical associations, which were strongly affected by the economic crisis of the 1980s (Abrantes Pêgo and Arjonilla Alday 2002). From the early 1980s, civil servants, including physicians, experienced significant reductions in salary. The same lack of financial resources undercut the public health sector's ability to deliver quality services in a timely fashion, eroding the prestige of health professionals and their organizations. Salary losses forced physicians to devote more time to their private practices to augment income or to work for private insurance programs, according to a member of the Medical College of Sonora. The same informant states that physicians resent the work conditions in the private insurance programs and adds that, until the 1994 physicians' strike, each private health insurance program negotiated with each physician to see "who could pay physicians the least" [E:11], with no consideration given to the physician's training or the quality of services rendered. This situation prompted physicians to organize in professional groups that could act as intermediaries in the negotiations.

Rumors and a lack of solid information about the direction of the health-sector reform have raised concern among physicians regarding the role the private sector will play in the new health system, how the reform will affect doctors' current employment status in the public sector, how the market is going to be regulated, and who will be responsible for enforcing the regulations. The president of the College of Gynecologists of Sonora expressed his concern as follows:

> Sector policies are forcing physicians to join together.... Physicians are starting to participate more [in the political arena].... Before, one could have counted on one hand the number of physicians who went into politics; now there is an effervescence. People want to participate, and not exactly in favor of the [PRI] government. Now they want to participate in opposition parties, because they feel attacked, they feel that the status they once enjoyed has been lost forever. When people talk about their political affiliations, I find that fewer of us belong to the PRI. When people were doing well, they didn't participate in politics, they left politics to the politicians. Now the physician is starting to want to participate, and this is an indicator that the government probably isn't doing things properly. And watch out! Policy issues are going to be difficult to deal with. [E:12]

Another characteristic of the physicians' associations is their distrust of the policies of the federal executive. This is largely due to the doctors' experience with decentralization. A representative of one medical association declared: "Decentralization should not be a policy for decentralizing problems; it should be a policy for decentralizing power to find solutions" [E:11].

Many physicians resent the fact that the decentralization initiative ignored the state medical associations, and they believe that the associations should be the institutions that regulate the medical labor market in the state [E:12]. They argue that state medical associations should evaluate and guarantee the quality of services, grant certificates, offer courses to keep health professionals up to date, and set the fees for services. Other factors that irritate physicians are the fees they must pay for a license to practice medicine and the costs associated with regulating private practice; the fact that foreign health professionals, health insurance programs, and hospital chains are beginning to set up in Mexico; and the creation of the National Medical Arbitration Commission (CONAMED).

The State Health Secretariat's decision to charge a fee for a license to practice medicine was interpreted by physicians as one more scheme to obtain additional resources: "more money, no matter what it takes" [E:12]. At the same time, there is the perception that NAFTA allows health corporations and professionals from the United States and Canada to establish themselves in Mexico, but these countries refuse to recognize Mexican physicians' qualifications—that is, these doctors perceive a lack of reciprocity. Mexican physicians are now considering ways to exert broader regulatory controls over foreign doctors practicing in Mexico.

Physicians also felt that the 1996 presidential decree that created CONAMED made them the "ugly ducklings" of the health care story. Medical associations see CONAMED as an organization of surveillance and persecution. After overcoming objections from the medical associations, the Sonora Health Secretariat created the State Medical Arbitration Commission in 1999 to bring arbitration cases closer into the purview of state physicians and thus dispel the mistrust in arbitration matters that CONAMED had created. However, this state-level initiative was not well received. A representative of a medical association thought that the state commission would "create many problems for the public sector, because the sector does not operate with all the needed safety requirements" [E:11]. According to the same interviewee:

> A main weakness of the public health sector is the crowded conditions of its centers, the lack of modern equipment, and its extensive coverage in a market where the private sector serves a very small number of users.... The result is that when a doctor enters an operating room, the patient will not have received all the required tests. At the same time, the doctor is trying to address the suboptimal conditions he confronts in the surgical room, such as lack of sutures, medicines, and so on.

This informant postulates that the State Medical Arbitration Commission will lead physicians to demand that public hospitals be equipped appropriately, and that the hospitals, not the physicians, be responsible for medical errors. Aware that such demands are unlikely to be met, medical associations have decided to send four of their members to law school so that they can then defend their medical colleagues.

The medical associations are fighting to reclaim the social status and political influence in health policymaking that physicians have enjoyed in the past. To this end, they are attempting to control the regulation of the medical profession and are opposed to leaving the professional status of physicians in the hands of the marketplace. They are also seeking alliances with the state bureaucracy in order to achieve these objectives. And medical associations, like state officials, are requesting greater clarity with respect to the reform policies. In sum, for many physicians, decentralization goes against their professional interests and needs, and the undefined nature of the reform raises serious concerns about the future.

DISCUSSION

Mexico's federal government launched an ambitious health reform, a reform designed in secret and without the participation of key groups such as state governments, professional groups, labor unions, and consumers. In addition, this reform has been implemented at a time of economic crisis, to the detriment of health care providers' working conditions, the health of certain social groups, and conditions in public health institutions. Despite official discourse that portrays decentralization as a means to democratize decision making, the reform has been designed and imposed from above and its implementation has been complicated by a lack of details about how it should be carried out.

Even though the federal government controls the great majority of the resources and continues to have significant power over the states' authority, its relationship with the states has changed as it has tried to implement decentralization. There is now a movement at the state level to influence how the health sector is redesigned. Even if decentralization remains incomplete and continues to be a policy of the national executive, governors and state political forces are no longer in the positions of subordination that they previously occupied. The new political scene that allows regional stakeholders to assume a more forceful role appears to be an unintended consequence of decentralization. In Sonora there has been a power shift from federal policymakers to the state's stakeholders.

The federal government has encountered difficulties when trying to impose its reform model, and it has engendered unanticipated ambivalences and dynamics. State-level decision makers find themselves without the resources to address the problems that have been transferred to them from the federal level, and they resent the control that the Health Ministry continues to exert over many financial and human resources, as well as their exclusion from discussions about how decentralization is defined.

Professional associations, especially physicians' organizations, which had been loyal allies of the PRI and the central government since the Mexican Revolution (Cleaves 1985), note that the federally imposed health reform and decentralization disregard their economic and professional interests. They see a loss in both their salaries and status and fear that the market opening under NAFTA, which allows the entrance of powerful foreign health corporations, could threaten their salaries and benefits even more. All of these events have heightened physicians' sense of insecurity and their distrust of federal health policymakers.

The state's political forces reacted to decentralization by trying to assume the limited decision-making authority that the federal government had relinquished and using it to influence the organization of the state's health sector. State health authorities and physicians are unwilling to subordinate their interests to the decisions of the federal government, and they are demanding more power, resources, and autonomy. This explains why state stakeholders sometimes come together to shape policies that strengthen their position vis-à-vis central authorities and at other times fight among themselves for control of the existing scarce resources.

In Sonora, decentralization has brought a transition from a rigid, centralized system to a situation of ambiguity, where the different stakeholders try to find ways to legitimize their role without the need to spell out or share the principles on which the system is to be sustained. Another complicating factor is that these changes have occurred during an economic crisis, a time when it is particularly important to draw maximum benefit from scarce resources. All reforms cost money, and the public health sector is responding by extracting money from both health professionals and patients. In the process, it is diminishing health professionals' loyalty to the public sector. The patient, meanwhile, who is in the care of disgruntled medical professionals and is inconvenienced by a bureaucracy that is increasingly empowered to extract resources through user fees and other mechanisms, may receive lower quality of care at a higher cost.

References

Abrantes Pêgo, R. 1998. "Conflictos de poder y el efecto perverso sobre la salud de la población campesina en México: un problema en el ojo del huracán. Comentarios al programa de seguridad social campesina sometidos a la consideración de la Secretaría de Salubridad y Asistencia," *Relaciones* (El Colegio de Michoacán) 74, no. 19: 237–44.

Abrantes Pêgo, R., and S. Arjonilla Alday. 2002. "Descentralización del sector de salud y conflictos con el gremio médico en México," *Revista Saúde Pública* 363: 324–29.

Brachet-Márquez, V. 2002. "Elementos para investigar la capacidad estatal político administrativa en materia de salud pública: los casos de Guanajuato, Oaxaca y Sonora," *Estudios Sociológicos* (El Colegio de México) 20, no. 58: 239–52.

Cadena Pelarde, L. 1989. "La descentralización de la salud al estado de Sonora." Bachelor's thesis, Universidad de Sonora.

Cleaves, P. 1985. *Las profesiones y el Estado: el caso de México*. México D.F.: El Colegio de México.

Haro, J. A. 1998. "El sistema local de salud Guarijió-makurawe: un modelo para construir." Hermosillo: El Colegio de Sonora/CIAD/CONACULTA.

Hernández Llamas, H., ed. 1984. *La atención médica rural en México, 1930–1980*. México, D.F.: IMSS.

IMSS (Instituto Mexicano de Seguro Social). 1984. "Extensión de la seguridad social en el medio rural." In *La atención médica rural en México, 1930–1980*, ed. H. Hernández Llamas. México, D.F.: IMSS.

Jasís, M., and S. Guendelman. 1991. "Uso de servicios de salud en la frontera México–Estados Unidos," *Salud Pública de México* 335: 463–74.

Pérez Duarte, F. 1988. "La Jurisdicción de Salud en el Estado de Sonora." In *El cambio estructural: desafíos ante la consolidación del Sistema Nacional de Salud*. México, D.F.: Secretaría de Salud y Asistencia/OPS.

Pineda Pablos, N. 2000. "Introducción." In *Agenda de la Reforma Municipal en Sonora*, ed. J. Poom Medina and N. Pineda Pablos. Hermosillo: El Colegio de Sonora.

Presidencia de la República, Gobierno de Miguel de la Madrid. 1985. "Crónica del sexenio 1982–1988, segundo año." Unidad de la Crónica Presidencial. México D.F.: Fondo de Cultura Económica.

Soberón, G. 1987. "El financiamiento de la salud para consolidar el cambio," *Salud Pública de México* 29, no. 2: 169–77.

SSA (Secretaría de Salubridad y Asistencia). 1982. *La salud pública en México, 1959–1982*. México, D.F.: SSA.

7

Guanajuato: Invisible Results

SOFÍA ARJONILLA ALDAY

This chapter examines decentralization in the state of Guanajuato and the capacity of the State Health Secretariat (SSG) to obtain and administer financial resources, to manage human resources, and to design and implement new health programs. The study analyzes the decentralization process, the role played by professional associations and community groups, and the perceptions of health care providers and users regarding decentralization's impact on the performance of the SSG.[1]

The state of Guanajuato is located in the east-central part of Mexico. In 2000, Guanajuato had a total of 4.7 million inhabitants distributed over an area of 30,494 square kilometers in 46 municipalities with 9,007 localities. Some basic socioeconomic indicators are presented in table 7.1.

Guanajuato is rapidly being transformed from a rural to an industrial state. Forty-six percent of the population lives in four cities that form an industrial corridor, while the state's northeast and south are primarily farming areas. According to the official Mexican classification of socioeconomic exclusion, 74 percent of Guanajuato's municipalities are classified as extremely or highly marginalized, 24 percent are at mid-level, and only 2 percent rank at the lowest level of exclusion. Among the economically active population, 15 percent are unemployed, 16 percent earn less

This chapter is part of the qualitative analysis portion of a study entitled "Macroeconomic Adjustment Policies, Health-Sector Reform, and Access, Utilization, and Quality of Care in Mexico," conducted by the Instituto Nacional de Salud Pública de México and financed by Canada's International Development Research Centre (IDRC).

[1] For more on this topic, see Arjonilla and Parada 2003, 2005.

than the official minimum wage, 31 percent earn between 100 and 200 percent of the minimum wage, 23 percent earn between 200 and 500 percent of the minimum wage, and 15 percent earn more than five times the minimum wage.[2] In 1998, 64 percent of the economically active population did not have health insurance. The uninsured population can access the services offered by the State Health Secretariat, but only 47 percent of the eligible population utilizes these services.

Table 7.1. Selected Socioeconomic Characteristics of Guanajuato State

Life expectancy, years (2000)	75
Fertility rate (1996)	30.6
Infant mortality per 1,000 live births (1996)	22.4
Indigenous population as percent of total population (1997)	0.11
Migratory balance, percent (1997)	−7.3

In the rural areas, a fundamentally agricultural subsistence economy predominates, and it is heavily dependent on remittances from migrants living and working in the United States. Housing conditions are poor and crowded, and homes have little ventilation. Chlorinated water is usually piped to the houses, but few rural dwellings have toilets. Education levels are low; Guanajuato's 15 percent illiteracy rate (in 1997) ranks the state as the eighth-lowest in the country (INEGI 1994, 1997, 2000).

The data presented here regarding decentralization were obtained from thirty semi-structured interviews. Respondents included mid- and top-level administrators of the State Health Secretariat, the Mexican Social Security Institute (IMSS), and the Social Security Institute for State Employees (ISSSTE) with a minimum of ten years of service; leaders of civil society organizations that carry out health-related activities; representatives from labor unions and political parties; news media executives; and members of teaching and research institutions.

Two guides were prepared for the semi-structured interviews—one for use with public health personnel and the other with interviewees from civil

---

[2] In 1999, the minimum daily wage in Guanajuato was 33.50 pesos (approximately US$3.52).

society and the private sector. Interviews lasted an hour on average, though two continued for more than two hours. The interviews were tape recorded and transcribed.

In the second stage of research we studied the perceptions of the users and providers of health services. For the users of health services, we organized eight focus groups of mothers in order to ascertain their level of knowledge about accessibility, utilization, and quality of care in the various types of health services. The majority of the women who participated in the focus groups were users of Health Secretariat services. Four focus groups were held in rural areas and four with residents of urban areas. Rural sites included communities that differed in size, geographical location, governing political party, and socioeconomic characteristics. The urban focus groups took place in León, Guanajuato's largest city. The focus groups included people from high, middle, low, and marginal socioeconomic classes. The focus groups ranged in size from four to sixteen persons.[3]

To determine attitudes about the health-sector reform, perceived changes in working conditions attributable to decentralization, and perceptions about access, services utilization, and quality of services, we carried out fifty-seven semi-structured interviews. Our interviewees worked in both the private and the public sectors and included general practitioners, specialists, general and intensive-care nurses, laboratory technicians, and social workers. All participants gave informed consent and were guaranteed anonymity. With very rare exceptions, the informants were very open and willing participants.

---

[3] Group size was to be between eight and ten persons. For the middle socioeconomic stratum, which was the last group studied, only four of the people who had agreed to participate were present for the discussion. This limitation was eased somewhat by the many informal conversations we had with people from this stratum during fieldwork, when we talked about the same topics that were to be covered in the focus group. On the other hand, sixteen women came to the session for the marginalized socioeconomic group, and we decided to include all of them. Their participation was very orderly, and we did not encounter problems when transcribing the tape.

THE FIRST PHASE OF DECENTRALIZATION, 1986–1995

Guanajuato began the decentralization process in 1986. Since then the State Health Secretariat has had four secretaries: Dr. Adolfo Mata (of the Institutional Revolutionary Party, or PRI); Dr. Marta Esquivel (no political affiliation); Dr. Carlos Tena Tamayo (of the National Action Party, or PAN), who was secretary of health in 1999 when the fieldwork for this research was conducted; and his successor, Dr. Éctor Ramírez (independent).

Informants from the State Health Secretariat observed that negotiations between the federal government and the state of Guanajuato on the decentralization agreement signed in 1986 proceeded much more slowly than was the case in the other states that decentralized during the first phase. The prolonged negotiations allowed for a very detailed decentralization accord. There were activities that the federal Ministry of Health (SSA) wanted to decentralize (such as the immunization program) but which the state refused to accept.

Until 1985, in Guanajuato, as in other states, the Coordinated Public Health Services were responsible for providing preventive and curative health services for the uninsured population. Then in 1985 the State Health Secretariat was created, and in March 1986 the decentralization agreement between the state and the federal government was signed. The principal points of this agreement were: (1) decentralization of the execution of certain federal programs to the state, and (2) clarification of the roles of the Health Ministry and the State Health Secretariat. A system of coordination between the SSA and SSG was also instituted. The second stage of health decentralization in Guanajuato began in November 1996, and it is the focus of this chapter.

THE SECOND PHASE OF DECENTRALIZATION, 1996–2000
Financial Decentralization

Historically, health allocations from the federal government to the states did not take into account how much each state budgeted for health services. After decentralization, the federal government continued to allocate health funds according to historical budget patterns, with only one minor change: a very small amount began to be distributed to the states based on a principle of solidarity. According to Guanajuato's health secretary:

> It is unfortunate that the [solidarity] formula does not apply
> to 100 percent of the fiscal resources.... It is clear that when
> they distributed the national pie [in the past], they did not do
> it in an equitable manner across the states. They based the
> distribution of funds on the managerial capacity of the gov-
> ernors.

Guanajuato increased state support for health services following decentralization (see table 7.2), raising its allocation from 408,000 pesos in 1990 to
3,960,000 pesos in 2000 (in constant 1994 pesos). The state's highest allocation (more than 4 million pesos) was in 1994, but it dropped to 2.9 million
pesos the following year as a result of the economic recession. In 1990, the
state's contribution represented only 6 percent of the total health budget;
this share increased steadily to reach 29 percent in 1996, the year of the
second decentralization, after which it began to decline. By 2000 the state
contribution was only 13 percent, and this state contribution included a
significant inflow of funds generated through user fees, also referred to as
self-generated funds (see table 7.3).

Apart from its contribution to the State Health Secretariat's budget,
Guanajuato also provides some resources to the private sector. For example, in 1998 the state government donated ambulances, oxygen tanks, and
emergency equipment to the Red Cross, which together were valued at 1.2
million pesos.

Officials at the State Health Secretariat were well aware that effective
decentralization would only result if the Health Ministry put federal funds
at the free disposition of the state. One official pointed out that, because
between 70 and 80 percent of federal funds went to pay salaries and most
operating expenses went to vertical programs, very little remained for the
Health Secretariat to develop programs targeted to local needs. Among the
few efforts the state had taken in response to perceived local needs was the
establishment of 104 medical care facilities, including two new hospitals
built between 1994 and 1999, and four blood banks.

In 1997 the State Health Secretariat dedicated 16 percent of its resources
to constructing new facilities, procuring specialized equipment, and rehabilitating hospitals; this fraction rose to 63 percent in 1998, fell to 50 percent
in 1999, and rose again to 60 percent in 2000. Much of this funding was

Table 7.2. Federal and State Contributions to Guanajuato's Health Budget (1000s of 1994 pesos)

Fiscal Contribution	1990	%	1991	%	1992	%	1993	%
Federal	6,477.89	94	7,802.56	90	8,887.75	82	9,725.08	76
State[a]	408.00	6	860.12	10	1,936.18	18	2,849.00	23
Total	6,885.89	100	8,662.68	100	10,823.93	100	12,574.08	99

	1994	%	1995	%	1996	%	1997	%
Federal	10,441.42	72	8,676.42	72	9,338.60	71	10,974.13	63
State[a]	4,070.16	28	2,998.45	28	3,877.45	29	3,959.67	27
Total	14,511.58	100	11,674.87	100	13,216.05	100	14,933.80	100

	1998	%	1999	%	2000	%
Federal	13,401.64	76	16,898.47	82	26,308.38	87
State[a]	4,126.12	24	3,717.70	18	3,960.52	13
Total	17,527.76	100	20,616.17	100	30,268.90	100

[a] The state contribution includes user fees.

invested in secondary and tertiary health care services, not the primary health care network that treated 80 percent of illness events and that had been identified as the target of the health reform. This allocation of a large share of available resources to high-tech medicine in urban areas meant that the majority of the rural population could not access them because of economic, geographical, or cultural barriers.

Table 7.3. User Fees in Guanajuato State, 1995–2000

User Fees	1995	1996	1997	1998	1999	2000
User fees collected (1000s of 1994 pesos)	1,476.94	1,584.38	1,857.11	1,853.72	1,927.79	2,092.58
User fees as % of state contribution to health budget	49	41	47	45	52	53
User fees as % of total health budget	13	12	12	11	9	7

User fees increased the resources that the Health Ministry could expend at its discretion. According to one informant, Guanajuato collected the second-highest amount in user fees in the country (after the richest state, Nuevo León). Ignoring a national structure that set user fees, the State Health Secretariat set these charges according to the type of service (primary and specialist consultations, hospitalization, and clinical laboratory work). The Health Secretariat determined the minimum amount that clinics and hospitals should collect in user fees,[4] and any revenue collected above this minimum was returned to the unit for the purchase of supplies and medicines. For fiscal control purposes, the funds generated through user fees were first sent to the state treasury and then returned to the State

---

[4] This could be seen as an effort to create demand for services in order to augment state resources, a point that deserves further study.

Health Secretariat. Because hospitals generated the majority of the fees, hospitals reaped the greatest benefit.

The general sentiment among the participants in our focus groups was that user fees were inexpensive when compared to the cost of private services. This does not imply that these fees did not represent a sacrifice for the consumers, the vast majority of whom are poor. Knaul (2000) states that the cost of health care has been rising as a percentage of Mexicans' total household budgets, especially for those in the lower socioeconomic classes. Our fieldwork found that the user fees for a medical consultation— and for medicines, when these were available—varied between urban and rural zones and ranged from 11 to 30 pesos per primary-care visit (approximately US$1 to US$3). In rural areas and marginalized urban zones, where families commonly subsist on 100 pesos a week, user fees imply a significant reduction in a household's ability to purchase food and other basic necessities. It is very likely that poor families had to reduce their food purchases and forgo other necessities to pay these fees. If this was indeed the case, we can conclude that user fees had a negative health impact and could create a vicious circle of poverty and illness. Theoretically, indigent persons were to be exempted from paying user fees, but studies have shown that, whether intentionally or in error, many who should be exempted are not, while some who are able to pay are not charged (Cruz Rivero and Domínguez Villarreal 1990). In Guanajuato, the State Health Secretariat decided that the health centers should charge user fees for the services included in the Program to Expand Coverage (PAC) even though a loan agreement between the Health Secretariat and the World Bank stipulated that PAC services should be provided free of charge.[5] Thus this measure contravenes both a key program aim and equity as well.

Federal health funding that went unspent (because of state workers' absenteeism) was an additional source of revenue for the State Health Secretariat. Prior to 1996, these funds stayed with the Health Ministry, but after the second decentralization the State Health Secretariat could retain them and use them as it deemed appropriate.

---

[5] The PAC consists of fourteen health interventions for the very poor and for rural inhabitants who have no access to health care.

With decentralization, the states could, in theory, transfer program implementation to the municipalities, but the lack of resources made this transfer difficult to achieve. After President Zedillo created the Health Care Savings Fund (FASSA) in 1997 (see chapter 2 in this volume), the state was free to transfer some of these funds to the municipalities, and the process to accomplish this was simplified. Guanajuato's State Health Secretariat transferred small health initiatives to twenty-six municipal governments; the transferred functions included sanitary control of open markets and public swimming pools, and levying fines on factories, stores, and other businesses such as restaurants and supermarkets for noncompliance with sanitation codes. For fiscal control reasons, funds obtained from fines were remitted to the Health Secretariat to be forwarded to the state treasury. Eventually, the funds were to be returned to the municipalities.

Decentralization of Physical and Human Resources

The transfer of buildings and equipment from the federal Health Ministry to the Guanajuato Health Secretariat began in the late 1990s. It was a slow process, marred by legal problems that surfaced over ownership issues. For example, some properties had been lent to the Health Ministry by the municipalities or other owners, and ownership could not be transferred. Legal complications hindered a renegotiation of contracts that the federal government had signed with municipalities, foundations, or private individuals many years previously.

Opposition from the National Union of Health Ministry Employees (SNTSSA) further delayed the decentralization of human resources. Before decentralization, Health Ministry employees in Guanajuato (the vast majority in the state's health sector) had higher salaries and better benefits than state health employees. Making these federal employees state employees would have meant a cut in their pay and benefits and/or a loss in their seniority status, gains they had made over the course of years and which they refused to relinquish. The only solution, then, was to raise state workers' salaries and benefits to the level of federal employees, a process known as homologation. By 1999, the salaries of state employees had been raised even with those of federal employees, but problems persisted with respect to matching seniority and other benefits.

In Guanajuato, authorities from the State Health Secretariat and/or union leaders informed the employees about the health reform, but neither sought workers' opinions on these matters. Interviewees affirmed that the decentralization process was imposed from above, with no one seeking the health workers' input. The health authorities consulted only with labor leaders, and the majority of the personnel were totally unaware of the potential consequences of decentralization. With very few exceptions, Mexico's labor unions were controlled by the PRI and characterized by bossism, authoritarian and undemocratic leadership, and corruption (Bizberg 1990; Novelo et al. 1989). The "white unions," which were generally allied with employers, suffered from the same ills. Until 1999, all health workers employed through the Health Ministry had to join the PRI-controlled union. In 1999 a court decision broke the union's monopoly and allowed workers to affiliate with new, independent labor unions,[6] but no new labor unions of health workers were organized in Guanajuato.

Top officials at Guanajuato's Health Secretariat affirmed that employees were working harder and were more productive after decentralization, but they also admitted there was strong resistance to change among the rank and file. There was little consensus among officials regarding the cause for this state of affairs. One suggested it could be attributed to low salaries; another felt that resistance to change is simply part of human nature.

Under decentralization, the SSG was authorized to create new permanent positions—if the state had the resources to cover them. Otherwise, the state could only hire workers on temporary contracts. If a position paid by the federal government was vacated, the State Health Secretariat was supposed to fill it in the same fiscal year or the position could be forfeited:

> Of course the creation of positions is restricted ... because a position is for life, it creates seniority and entitlements. A job is forever; this is the problem.... This is why there are restrictions, and these restrictions come from the federal level, along with a recommendation to not fire anyone because then the position could be frozen and lost.

---

[6] This political opening responded in part to the national democratization process initiated by the Zedillo government (1994–2000).

State Innovations under Decentralization

When implementing federal programs, states must comply with Health Ministry rules and regulations. States issue their own rules for state programs, provided that these do not contradict those issued by the Ministry. For example, the Guanajuato Health Secretariat wrote a regulation setting the norms for private ambulances during road emergencies and accidents. There were no federal rules covering this situation and, after consultation with the Health Ministry, the State Health Secretariat issued the new protocol.

Administrators at the Guanajuato Health Secretariat pointed to an agreement between the Secretariat and IMSS to jointly manage an IMSS hospital as an example of what could be achieved with decentralization. The State Health Secretariat needed a hospital in San Luis de la Paz, and IMSS had one in this city with a low rate of occupancy. The two institutions concluded that sharing the hospital would be to their mutual benefit. According to a high official in the SSG, this was the only shared hospital in Mexico at the time that the agreement was made:

> San Luis de la Paz is an example of true coordination with IMSS.... [We were able] to take over ... half of the hospital and maintain the clinic.... It is an example of how at the local level and in coordination ... we could find a formula that, instead of benefiting 120,000 people, now benefits more than 300,000, and instead of having another hospital and duplicating beds, we use those of the IMSS. Now we are providing services to more municipalities and more people.

Decentralization gave the SSG hospitals some degree of autonomy and also allowed the health districts to become a little more autonomous. But decentralization to the health districts did not begin in Guanajuato until 2001, and vertical programs continued to be considered an interference with local decision making on health issues. One health district director complained that vertical programs could be problematic:

> [It is difficult] to change a program or health campaign ... for another that better fits the needs of the state—for example, to

replace the campaign against malaria, which is not a health problem in Guanajuato, with one against scorpion stings, which are a problem.[7]

The Guanajuato Health Secretariat has managed to finance and carry out a few health programs of its own. For example, the SSG funded health education programs via radio to reach distant rural areas. Decentralization also permitted a few innovations in some programs. For example, in the area of sanitation, the State Health Secretariat:

- developed a computer program to randomly select food samples for laboratory analysis;

- raised personnel qualification levels (for example, technicians, who previously only needed a primary school education, now must have completed secondary school);

- increased salaries as a strategy to reduce wrongdoing; and

- raised the fines for violations of sanitation codes to increase compliance (and to garner more resources for an underfunded division).[8]

Some members of the Sanitation Department were concerned about the social impacts of these innovations. According to one official:

> If we go right now to all the establishments where there are contaminated products and we take samples, we could cause a food shortage [because we would have to close them all].

IMPACTS ON EFFICIENCY, QUALITY, EQUITY, AND USER SATISFACTION

This section compares the results of decentralization with some of the anticipated outcomes. As discussed earlier in this volume, one assumption

---

[7] Health campaigns are carried out by State Health Secretariats but are usually ordered by the Health Ministry to address a specific health problem. Health promotion interventions and vaccinations are the most common activities.

[8] The operational budget of the Sanitation Department was very low, at between 2 and 5 percent of the operational expenditures of the Guanajuato Health Secretariat, or about US$35,000 in 1995.

regarding decentralization is that bringing decision making closer to users increases efficiency and equity and also improves the quality of services and user satisfaction.

Efficiency and Quality Improvement

The information for measuring changes in efficiency in Guanajuato was very limited. The percentage of the total population that utilized SSG services had increased, and the SSG authorities felt that the increase suggested a better utilization of resources and improved quality of care. In 1993, 38 percent of the population used SSG services; by 2000 the share had increased to 51 percent. State Health Secretariat officials claimed that social security beneficiaries had begun to access SSG services, which they interpreted as a further sign of improvements in quality of care.

However, it is questionable whether an increase in the number of users meant higher efficiency, given that the budget had more than doubled over the same period. Also, an unknown number of workers lost their jobs due to the 1994 economic recession, meaning that they also lost their social benefits and access to IMSS services. Some of the increased utilization of SSG services by beneficiaries of social security programs (IMSS, ISSSTE, and others) may also have reflected the convenience of using the newly built (and closer to home) SSG centers.

The fact that the Guanajuato Health Secretariat could not curb the inappropriate use of their services by social security beneficiaries suggests poor administrative practices on the part of the SSG and created a drain on funds earmarked for the uninsured population. This misuse was also the result of the fragmentation of health services in Mexico and the lack of coordination between public institutions. According to one SSG official:

> Our own statistics show that 20 percent of the population we treat is entitled to IMSS services; in addition, another 7 percent is entitled to ISSSTE. And this is only an observation; I believe that the real number is even higher.

The reduction in the number of administrative personnel in the Guanajuato Health Secretariat is indicative of better resource utilization. Between 1986 and 2000, the SSG decreased administrators from 39 to 19 percent of personnel. On the other hand, between 1995 and 2000 the number of attending physicians increased by 40 percent and the number of nurses rose by 45 percent, but physician productivity improved only marginally and continued to fall below the national average.[9] SSG physicians in Guanajuato averaged 7.8 general consultations per day in 1996 and 12.8 per day in 1999,[10] but the average number of the more expensive specialty consultations dropped from 1.6 to 1.1 per day. This low productivity cannot be attributed to a need for lengthy consultations; the average time spent with a patient was less than the SSG standard of 15 minutes per general consultation. It is possible that many physicians in Guanajuato were underutilized, which would negatively affect physician productivity data.

At the time of this research, the State Health Secretariat had not conducted evaluations of the quality of its services and did not perform medical audits, making it impossible to assess clinical improvements in service quality. Guanajuato has more than 9,000 rural localities served by 446 primary-care centers. Focus group participants considered that the quality of the services offered at these centers was good, despite the fact that the infrastructure appeared to be in poor condition. One possible explanation for the tendency to judge the centers favorably is that rural residents seldom had the opportunity to compare the services they received with other public or private services, and they do appreciate the free medicines, when these are available.

In interviews, the physicians and nurses who work in secondary- and tertiary-care settings complained about the tension between the patients' needs for care and the health centers' continual shortage of supplies and equipment. They were very aware that these conditions had a negative impact on the quality of care.

Without baseline data, we cannot conclude that decentralization either improved or worsened the quality of care. What is clear, however, is that many years after decentralization was initiated in Guanajuato, important

---

[9] In 1995 the national average of daily consultations for general physicians was 14.8 and for specialists, 3.2. In 1999, the respective averages were 17.4 and 3.3.

[10] General consultations are very inexpensive because the physicians in rural areas are recent medical school graduates doing their obligatory social service, for which they receive only a token stipend.

aspects that negatively affect quality of care had not been resolved. These include problems regarding the availability and quality of equipment and supplies, quality of supervision, referral systems, availability of medicines, and continuity of care.

User Satisfaction

The Guanajuato Health Secretariat emphasized improving user satisfaction by improving the interaction between patients and health center personnel. Users had long complained of excessive wait times to see a doctor, and an effort was made to shorten the waiting time. According to hospital directors, physicians, and SSG officials, the waiting time for ambulatory care had been reduced from two hours to thirty minutes.

The urban participants in our focus groups complained about occasional refusals to provide medical attention and criticized the clinics' hours as inconvenient for clinic users. Both rural and urban group participants agreed that user fees were inexpensive given that medicines were provided free of charge. On the other hand, focus group participants expressed distrust of physicians and questioned the quality of the medicines dispensed.

Another frequent complaint mentioned in the rural focus groups was the continuous turnover in physicians, who tended to move on after completing their year of required social service. This system places a burden on patients because there is no continuity, which is one of the basic principles of primary health care. The result was that patients had more confidence in the nurse's aide, whom they knew well; aides were often from the community and had more empirical experience than the doctor who had just graduated from medical school. For their part, these new doctors complained about the number of programs they had to implement and oversee, the onerous paperwork, and the long hours (even though the number of consultations they provided was very low).

The focus group participants were unhappy about difficulties, many of them bureaucratic, in accessing the secondary level of medical care. Rural participants explained that the few who had sufficient resources would travel to the city and begin the hospital admission process, but, because of hurdles they did not understand, they were asked to leave and return later. After making several such trips but never gaining admission to the hospital, they gave up. Although a National Medical Arbitration Commission (CONAMED) was created in 1994 to adjudicate malpractice demands, people rarely make use of it; focus group participants said they did not know how to use it or were afraid to file a complaint. This was especially true of the poor, who were fearful of retaliation and had no alternative source of health care services.

Equity

It is difficult to assert that decentralization produced equity in Guanajuato. The decisions that state health authorities made did not favor the poor. To the contrary, people now had to pay for services that had previously been provided free of charge. As indicated, the SSG had introduced very few new programs, but most of those few favored hospital infrastructure, that is, the brick-and-mortar projects that political leaders tend to favor. Given the health conditions of the state's poor, their needs would have been better served by preventive and primary-care services.

Rural and urban focus group participants felt that providers treated people differently based on appearance. The poor believed that they were treated with less respect than the more educated. They also claimed that those who accessed the health services with recommendations from SSG personnel, officials of the incumbent political party, or influential persons in the community received better treatment.

Community Participation

Community participation is seen as a prerequisite to tailoring decisions to fit local needs and to improving efficiency and user satisfaction, but experts differ in their understandings of community participation (Morgan 2001). Documents regarding Mexico's health reform posit that participation is achieved through the Healthy Municipalities Program, user fees, and the participation of nongovernmental organizations (NGOs).

Healthy Municipalities was a Ministry of Health strategy to involve communities in resolving their local health problems. Community leaders would first meet to discuss options and decide which programs they felt would be most beneficial to the health of their community. Once they had identified some projects, they could apply (through the State Health Secretariat) for federal funding for one of them. After the municipality fulfilled all requirements, the SSG gave it a white flag to symbolize that it was a "healthy municipality." In 1999, according to an assistant director of the SSG: "almost 80 percent of the municipalities are already included in the program and have selected specific projects." Project themes were chosen by community leaders, and in Guanajuato health education projects were the preferred choice.[11] According to SSG officials, communities also participated by paying the user fees. Contributing to the SSG budget was a form of participation, notwithstanding the fact that the fees were imposed without community consultation and the community had no voice in how the funds were spent.

Our interviewees concurred that Governor Carlos Medina Plasencia (PAN, 1991–1996) encouraged NGO participation on health matters, the aim being to transfer part of the responsibility for health care to civil society. Medina Plasencia entrusted the organization of 120 rural communities to Rural Development of Guanajuato, an nongovernmental organization directed by Jesuits which had a variety of development projects, including some basic health interventions. One NGO director affirmed that Rural Development's activities created a social movement with "huge [community] participation."

In an interview, the director of Rural Development of Guanajuato pointed out that improving the health status of the population required intersectoral coordination:

> If people live in healthy homes, there are fewer gastrointestinal and respiratory diseases, which are a big problem. Therefore, the State Health Secretariat should invest more money in healthy housing. Moreover, assuming that care for each episode of respiratory or diarrheal illness costs 100 pesos, if people resided in better homes they would save a significant amount of money. How much, then, should be invested in housing to prevent or eliminate these diseases?... The SSG

---

[11] Of course, completing a single project did not mean that a municipality had acquired all of the services—sewerage, potable water, and so on—to be a truly "healthy" municipality.

> has not done it, but the state is doing it through the Housing
> Institute.... We have a public trust to improve rural living,
> and right now they have invested 27 million pesos.

The Guanajuato Health Secretariat financed other private projects. For example, it was the primary contributor, along with other state health secretariats, to an NGO-sponsored radio program entitled *Que viva mi tierra, radio campesina*, which provided health education and promoted the Healthy Municipalities Program. Through the radio program, the secretariats were able to provide broad rural coverage about activities and services of interest to rural residents. The program operated with a call-in format to help peasants resolve land, job-related, and health problems, and then interceded on the callers' behalf with the bureaucracy and political leaders.

Although there were no studies of the NGOs active in Guanajuato's health sector at the time the present research was conducted, it seemed that government institutions tended to finance NGOs that shared the ideology of the PAN, the party in state power at the time. Even so, civil society participation was largely limited to a token presence; the governor appointed only one NGO representative to serve on the State Health Council, which was created in 1996 to coordinate activities with other public health institutions and with civil society.

In Guanajuato, social movements have been more successful than formal civic organizations in influencing the outcome of some health decisions. In the 1980s, following a health needs assessment, the State Health Secretariat decided to build a maternity hospital in León, and construction began during the tenure of State Health Secretary Dr. Marta Esquivel. However, her successor, Dr. Tena Tamayo, felt that León had a greater need for a pediatric hospital and proposed converting the maternity hospital to pediatric care (Arias 1999). According to Tena Tamayo (1999), most deliveries at the now-completed maternity hospital were vaginal, and expensive hospital care for uncomplicated deliveries could not be justified in a poor region like Guanajuato.

Tena Tamayo's plan to convert the hospital mobilized a good part of the population, including women's NGOs, the political opposition, and physicians who worked in the hospital. To assuage the protesters, the health secretary offered to open four clinics on the outskirts of León, but this did not satisfy the movement's leaders, who brought the case before the Court of Appeals, which compelled the Health Secretariat to withdraw its proposal.

In a similar case, in 2000 the government sought to penalize all types of abortion. Women's associations, representing a range of political affiliations, quickly organized a social protest movement and succeeded in halting the government initiative.

CONCLUSIONS

Decentralization of the Guanajuato Health Secretariat accomplished very little. The state was authorized to issue a few regulations, could decide how to spend self-generated funds, and was given flexibility in the use of the federal funds transferred through FASSA; the small gains in financial decision making were centralized in the SSG. Decentralization to the municipal level consisted of transferring supervision and funding for twenty-six health-related programs. Decentralization to the health district level remains a challenge for the SSG.

The limited increase in the state's decision-making power produced some decisions of questionable merit. The State Health Secretariat spent most of the investment funds in building and rehabilitating hospitals, rather than in preventive programs and improvements in the primary-care facilities that were the object of health-sector reform and where 80 percent of health problems can be treated. The SSG imposed user fees for services offered by the World Bank–funded PAC program, a decision that violated the loan contract the federal government had signed with the World Bank. The decision to invest in hospitals without addressing the access barriers that prevented the rural population from using these facilities increased inequity. In sum, the assumption that local decision makers are better able than the central government to assess the health needs of their community is not always correct.

The Guanajuato Health Secretariat did not incorporate health service users, representatives of rural residents, or neighborhood associations in its decision making. Only one NGO (with close ties to the governor) was invited to participate in the State Health Council. The complexity of the health sector may limit the roles that NGOs and social movements can play in decision making. For example, the social movement that blocked conversion of the maternity hospital, whose primary function was to attend uncomplicated births in the state's most prosperous city, raises questions about the appropriateness of citizen participation in decisions regarding health care. The health secretary's view that high-tech hospital care for uncomplicated deliveries represents an excessive cost may be a valid point when resources are limited and there are more economical care alternatives that do not endanger the health of the newborn or mother. This social movement included physicians from the maternity hospital who had a personal interest in keeping the hospital open, along with members of opposition parties who may have been motivated more by partisan interests than by concern for the common good of the population. One can also argue that many of the women who participated in the protests lacked the technical knowledge to judge whether a pediatric hospital and four peri-urban clinics could produce more health benefits for the citizens of León and the surrounding rural areas than would the maternity hospital.

Another foreseeable problem as districts assume decision-making powers is the politicization of decisions. The geographic boundaries of municipalities and health districts do not coincide. Health districts include several municipalities, a fact that can complicate decision making when the municipal presidents and governor belong to different political parties. One example of such a conflict occurred in a municipality governed by the Party of the Democratic Revolution. The municipal council wanted to construct a new clinic, but the director of the health district, who belonged to the PAN (as did the governor), did not support the request, alleging that the proposed clinic was intended to give work to friends of the mayor. Nobody debated the technical need for the clinic; the decision was based totally on partisan rivalries.

The conclusion from our study of Guanajuato is that, fifteen years after the decentralization process was begun in the state, equity has not increased,[12] the rural poor continue to receive fewer services than the more affluent urban classes, and users perceive many deficiencies that call into

---

[12] Indeed, the fact that users must now pay for services that they formerly received free of charge may represent an increase in inequity.

question the quality of services and prolong user dissatisfaction. In Guanajuato, decentralization did not reduce public expenditures on health, nor did it result in increased efficiency.

References

Arias, A. 1999. "El Hospital Materno Infantil se creó para atender a un sector desprotegido," *El Correo*, March 17.

Arjonilla, S., and I. Parada. 2003. "¿Qué piensa la población de los servicios de salud? Accesibilidad, utilización y calidad de la atención," *Cadernos Saúde Coletiva* 11, no. 2 (July–December): 159–82.

———. 2005. "Reforma del sector salud y las condiciones de acceso, utilización y calidad de la atención de los proveedores de servicios de salud." In *Salud y sociedad: sus métodos cualitativos de investigación*, vol. 2. Estado de México: Universidad Autónoma del Estado de México.

Bizberg, I. 1990. *Estado y sindicalismo en México*. México, D.F.: El Colegio de México.

Cruz Rivero, C., and M. Domínguez Villarreal. 1990. "Equidad en el cobro por servicios médicos hospitalarios: el caso de las cuotas de recuperación en la Secretaría de Salud," *Salud Pública de México* 32, no. 4: 449–64.

INEGI (Instituto Nacional de Estadística, Geografía e Informática). 1994. *Anuario estadístico del Estado de Guanajuato, 1994*. México, D.F.: INEGI.

———. 1997. *Anuario estadístico del Estado de Guanajuato, 1997*. México, D.F.: INEGI.

———. 2002. *Anuario estadístico del Estado de Guanajuato, 2002*. México, D.F.: INEGI.

Knaul, F. 2000. "Financiamiento justo en salud: crisis económica y reforma financiera en salud." Lecture presented at the Instituto Nacional de Salud Pública, Cuernavaca, July 18.

Morgan, L. 2001. "La participación comunitaria." Presented at the conference of researchers of El Centro de Investigaciones en Sistemas de Salud of the Instituto Nacional de Salud Pública, July.

Novelo, V., et al. 1989. *Democracia y sindicatos*. Mexico: Centro de Investigaciones y Estudios Superiores en Antropología Social/Ediciones El Caballito.

Tena Tamayo, C. 1999. "1999 año de la salud." Press conference, Guanajuato.

8

Nuevo León and Tamaulipas:
Opening and Closing a Window of Opportunity

NÚRIA HOMEDES AND ANTONIO UGALDE

The states of Nuevo León and Tamaulipas are located in northeastern Mexico and share a border with the United States. Their decentralization processes provide additional insights because both states view themselves as having greater independence from the federal government than do other Mexican states. In this chapter we describe the decentralization process in these states; discuss its impact on access, equity, and efficiency of services; and draw lessons to guide future steps in the decentralization effort.

The fieldwork for this study took place in two phases. The first phase was carried out between June 22 and October 30, 1998, and was conducted by two social scientists and one public health physician. In addition to reviewing archival information, we interviewed a total of thirty-four individuals. The semi-structured interviews were conducted at the interviewees' offices and lasted between one-half and two hours. We were interested in eliciting the opinions of four categories of respondents: elected officials and officers from the four largest political parties;[1] representatives of groups that influence the policy process such as professional associations (of physicians, dentists, nurses, and pharmacists) and labor unions; experts from academic institutions; and health professionals (see table 8.1).

The sample was selected with the help of two academics (one in each state) who were contracted as facilitators. Their role was to collect documents, identify interviewees according to guidelines from the principal investigators, and schedule appointments.

---

[1] These are the Party of the Democratic Revolution (PRD), National Action Party (PAN), Institutional Revolutionary Party (PRI), and Labor Party (PT).

Table 8.1. Characteristics of the Interviewees: Nuevo León and Tamaulipas, 1998 and 2001

Interviewee	1998		2001	
	Nuevo León	Tamaulipas	Nuevo León	Tamaulipas
Union representative	3	1	1	1
Representative of a political party	2	7	2	1
Member of a professional organization	2	3		1
Academic	3	1	1	1
Social insurance administrator	1	3	2	2
From the private sector	2	1		
State Health Secretariat personnel	2	6	18	8
Member of an NGO				2
Total	15	22	24	16

Note: A total of thirty-four interviews were conducted in 1998 and a total of thirty-five in 2001. Column totals are higher because some interviewees are represented in more than one category.

The interviews were not taped. Two researchers were present at each interview—one asking the questions and the other writing the responses. The research team transcribed and analyzed the notes immediately following the session, and questions raised during the analysis were clarified in a second interview by telephone or e-mail.

In August 2001, after the first phase of data collection and analysis was completed, we examined additional archival materials and documents and conducted thirty-five additional interviews. The aim of the second phase was to ascertain how decentralization was working; most interviewees were public health officials at the Tamaulipas Health Secretariat (SST) and Nuevo León Health Secretariat (SSNL), a few members of the state legislature, members of the health workers' union, academicians, and administrators of the Mexican Social Security Institute (IMSS) (table 8.1). The format of the interviews followed the same guidelines used during the first phase.

Informed consent was obtained from all participants, and no one refused to be interviewed. In order to maintain confidentiality, we provide only the position occupied by the interviewee but not his or her location. All direct citations are our own translations of the notes taken immediately after the interviews.

NUEVO LEÓN AND ITS HEALTH SYSTEM

Nuevo León is one of Mexico's most important industrial regions, has some of the best medical schools in the country, and is the health referral center for the northeastern region. It is an entrepreneurial state, contributing more to the national economy than it receives from the federal government.[2] Nuevo León's sense of economic independence allows it to forgo adherence to federal mandates that run counter to state priorities.

The state is highly urbanized. Its per capita income is considerably higher than the national average, and basic sanitation characteristics are more favorable (the state's sociodemographic and economic characteristics are presented in table 8.2). Health indicators parallel the state's more developed economic conditions with higher life expectancy and lower child (under age five) and maternal mortality rates (table 8.3).

---

[2] Nuevo León, which has about 4 percent of the country's population, contributes 6.8 percent of Mexico's gross domestic product (GDP).

Table 8.2. Demographic, Economic, and Political Characteristics of Tamaulipas, Nuevo León, and Mexico as a Whole

Characteristic	Nuevo León	Tamaulipas	Mexico
Total population	3,834,000	2,753,000	97,483,400
Area, in square kilometers	64,742	79,686	1,959,248
Population density (hab/km²) (2000)	59	35	50
Population with no public health insurance (%)[a]	34.1	48.8	59.9
Population growth rate[a]	1.5	1.5	1.4
Total number of municipalities >100,000 inhabitants	7	6	114
Total number of villages	5,726	8,824	199,369
% population in communities with <2,500 residents[b]	7	17	n.a.
% population in communities with >100,000 residents	82	66	47
Contribution to GNP (%) (1999)	6.8	3.0	—
% residents >15 years who are illiterate	3.3	5.1	9.5
Per capita income (pesos) (1999)	24,996	15,518	14,396
% households with a total income below two times the minimum wage (2000)	27	43	43
% households with running water	94	90	84
% households with sewerage systems	91	74	78
Political party in state government	PRI (2003–09) PAN (1997–03)	PRI (2004–10)	PAN (2000–06)
Previous administration	PRI since 1929[c]	PRI since 1929	PRI (since 1929)

Sources: SEGOB n.d. [a] Secretaría de Salud 2001. [b] INEGI 2000.

[c] In 1929, today's PRI was called the PNR; it was renamed the PRM in 1938 and the PRI in 1947.

Table 8.3. Health Indicators and Utilization Rates for Nuevo León, Tamaulipas, and Mexico as a Whole

Indicator/Utilization Rate	Nuevo León	Tamaulipas	Mexico
Fertility rate	2.1	2.1	2.4
Life expectancy (in years)			
Males	74.7	73.5	73.1
Females	78.8	77.6	77.6
Mortality rates (per 100,000 population) due to:			
Transmittable, nutritional, and reproductive health problems	46.3	48.5	72.5
Nontransmittable diseases	323.4	323.1	314.6
Accidents	39.7	51.9	55.6
Percent of women obtaining prenatal care during first trimester of pregnancy	38.5	31	33.6
Percent of institutional deliveries	100	100	80
Maternal mortality (per 10,000 live births)	3	5.3	5.1
Under-five mortality rate due to diarrheal diseases (per 100,000 children under age 5)	7.9	9.6	25.3
Under-five mortality rate due to respiratory infections (per 100,000 children under age 5)	10.3	16.2	47.3

Source: Secretaría de Salud 2001.

Table 8.4. Health Resources and Productivity: Nuevo León, Tamaulipas, and Mexico, 1999

Resources/Productivity Measures	Nuevo León	Tamaulipas	Mexico
Resources of the State Health Secretariat[a]			
Number of beds per 100,000 uninsured	34.39	136.58	78.53
Number of physicians per 100,000 uninsured	75.71	173.71	126.42
Number of nurses per 100,000 uninsured	100.91	273.52	175.09
Hospital occupancy rate (1999)	72.5	60.5	66.5
Adjusted hospital mortality rate (1999)	11.4	17.7	14.1
Health Resources of the Public System[b]			
Number of beds per 100,000 population	100	100	79
Number of practicing physicians per 100,000 population	123	135	117
Number of practicing nurses per 100,000 population	243	216	188
Number of dentists per 100,000 population	8	8	9
Total Public Expenditure per Capita[b]	1465.3	1240.2	1214.8
Productivity of the Public System[c]			
Number of deliveries per 1,000 hospital discharges	302.7	333.1	346.4
% of Caesarean section births	41	33	30
Number of daily surgeries per surgery room	3.8	2.6	3.9
Average number of daily consultations per physician	9.4	9.2	7.6
Hospital occupancy rate (%)	80	66	66

Sources: [a] Salud Pública de México 2000a; the denominator used to calculate the rates for infrastructure and services provided includes all the residents who do not have public insurance—that is, the uninsured and those covered by private insurance. Nuevo León has a high proportion of residents covered by private insurance, which can explain, at least in part, the low rate of health infrastructure per population for the residents of Nuevo León. People covered by social insurance (IMSS, ISSSTE, and so on) are not included in the denominators of this table.

[b] Secretaría de Salud 2001; these data include SSA, IMSS-Solidaridad, IMSS, ISSSTE, and PEMEX.

[c] Salud Pública de México 2000b.

Two-thirds of Nuevo León's residents are enrolled in a social security system, which reflects the state's high level of formal employment. The health infrastructure of the public sector (State Health Secretariat and social security programs) is also more favorable than in Mexico as a whole, with more beds per capita, more contacts with physicians and nurses, and higher per capita expenditures. However, productivity comparisons show both higher and lower rates for selected indicators. On the one hand, the hospital occupancy rate is higher, suggesting a better use of one of a health system's most costly components. And the number of deliveries as a percentage of discharges is lower than for the nation overall, indicating a more appropriate use of hospitals. On the other hand, the number of Caesarean births as a percentage of total births is very high (higher than in the rest of the country), which may indicate an undesirable and unnecessary use of hospital resources. It is possible that the relatively high hospital occupancy rate would drop if the percentage of Caesarean sections were reduced to recommended target rates. The number of daily consultations per physician is very low by international standards but higher than in other regions of Mexico (table 8.4).

The health infrastructure of the Nuevo León Health Secretariat (SSNL) falls below the Mexican average, but it cannot be suggested that the SSNL has insufficient physical resources.[3] According to studies conducted by the School of Public Health at the Autonomous University of Nuevo León in Monterrey, the available health infrastructure could cover twice the currently eligible population covered by the SSNL (Zacarías Villarreal Pérez 1999). The SSNL has a health center within a one-hour distance of any population concentration, as well as fourteen mobile units (each with a physician, nurse, and health promoter) that regularly travel to remote areas to deliver the basic package of services mandated by the federal government.

According to the state's health secretary, the Health Secretariat's priorities are to strengthen second-level rural hospitals (Sabinas, Cerralvo, Montemorelos, Dr. Arroyo, and Galeana) and to facilitate rural dwellers' access to specialty care by improving transportation and communication systems

---

[3] The low rates of infrastructure per population are partly explained by the presence of private companies (beer and glass makers) that provide services to all employees and their families through their own network of professionals and facilities.

Table 8.5. Nuevo León: Resources Available to the State Health Secretariat, 1985–1991

	1985	1987	1989	1990	1991
Population	1,175,782	1,056,399	1,825,000	1,339,000	1,300,500
Infrastructure					
1st-level medical units	163	340	324	n.a.	322
2nd-level medical units	7	8	8	8	8
Human Resources					
Physicians and dentists	1,023	1,152	1,118	n.a.	1,115
Nurses	1,455	1,545	1,525	n.a.	1,655
Financial Resources					
Executed budget in millions of constant pesos (1985)	6,590	5,245	5,945	3,792	4,369
% federal budget	79.70	86.35[a]	66.15	n.a.	n.a.
% state budget	19.91	10.95[a]	29.21	n.a.	n.a.
% user fees	0.39	2.70	4.64	n.a	n.a.
Pesos executed per capita	5,605	4,965	5,027	2,832	3,359

Source: Cardozo Brum 1995: 150.

[a] The proportional decline in state contributions is due to a significant increase in federal capital investments for the construction of the General Hospital of San Nicolás de Garza and a central storage facility.

(including telemedicine) between the health centers, rural hospitals, and tertiary hospitals in Monterrey (Zacarías Villarreal Pérez 2003: 260).

THE FIRST DECENTRALIZATION ATTEMPT, 1985–1996

Nuevo León signed the first decentralization agreement on May 31, 1985, after which the Coordinated Health Services office became the Nuevo León Health Secretariat. On December 9 of the same year, all IMSS-COPLAMAR infrastructure (forty-two health centers and a rural hospital) and personnel were transferred to the SSNL. The State Health Law was approved two years later (December 1988), and its rules and regulations were approved on May 30, 1990. The State Health Law established the population's right to health protection, defined the state health system and how the population could access health services, and clarified the responsibilities of the state and municipalities in the area of public health and basic sanitation.

In the decentralization agreement, Nuevo León agreed to increase the state's contribution to the health budget to 20 percent of total health expenditures, which it did (table 8.5). However, total per capita health expenditures decreased in constant pesos, reaching their lowest level in 1990. As public contributions declined, the amounts recovered through user fees increased from 0.39 percent of total expenditures in 1985 to 2.70 percent in 1987 and 4.64 percent in 1989 (Cardozo Brum 1995: 150).[4]

According to several informants, the quality of services clearly worsened after decentralization. The state's health secretary noted the deterioration of the population's health status, attributing it to the insufficiency of federal funds and the state's inability to cover the increased cost of providing care. The increase in malaria incidence is a good example. According to the then-secretary of health, the state had the needed expertise but lacked the resources to control the spread of this disease. The manager of a private insurance company confirmed the deterioration in health care, noting: "The health care budget [the public budget] did not keep pace with population growth and the increase of poverty." He also suggested that the norms guiding the use of federal funds were very rigid, limiting the State

---

[4] In Mexico, as noted in chapter 2 on the history of decentralization in Mexico, user fees include income generated through contracts with the municipalities and social security plans, as well as fees for services, including medicines.

Health Secretariat's ability to administer the resources in more efficient ways and to respond more adequately to the needs of the state: "The central government wanted decentralization, but they didn't want to lose economic control." In contrast to the shortage of operational funds for health services during this period of economic crisis, there was a significant expansion in infrastructure. The number of primary-care units doubled, from 163 in 1985 to 340 in 1987, and a 200-bed hospital, the Hospital de San Nicolás de Garza, was built in 1987 (Cardozo Brum 1995: 147).

In the area of public sanitation, the General Health Act of 1985 defined the twenty-seven public health regulatory activities that would be decentralized to the states, and the State Health Law specified which tasks would be the responsibility of the SSNL and which would fall to the municipalities. The implementation of these changes was very slow, and little was accomplished during the first decentralization wave. For instance, the Nuevo León Health Secretariat would carry out inspections (hygiene and safety control of commercial establishments), but the federal government continued to issue warnings and levy fines. The decentralization of state responsibilities to the municipalities followed a similar pattern; most municipalities, especially those in rural areas, did not want to accept the new responsibilities because they felt that, in carrying out sanitary inspections and enforcing regulations, they would have to confront their neighbors and risk losing their friendship and political support.

In the opinion of our interviewees, in Nuevo León the first decentralization produced no significant impact. As an official of a political party explained:

> Decentralization of the Ministry of Health did not impact any of the programs until 1997. [Before that date] the programs were all designed in Mexico City, and the objectives [benchmarks] were the same for all the states. They were much below our ability to perform; [our indicators were already above those set by the SSA] so they were useless. Everything was determined at the federal level, and it was unrelated to our reality.

As in the rest of Mexico, the decentralization effort was interrupted during the presidency of Carlos Salinas de Gortari (1988–1994).

THE SECOND DECENTRALIZATION, 1997–2001

The state of Nuevo León signed a second decentralization agreement with the federal government during the administration of President Ernesto Zedillo on December 18, 1996. In 1998, when this study began, reaction to this new agreement was mixed; some respondents felt that the federal government was committed to devolving responsibilities to the states and that the latters' accomplishments would depend on their managerial capacity and the risks they were willing to take, but others remained skeptical. A university professor alleged that Zedillo and his health minister sincerely wanted to decentralize, but he doubted whether mid-level federal bureaucrats shared this commitment:

> Nobody wants to lose power, and the lower you are in the hierarchy, the more you resist losing power. Some people measure their power by the number of employees that report to them [which presumably would decrease after decentralization], and others fear losing their jobs.

The following paragraphs discuss the changes implemented by the Nuevo León Health Secretariat as a result of the second round of decentralization—organizational changes and an increase in the number of people eligible to receive services through SSNL; changes in the management of financial and human resources; and impacts that the changes had on delivery of care.

Organizational Changes and Expansion of Coverage

Between the first and second decentralizations, the Nuevo León Health Secretariat was under the Ministry of Social Development (SEDESOL), but in January 1999, as a result of the November 1998 Public Administration Reform, the SSNL was reinstated as an independent secretariat. Accordingly, the state's secretary of health is the state's highest health authority and is also the chief executive officer of the decentralized public agency (OPD) that is responsible for providing services to the uninsured (see chapter 2 in this volume).

Dr. Jesús Zacarías Villarreal was the state health secretary responsible for leading the decentralization process. He is a well-respected physician who, at the time of his appointment, was dean of the prestigious medical school of the Autonomous University of Nuevo León and a leader in the medical community. His appointment was a rare event in Mexican politics because he was not a politician. He was appointed in recognition of his professional accomplishments, and he accepted the position hoping that he could improve health conditions in the state. He indicated during an interview that he was ready to resign at a moment's notice if political pressure and interest groups unduly interfered with the SSNL's operations.

Significantly, and contrary to the prevailing custom of replacing high-level administrators appointed by the previous administration, Zacarías Villarreal chose to retain them and benefit from their technical skills. His two major initiatives were: (1) to increase the productivity of the OPD by selling its services to social security institutes for their beneficiaries who resided in areas where the institutes lacked health infrastructure, as well as to municipalities for their employees and employees' families; and (2) to transfer resources and decision making to the health districts and hospitals (see chapter 9 for a detailed discussion of the health districts).

The Nuevo León Health Secretariat has signed agreements to provide health services to beneficiaries of ISSSTE, ISSSTELEON, and IMSS, and for municipal employees. However, according to the health secretary, the contracts are a useful tool but in need of improvement:

> We need to have better estimates of the cost of our services and use that information in our contracts. We do not have this information. The only way to have a seamless system of health care delivery is to have a system to identify who is responsible for the care of a particular client, and then being able to bill that entity for the cost of the services rendered.

Many State Health Secretariats have contracts with social security institutes, but contracts with the municipalities are more unusual. In August 2001, employees and their families in twenty municipalities in Nuevo León received free health care services, including hospitalization and medicines, from health districts and SSNL hospitals. The municipalities pay a yearly premium per employee to the SSNL, and the SSNL distributes the funds to the districts. The health districts reimburse hospitals for expenditures incurred by the referred patients. The funds generated through these contractual arrangements are included in the "user fee" accounting category, reported to the legislature for control purposes only, and included in the following year's budget of the district that generated the funds under the category of "funds generated through user fees."

On some occasions the municipalities have also acted as intermediaries for *maquiladoras*.[5] Mexican law requires that all *maquiladora* workers be enrolled in the IMSS; where there is no IMSS infrastructure, the IMSS can contract private or public networks, including OPDs, for the provision of health services. In Nuevo León, at least one *maquiladora* asked the municipality to provide health services for its employees and their families; the municipality in turn asked the district to provide these services. As a result, the OPD is providing services to the workers. In this case, the municipality collected funds from the industry and used them to provide in-kind support (an ambulance and another vehicle) to the district. The director of the health district was satisfied with this arrangement because the district received additional resources.

The second decentralization did not introduce any major change in the area of sanitary regulation. The main difference was that the state was given the authority to issue official notices for sanitation violations and to collect and keep the fines. Additional efforts have been made to decentralize specific regulatory activities to the municipalities, but by the summer of 2001 only five municipalities had signed agreements accepting regulatory responsibilities, mainly for the same reasons expressed during the first decentralization wave and also because municipal governments were reluctant to accept new responsibilities without the transfer of sufficient resources to cover the costs.

Financial Resources

The state budget is composed of three main sources of funding: federal, state, and self-generated (funds generated through user fees, sales of medi-

---

[5] *Maquiladoras* are industries that are taxed only on the value added when converting materials imported from the United States into finished products, primarily for export to the United States. These plants do not pay taxes, and the United States pays import tax only on the value added. Mexico's *maquiladoras* are generally located along the country's northern border.

cines, and contracts with social security institutes or municipalities). Most of the financing (about 70 percent) for the sanitary regulation department comes from fines imposed for violations of the sanitary code. All federal and state funds must be spent according to state regulations, and the state comptroller audits the departments. All self-generated funds are included in the state budget under the category of user fees and can be used at the discretion of the SSNL. Following subsections describe the level of funding from each source and how funds can be used.

Federal funds. As noted in chapter 2, all federal funds are deposited in the state treasury, and from here the funds are transferred to the SSNL once the State Board of Health approves the health budget. The SSNL can move funds across all budget categories except for salaries, which represent about 79 percent of the federal funds.

In January 1998, the state began issuing the payroll checks for federally funded positions and was allowed to keep any funds that went unspent because of unauthorized staff absences or authorized unpaid leaves. These funds, which previously reverted to the federal government, allowed the Nuevo León Health Secretariat to cover new expenses incurred as a result of the decentralization and not covered by the federal government. According to the state health secretary:

> The federal government is responsible for paying the salary differential for the state employees whose salaries were homologized to those of federal workers, but they do not pay for special bonuses [such as the end-of-year bonus] that are regularly given to federal employees. It is up to the state to find the funds…. The lawyers do not agree on whether these payments should be made with federal or with state funds…. For the moment we are using SSNL funds. In some cases this means that we leave positions open so that we have enough "unspent funds" in the personnel budget.

Another high-level SSNL officer expressed his frustration with this system:

> One of the most troubling issues for the state government is that personnel bonuses to be paid by the states are negotiated

between the federal government and the National Union of Health Ministry Employees [SNTSSA], without involving the states or considering whether the states can shoulder those commitments.

The per capita federal health allocation to Nuevo León is below the national average, and, as reported in chapter 2 (table 2.5), the uneven distribution of federal health funds to the states does not follow a clear logic. The National Health Council is trying to establish specific criteria to make the distribution of federal health funds to the states more equitable. Nuevo León's health secretary is a member of a taskforce created by the National Health Council to oversee a more equitable allocation of federal funds. In his opinion, the new formula should reward the states that are investing in the health sector and are using their funds efficiently. This would reverse the current situation, which, according to him, punishes the states that make efficient use of their resources and rewards inefficient states, perpetuating their dependence on federal handouts.

State financial flows. The state's contribution to the health budget has increased substantially in recent years. In 1997 it represented 5.8 percent of the total budget; by 2001 it amounted to almost 20 percent, and it continues to increase (table 8.6). Among the governor's commitments was a pledge to refurbish all health units during his tenure.

Self-generated funds. Self-generated funds include user fees, income generated through the sale of medicines and contracts for the delivery of health service, and donations.[6] Nuevo León gained total control of these funds during the first decentralization, and their amount has been rising, from 6.5 percent of the budget in 1997 to 7.6 percent in 2000 (SSNL 2001). Unfortunately, the accounting system does not break self-generated funds down by category; it may be that the increases are due mainly to rising income from user fees and municipality contracts.

User fees have been collected in Mexico's public health system for decades. In 1984 the federal government developed a fee scale to guide health

---

[6] For example, the Rotary Club financed an immunization campaign against Haemophilus influenzae.

Table 8.6. Nuevo León: State Health Secretariat 1997–2001 Budget, by Funding Source (in millions of pesos)[a]

Funding Source	1997 $million	%	1998 $million	%	1999 $million	%	2000[b] $million	%	2001[b] $million	%
Federal level	340	87.9	426	83.0	573	80.0	663	74.0	773	73.2
State level	22	5.7	34	6.6	71	9.9	165	18.4	212	19.9
Self-generated	25	6.4	51	10.0	72	10.0	69	7.7	71	6.7
Total[c]	387	100.0	512	99.6	716	99.9	896	100.1	1,056	99.8

Source: SSNL 2001.
[a] Excluding the state budget for the university hospital.
[b] Includes state capital investment funds (117,000 pesos in 2000 and 148,000 pesos in 2001).
[c] Percentages do not add to 100 due to rounding.

Table 8.7. Allocation of Self-Generated Funds according to SSNL Regulations

User Fees and Sales of Medicines	Funds Generated through Contracts with Municipalities and Social Insurance
50% returned to the health center where they were generated: 30% for personnel incentives and 20% for other expenditures	30% returned to the health centers that have the contracts as incentives for personnel
	10% used for personnel incentives in regional offices
30% spent by the regional office for infrastructure, maintenance, and equipment	40% used to purchase medicines (provided without cost to clients covered by those plans)
10% used for personnel incentives in the regional office	20% transferred to hospitals for services rendered to clients covered by these schemes
10% sent to SSNL	

establishments such that charges for services would vary according to the patient's income. The Ministry of Health also mandated that all services linked to priority programs be provided free of charge; these include maternal and child care, family planning, and treatment of tuberculosis, hypertension, and diabetes, among others. Today all the services included in the basic package are to be provided free (including medicines and vaccines). States' adherence to the federal fee scale is no longer mandatory. In Nuevo León, by the decision of a former governor, Health District Number 8 cannot charge user fees, due to the region's poverty. In the other districts, the district director can waive the user fee when she or he judges that a patient is unable to pay; generally this responsibility is delegated to the directors of the health centers and members of the staff (see chapter 9 for a detailed discussion).

Health providers and administrators believe that those who can pay should pay for services. This view is shared by some state legislators. A Labor Party legislator mentioned that user fees were desirable and that the State Health Board had recently approved a 15 percent increase in the cost of contracts with social insurance funds and municipalities and a 26 percent increase in user fees. A member of the PRI was somewhat more critical:

> The PAN now charges for everything.... The health sector has been dehumanized, and the physicians have lost their dignity.... The SSNL health centers are empty because everybody has to pay, and the user fees are higher than in the private sector. Thus people prefer to use a private provider closer to home than go to the health center.

When asked if the PRI had made any specific proposal to remedy the situation, he said that they had not done anything at the structural level but that the party was providing free services and delivering free medicines in some marginalized areas and obtaining fee waivers for people unable to pay for services. This PRI member also expressed concern about the substantial fines imposed on street vendors who violated sanitary codes, and he mentioned that the PRI's health committee was spending a considerable amount of time doing the following:

helping the street vendors because the fines are too high. The fines can amount to several times the weekly income of those workers, causing them to go out of business. For example, a street vendor was charged 300 pesos, and the value of her goods was about 50 pesos.

Most states send a percentage of the self-generated funds to the Federal Welfare Agency, but the SSNL refused, arguing that it would never receive any benefit from the Welfare Agency. On the other hand, the SSNL sends a portion of its self-generated funds to Health District Number 8, the only health district that is not allowed to collect user fees. Table 8.7 presents the regulations that the Nuevo León Health Secretariat issued regarding the use of funds generated by user fees and sales of medicines at the health centers and from contracts with municipalities and social security programs.

Self-generated income can only be used for personnel incentives in those health districts that complete the minimum average number of consultations per day. When this is not the case, the funds are transferred to the Reform Fund (Fondo de Reforma). The health workers' union and the SSNL manage the Reform Fund jointly, and it is used for social events (such as a Mother's Day celebration) and other activities such as the construction of a recreation center in the countryside for all health workers. In 2001 there were about 10 million pesos in the Reform Fund (about US$1 million).

If a health district qualifies to receive incentive funds, these funds can be distributed to the health centers within the district that meet minimum productivity and performance standards. In the health centers, the funds are distributed to the employees who performed above established minimum standards (that is, physicians had to see at least ten patients a day, staff could not have unauthorized absences, all personnel had to comply with the work schedule), using a salary-based distribution formula (those with higher salaries, such as physicians, receive higher incentive bonuses).

A different allocation system prevails in the administrative offices of the health district: staff personnel receive a higher proportion of the incentive funds than do the professionals, provided that they do not have unauthorized absences and that they adhere to set work schedules. Some hospitals do not have a personnel incentive system, and the funds are used at the discretion of the directors.

The self-generated funds retained by the SSNL are used in the following manner: 30 percent is expended as staff incentives in the state office, 15 percent is spent at the discretion of the secretary of health, 15 percent is transferred to Health District Number 8, and 40 percent is used for infrastructure improvements.

In sum, there is a good deal of variability in the amount that workers receive as performance incentives paid out of the self-generated funds. Whereas some health districts and health centers (mainly urban) never meet the minimum standards and their workers never receive these bonuses, there are physicians (mainly in rural areas) for whom these incentives can increase their basic salary by about 30 percent.

Fines. Funds collected from fines for infractions of the sanitary code are spent in the operation of the sanitary regulation program. They represent about 70 percent of the SSNL budget for this program.

The Nuevo León Health Secretariat has a matching funds program with municipalities for capital investments (buildings, ambulances, radio communication systems, and other equipment). As a result, the municipalities increased health-sector investment allocations from 19 percent in 1994 to 23 percent in 1999.

Human Resources

The 5,000-plus employees of the State Health Secretariat fall into five categories: (1) those who have always occupied federal posts (the vast majority of workers); (2) employees hired by the state prior to decentralization and whose salaries and benefits were homologized with those of federal employees following the second decentralization (about 530 workers); (3) state employees who for various reasons could not (or chose not to) be homologized with federal employees (125);[7] (4) employees under temporary contract (not to exceed six months) who have no benefits; and (5) young medical professionals fulfilling their year of social service, who are paid by the federal government. Categories 1 and 2 are affiliated with the National Union of Health Ministry Employees; the others are not unionized.

---

[7] These 125 employees chose not to convert so as not to lose the benefits earned through their contributions to the state social security funds (ISSSTELEON).

The salaries, work conditions, and benefits of workers affiliated with the SNTSSA are negotiated between the labor union and the federal government, but the 1996 decentralization allows state secretaries of health to negotiate with the local chapter of the labor union regarding the recruitment and transfer of personnel within the state. SSNL administrators and SNTSSA local leaders felt very positive about this change, indicating that they could now demand greater accountability from their workers than they could when everything was decided in Mexico City. The state SNTSSA representative said:

> The union protects workers, but not the lazy ones.... We're changing the behaviors that gave us such a bad reputation. It is a question of survival; we need to provide good-quality services. There was one physician who had four jobs, and he would only be at the health centers for 45 minutes a day.... The secretary of health spoke with us and we agreed with him. The doctor was fired. We cannot protect union members who do not work or who engage in illegal activities.

The main frustration for the state health secretary is the inability to change federally funded positions. For example, if the State Health Secretariat needs x-ray technicians and has too many lab technicians, the SSNL cannot use funds freed up by a retiring lab technician to hire the needed x-ray technician. The secretary of health explained:

> In 1999 we had two hundred vacant federal positions that were no longer needed [such as drivers], but those positions could not be redefined to allow the hiring of other needed personnel [such as nurses]. I discussed this in Mexico City, and they would not convert the positions.

To satisfy its personnel needs, the SSNL had to hire mostly temporary workers. Between 1997 and 2000, the workforce was increased by 18.7 percent, and in 2001 the health planner requested the creation of 367 additional positions, which would represent a 25.8 percent increase in personnel in less than five years.

Decentralization has not significantly changed staff productivity, and the system continues to be inefficient. Physicians contracted by the State Health Secretariat are only required to see eighteen patients a day, and the actual number of daily consultations per physician is significantly lower. According to data gathered by the SSNL, in 1996 general practitioners were seeing an average of 11 patients per day, and in 2000 their average daily load was 13.5 patients.

The Decentralization of Physical Infrastructure

The 1996 decentralization agreement specified that the Ministry of Health would donate all infrastructure (except tertiary-level hospitals) and equipment to the states. By 1999 the SSNL owned 430 health centers and 9 hospitals. According to the director of the decentralization unit of the SSNL:

> Very often municipal or private buildings had been informally lent or given to the Health Ministry without any formalization of the transaction in a written or legal document; on other occasions the buildings had been lent for a limited period such as ten or twenty-five years. This process [of transferring the physical infrastructure] has been significantly more complicated than anticipated.... We had to work with the Public Property Registry, and it took a lot of time. In some cases we had to go to the Agricultural Property Registry because the land is owned by an *ejido*.

In 2001 the transfer of physical infrastructure had not yet been completed, and there were many issues that remained unresolved. According to the same informant, "Another unresolved issue was that of property taxes. The Ministry of Health had never paid them, but now some municipalities may want to charge property taxes to the SSNL."

The transfer of equipment is complete and has been very rewarding. Now, as one respondent indicated, "The disposal of obsolete equipment can be done within the state. Before, all surplus equipment had to be taken to Mexico City, and that was expensive." A district director corroborated the opinion of this decentralization officer: "Now, unnecessary equipment can be disposed of in Monterrey twice a year instead of just once every ten years."

Health Programs

As is the case in other states, the Nuevo León Health Secretariat has to deliver the basic package of services mandated by the Health Ministry and is encouraged to add other programs according to the state's priorities and resources. The SSNL has added programs to accomplish the following:

- Strengthen knowledge about healthy behaviors by providing continuing educational activities for health promoters and training high school students on basic health concepts.
- Immunize against Haemophilus influenzae.
- Develop a registry of neural tubal defects and provide folic acid supplements to women of childbearing age.
- Lower the risk of complications during childbirth and increase the number of ultrasound screens for pregnant women.
- Prevent accidents.
- Train primary health physicians to detect and treat basic mental health problems.
- Strengthen dengue prevention and detection activities (in collaboration with the Centers for Disease Control and Prevention in Atlanta, Georgia).
- Promote public health research through the implementation of nutrition surveys and studies of factors associated with the development of complications in children with acute respiratory infections.

Some of these programs, such as dengue prevention and the registry of neural tubal defects, have attracted international attention and support because they tackle problems that hold implications for U.S. border communities. This outside interest highlights the trust that international groups have in the SSNL's scientific standards and in Nuevo León's corps of researchers.

One problem many of our interviewees mentioned is the excessive time and resources invested in coordinating and supervising programs. According to one district director: "The program directors have monthly meetings in Monterrey.... They have too many meetings and they only discuss bureaucratic issues." The district directors also meet in Monterrey once a month, administrators from the State Health Secretariat regularly visit health centers and hospitals, and, as in the rest of the country, the State Health Secretariat and Ministry of Health supervise the vertical programs, including the basic package of services. Federal employees may inform the states about the dates of an impending visit, but they carry out the yearly supervision of health establishments independently.

In addition, all regulatory personnel travel frequently to Monterrey to deliver food and water samples for analysis in state laboratories. Per diems and other travel expenses are becoming a concern to health district directors, who are beginning to limit the frequency of travel and the number of staff members who attend administrative meetings.

TAMAULIPAS AND ITS HEALTH SYSTEM

Residents of Tamaulipas proudly point out their state's cultural, historical, and political differences from the rest of Mexico. Two-thirds of the population reside in cities with more than 100,000 residents, though a relatively sizable number reside in villages with fewer than 2,500 inhabitants (some basic sociodemographic variables are presented in table 8.2).

The average per capita income in the state is slightly higher than the national average, and about the same percentage of families earns less than twice the minimum wage as at the national level. These numbers suggest that the distribution of wealth in Tamaulipas is relatively comparable to Mexico in general, but there is much less wealth overall than in Nuevo León. In Tamaulipas, a small number of workers employed by the oil industry receive a high salary by Mexican standards, and a significant percentage of underpaid agricultural workers or subsistence peasants have few economic resources.

Illiteracy in Tamaulipas is below the Mexican average. The sanitation system and health indicators compare favorably with the national average (see table 8.3). Tamaulipas has a lower fertility rate, lower mortality rate from transmittable diseases and nutritional and reproductive health problems, and lower under-age-five mortality rate due to diarrhea and upper respiratory infections than found in the nation overall. Life expectancy for both men and women in Tamaulipas is similar to national figures but lower than in Nuevo León. The maternal mortality rate is high, and higher than in Nuevo León, despite the fact that all women deliver in health establishments. A possible explanation may be that in Tamaulipas a higher proportion of women do not seek prenatal care during the first trimester of pregnancy, which may be the result of lower incomes, especially in remote rural areas. Also worrisome for Tamaulipas are the state's high hospital and accident mortality rates.

Half of the residents in Tamaulipas are covered by social security (51 percent) and the state is well endowed with health infrastructure (see table 8.4). If we consider the infrastructure of the Tamaulipas Health Secretariat (SST), the state appears to have significantly more per capita resources than is the case nationwide. The occupancy rate for SST hospitals is very low, as is the number of surgeries per operating room. The number of consultations per physician is low but above the national average.

Yet despite high per capita infrastructure and its underutilization, state legislators consider that the rural population lacks adequate access to health services because residents in remote areas are only served by mobile units and, as one political leader explained, "they do not get sick on schedule"—that is, when the mobile units visit the communities. According to one legislator we interviewed, purchasing ambulances is the highest priority for Tamaulipas, followed by health education and teaching citizens how to use available services. In his view, the people do not know about available services and therefore cannot take advantage of them. The low number of pregnant women who access prenatal care during the first trimester supports this perception.

DECENTRALIZATION IN TAMAULIPAS

As mentioned in chapter 2, Tamaulipas did not decentralize during the Miguel de la Madrid administration; not until 1997 did the state accept the decentralization of its State Health Secretariat. This section presents the aspects of its decentralization that differ from those of Nuevo León—namely, decentralization's impacts on state hospitals; fiscal management, especially of self-generated funds; and the role of the state legislature and nongovernmental organizations (NGOs).

The Autonomous State Hospitals

During the 1980s, Tamaulipas developed a network of eleven autonomous hospitals financed by the state and each governed by a hospital board. All hospital boards were presided over by the governor. Each hospital functioned independently, and the amount of state funding that each received was determined by the governor. State funds were transferred in bulk, allowing the hospital directors and hospital boards to manage the resources in response to prevailing needs. Critics assert that the financing system was highly inequitable and that the allocations depended heavily on the negotiating skills and political connections of hospital directors and board members. One interviewee noted, "the General Hospital had the highest salaries because of the political connections of its physicians." Hospital directors could even set the salary levels of their employees.

The eleven state hospitals varied widely in size and quality. Two—the General Hospital and the Pediatric Hospital—are located in Ciudad Victoria, the state capital, and operate as research and teaching hospitals for training specialists. They are considered top-rank and serve as referral centers for the region, and they also treat patients from the southwestern United States. These hospitals are well equipped; the General Hospital has hemodynamic equipment, and its surgeons can perform open-heart surgery and heart transplants. Some of the physicians in these two hospitals, especially those working there before decentralization, trained abroad, including formal training and research collaboration with U.S.-based institutions, and had international networks of associates. According to the former fourteen-year director of the General Hospital:

> The General Hospital opened at the end of 1985, and during those days we had a lot of interest in academic medicine. We hosted a number of international meetings in different fields: medicine, nursing, social work…. We had an international reputation and many contracts. At one point we had fifty agreements with foreign training institutions, and when I left the directorship in January 1999 we were about to sign an

agreement to exchange residents with the University of Maryland, under which some of our residents would go to Maryland and some U.S. residents would come here. We also allowed our workers to spend some of their time in the hospital to study....

We also extended our services to the rural areas.... At the request of the governor's wife, we launched a series of rural campaigns.... A group of hospital physicians and nurses would go to rural areas on Saturdays to deliver quality services. We conducted about 160 campaigns in ten years. Later the Pediatric Hospital and other hospitals adopted the same model. When I left, the budget for the General Hospital was higher than the budget of eight state hospitals.

In addition to the state funds, these autonomous hospitals derive revenue from contracts with IMSS and ISSSTE, and from fees paid by private clients. Private patients and the beneficiaries of social insurance programs occupy a specific section of the hospital and are separated from the uninsured patients.

With the signing of the decentralization agreement in 1997, all eleven state hospitals were transferred to the State Health Secretariat, and their organization and management were completely overhauled. All state personnel (2,124) were homologized and began to receive salaries and benefits equivalent to those of federal employees. All eleven independent labor unions—one per hospital—were merged into a single union. The merging of the unions and the negotiation of salaries and benefits were the most time-consuming and difficult aspects of the decentralization process in Tamaulipas.

The transfer of the autonomous hospitals to the OPD was not completed until January 1999. At that moment the hospital directors were replaced, and from that point forward all administrative procedures had to comply with SST regulations, severely constraining the decision-making authority of the new hospital directors. Thus, for the eleven autonomous state hospitals, the 1997 decentralization agreement brought a loss of autonomy and a centralization of power in the SST. Many physicians, resentful of their loss of autonomy and a reduction in income, resigned. For them, decentralization meant the politicization of hospital management. The former hospital director commented:

> The working environment has deteriorated tremendously; the hospital cannot operate efficiently under SST control. The State Health Secretariat could develop organizational and delivery models, but they should allow certain freedom of movement to hospital directors. The current administration is only concerned with image.... They look for photo opportunities, but they don't care much about solving the problems that are affecting the population.... The quality of care will deteriorate progressively.... You can already see it with the two malpractice cases that have been reported in the news [one case involved the death of a woman from infection following gallbladder surgery, and the other, a patient who was mistaken for another and had an unnecessary amputation].... The mortality rate has increased significantly since the hospital was transferred to the SST.... We had a mortality rate of 2.8 percent; now it is much higher.

Several physicians who left the General Hospital explored the possibility of building a private hospital where they could continue to provide quality care. One physician in this group explained:

> Market studies indicate that there are enough people in the state to justify the building of a private hospital in Ciudad Victoria. We can attract private patients who are now treated at the General Hospital or the Pediatric Hospital and also the patients who travel to Monterrey. We are looking for investors. We started looking for Canadian and American capital, but it appears that there is a group in Monterrey that is willing to finance us. The fees at the General Hospital are very high for private patients; we could offer the same services at a lower price.

Financial Management and the State Legislature

As in Nuevo León, the health budget in Tamaulipas receives funding from the federal and state governments. These funds are complemented with

Table 8.8. Sources of Funding of the Tamaulipas Health Secretariat, 1997–2001 (in millions of pesos)

Funding Source	1997		1998		1999		2000		2001	
	$million	%	$million	%	$million	%	$million	%	$million	%
Federal level	212	92.48	396	68.96	644	73.31	725	74.29	929	70.51
State level	1	0.23	78	13.60	110	12.47	129	13.25	249	18.87
Other	17	7.29	100	17.44	125	14.22	122	12.45	140	10.62
Total	230	100.00	574	100.00	879	100.00	976	99.99	1,318	100.00

self-generated funds (see table 8.8). The state's share has been increasing in recent years. The federal funds are deposited in the state treasury and, once the State Board of Health approves the budget, are transferred to the State Health Secretariat. A legislator from the National Action Party (PAN) who is a member of the State Health Commission complained that the Commission did not have any input in deciding how health funds should be allocated. Multiple requests to the SST for information about the execution of the budget had gone unanswered. This legislator interpreted the secrecy surrounding public health expenditures as indicating that decisions did not respond to technical considerations and that rural areas received less than their fair share.

The third major source of funding, after federal and state allocations, is revenue generated by each health establishment from contracts with the IMSS and ISSSTE, from user fees, and from the sale of medicines. As in the case of Nuevo León, there is pressure to increase self-generated funds, especially in hospitals.

The Tamaulipas Health Secretariat is encouraging hospitals to become self-supporting, except for personnel expenditures, which continue to be paid from federal and state allocations. In 2000 the state legislature, concerned about the accumulation of unpaid hospital bills, passed a law requiring hospitals to forgive outstanding bills of patients who, twelve months after discharge, had not been able to pay.[8] According to the director of the General Hospital, the amount of uncollected funds has been rising, and he thought the law would have a severe impact on the hospital's ability to obtain the resources needed to remain operational. In his view, the SST would have to cut services for the indigent and for those who could not afford to pay user fees.

In 2001 the General Hospital was under financial pressure, and its administration adopted the following policies: raising fees for private patients, requiring inpatients to purchase their medicines in the hospital pharmacy, increasing outpatient user fees, and establishing incentives to increase the number of outpatient visits. It is worth noting that, as in Nuevo León, the level of user fees had to be approved by the State Board of Health, but in 2001 the General Hospital raised outpatient fees from 22 to

---

[8] This could explain some of the drop in self-generated funds (see table 8.8).

40 pesos without consulting with the board or the SST. Although the state health secretary and other members of the board were aware of the increase, no action was taken.

The General Hospital's new policies were controversial. According to some private physicians, the hospital's fees for private patients had risen above those charged in private hospitals in Monterrey, and they feared that their patients would opt for out-of-state care in neighboring Nuevo León. The requirement that inpatients purchase their medications in the hospital pharmacy raised questions about quality of care because, according to the hospital director:

> If a patient is unable to purchase the medication, the hospital will not provide it, even if skipping a dose compromises the patient's prognosis. The only exception is if the patient is classified as extremely poor, in which case all fees are waived.

The impact of increased outpatient fees was hard to predict. For some people, it could limit access to needed services. But according to the hospital director, it could also encourage patients to make better use of state resources because they would go first to primary health clinics, where the services are cheaper. When interviewed in 2001, the director estimated that "about 30 percent of the patients who use the hospital's outpatient facilities could be seen in a health center at one-third of the cost."

The state budget for health districts and hospitals is preset, and it is difficult to move funds from one category to another. All procurement of goods and services with federal or state funds is carried out by the state, but SST officials claimed that if they could have more control over purchases, they could respond better to the needs of the health districts and hospitals. On the other hand, contrary to the situation in Nuevo León, hospital and district directors have full control over 85 percent of the self-generated funds. The remaining 15 percent is deposited in SST accounts; the SST uses 10 percent of these funds at its own discretion and transfers the remaining 5 percent to Federal Welfare Agency.

The self-generated funds cannot be used to purchase equipment. They can only be used for maintenance, to purchase supplies and medicines, and for personnel incentives. Each hospital and district director has full discretionary power in spending these funds. The director of one health district explained:

> I do not use the self-generated funds to complement person-
> nel salaries because this is very complicated and would give
> me headaches. You are bound to receive complaints and to
> generate jealousies. I use most of these funds to purchase
> medicines and supplies.

Members of the legislature's State Health Commission asserted that health was a priority for the governor, but they acknowledged that it was not at the forefront of his agenda. The Health Commission and the SST were working on a bill to ensure that the next administration would not be able to cut state health funding.

Some legislators felt that they could not gain an understanding of the complexities of the health system in their brief three-year terms in office (the Mexican system does not permit reelection), much less make any sig-nificant legislative changes. Instead, they spend their time responding to their constituents' requests, such as helping them get appointments with a specialist or obtaining SST reimbursements for rural patients for the costs of transportation to hospitals.

The Role of NGOs

In Tamaulipas, the State Health Secretariat created a Health Council that includes representatives of major health providers, self-help groups (there are more than one hundred of these, mostly for patients with high blood pressure and diabetes), and NGOs. The Council's role is to promote inter-agency coordination and increase participation in defining state health priorities. In practice, the Council is not very representative of consumers. For example, two NGOs, one working with cancer patients and the other with the disabled, were appointed to the Council by the state secretary of health. According to the director of Volunteers Against Cancer, no effort was made to allow community groups to select representatives to the Health Council. Although the two NGOs on the Council could in theory represent the concerns of other NGOs, they made no attempts to contact other groups in order to share information or engage them in the decision-making process. These two NGOs viewed their inclusion on the Health Council as an individual privilege and not as a means of encouraging true community participation. The director of one NGO confided:

> In times of crisis the State Health Secretariat should recognize the work that many volunteer agencies and NGOs are doing. We are helping them, and we are doing a better job than the SST. There are many of us; with a little help we can achieve a lot for the people of Tamaulipas.

Volunteers Against Cancer receives funds to treat cancer patients in the Pediatric Hospital, and the SST sends medicines directly to the hospital for the patients identified by this NGO. Its director affirmed that they made sure that "patients receive state-of-the-art treatment and that they are not experimented upon." It would be interesting to know why the SST chose this NGO for support, to determine what proportion of children with cancer receive treatment through the NGO, and which are the criteria used to select them. The program, which has been operating since 1993, began to receive government funds after decentralization in 2000, but we were unable to locate any evaluation of its performance.

DISCUSSION

The study of decentralization in Nuevo León and Tamaulipas confirms that Mexico's Ministry of Health continues to control many aspects of the health care delivery system and that the transfer of power to the states has been limited. The number of vertical programs controlled by the federal government has not changed significantly following decentralization. The Health Ministry decides the type and number of personnel that can be hired with federal funds and has shown little flexibility in responding to requests from the Nuevo León Health Secretariat to substitute some categories of personnel with others. The Health Ministry's reluctance to incur additional expenditures is easy to understand, but it is difficult to understand its unwillingness to accommodate states' requests to hire more nurses or health educators and fewer drivers, or to make any other types of occupational exchange, when those changes would have no financial implications. Because salaries represent more than 70 percent of the health budget, the states' ability to make decisions and organize health care is severely compromised.

Hiring and firing of personnel now takes place at the state level, and this change could be positive if political patronage, which tends to be intense at the local level, does not override technical considerations in personnel selections or terminations.

In Nuevo León and Tamaulipas by and large we have not found that the benefits promised by decentralization's promoters have resulted in increased community participation, gains in efficiency and improvements in productivity, or higher levels of equity and improved quality of care. In some instances, the reverse has occurred.

Community Participation

Officials at the Nuevo León Health Secretariat did not consider that participation by civil society or community organizations had any role in health planning. In Tamaulipas, the secretary of health handpicked two NGOs to participate in the largely symbolic Health Council, but these NGOs can hardly be considered representative of community groups. The Tamaulipas Health Secretariat did not share basic information with legislators and was secretive about how health funds were spent. Legislators did not play a significant role in health policymaking in either of the two states. The sole exception was the decision by the Tamaulipas legislature to require the SST to waive unpaid accounts that certain patients owed to the hospitals. Perhaps Mexico's limit on state legislators' terms is not conducive to such interventions, especially given the complexity of the health sector.

Communities and organized civic groups in the two states were not consulted on decisions regarding the level and use of user fees. Communities have kept silent even when fees were almost doubled, as occurred at the General Hospital in Tamaulipas.

Efficiency and Productivity Gains

It is not possible to calculate the costs of decentralization for the federal and state governments. But the price tag for increasing state employees' salaries and bonuses on par with those of federal employees was high, and the transfer of federal property to the states has been costly, if only in terms of the work hours invested. Over several years, administrators and staff of the Nuevo León Health Secretariat spent countless hours preparing manuals and regulations to facilitate decentralization, and state and district administrators had to travel frequently to meetings dealing with issues raised by decentralization.

The homologation of personnel eliminated differences in salaries and some benefits between federal and state employees. This welcome change produced greater equity in remuneration for workers performing similar tasks. Unfortunately, neither homologation nor staff incentives have translated into higher productivity, defined as the average number of daily consultations per physician. Despite having idle production capacity, there were substantial increases in personnel and infrastructure in the health sector.

Methods to ensure financial accountability among hospitals and health districts are weak and open to abuses in both states. In the case of Tamaulipas, self-generated funds are used at the discretion of district and hospital directors, and there is no mechanism to ensure that they are exclusively used to enhance the performance of health centers and hospitals or to benefit the system's users. Nuevo León has control mechanisms in place for state and federal funds, but the use of self-generated funds is not well regulated, and we heard of abuses in the use of state properties.

The contracts that the Nuevo León Health Secretariat signed with municipalities and social security institutes have generated more funds for the SSNL and have increased the utilization of health services. Due to the concomitant growth of the labor force, however, it is difficult to ascertain with available information whether the additional outpatient visits and increase in hospital utilization have served to improve the efficiency and productivity of the entire system.

Working conditions continue to be negotiated at the federal level with leaders of the National Union of Health Ministry Employees, which limits the states' capacity to introduce changes to increase productivity, but state health administrators are not even demanding compliance with the union-negotiated requirement that each physician see at least eighteen patients per day.

Officials maintain that decentralization has had a positive impact on morale and that their enhanced decision-making authority has been very positive. The administrators of a health district expressed this perspective:

> Since decentralization [in 1996] we have more responsibilities and work longer hours, but we prefer it because now we are in charge and we can expeditiously solve problems that before were handled by the Health Ministry and could take months to resolve.

Hopefully, this positive change will ultimately translate into higher productivity and better quality of services.

Quality Improvements

Quality of care is very difficult to assess, and federal surveys of quality assurance have not employed appropriate indicators. The result is that little is known about quality of care in Mexico, and attempts to make comparisons at two points in time must be undertaken with caution. Basic morbidity-mortality indicators could be used, but there are many factors outside the health care system that affect health indicators. In Nuevo León, the people we interviewed concurred that the quality of services decreased during the first decentralization attempt. During the second phase, user fees have been used to improve the physical infrastructure of administrative offices, health centers, and hospitals, and to ensure the provision of medicines. We can expect that administrators will produce more and better work if they are housed in air-conditioned offices rather than having to labor in hot and humid spaces, that better-equipped centers and hospitals will provide better quality of care, and that the availability of medicines will improve health centers' capacity to cure patients. These are only expectations, and it may be that the morale and commitment of attending physicians and supporting personnel play a more important role.

In Tamaulipas, the paradoxical centralization of the autonomous hospitals that followed decentralization of the State Health Secretariat appeared to lower the quality of hospital services. On the other hand, these hospitals also offer an example of the undesirable consequences of promoting hospital autonomy. Prior to decentralization, resources were concentrated in the General and Pediatric hospitals, both located in the capital city, and their budgets were developed by the governor. The salaries of some of the doctors in these hospitals were out of line with physicians' salaries elsewhere. Some of the autonomous hospitals were more interested in performing highly technical and impressive surgeries such as transplants and open-heart surgery, without considering whether the volume of cases ensured that the hospital teams could guarantee patients' safety or justify the investment in equipment and personnel. Tamaulipas has a very high hospital mortality rate, and the data suggest that the rural population lacks access to services. Thus, for Tamaulipas, investing in a good primary health care system and a secondary hospital network may be more appropriate. If this were done, the state could contract with Nuevo León for the provision of more sophisticated services.

One strategy for improving quality is to establish a federal accreditation system for hospitals, with the results made public so that patients could protect themselves by refusing service from an unaccredited institution.

Equity

Nuevo León and Tamaulipas do not have mechanisms to determine if patients are turned away or do not access services because they are unable to pay. State officials assert that health personnel are able to identify those who cannot pay and waive fees in these cases, but studies conducted in Mexico and elsewhere demonstrate that this generally is not the case (Ugalde and Homedes 2004), and these decisions are frequently very arbitrary.

In Nuevo León, using a good share of the user fees collected from the poor to increase the salaries of middle-class professionals equates to a regressive tax and a very inequitable policy. In Tamaulipas, the General Hospital's decision to deny medications to patients who cannot afford to pay for them is also inequitable. In as far as decentralization promotes greater dependence on local resources and the collection of funds extends to the very poor, we can conclude that decentralization has increased inequities in these two states.

Opening and Closing a Window of Opportunity

There are striking differences between Nuevo León and Tamaulipas in how they have used the limited decision-making authority that has been transferred from the federal government. There is significant variation in the collection and use of self-generated funds and in the transfer of power to the districts. The Nuevo León Health Secretariat, for example, took risks by adopting policies that the State Comptroller's Office considered illegal (such as allowing the districts to make direct purchases in excess of the quantities allowed by the state). Despite the limitations discussed above, and in part because of the many resources at its disposal and the entrepreneurial spirit of its leadership, this State Health Secretariat took advantage of the small opening that decentralization allowed, by, for example, signing contracts with municipalities and social security institutes and transferring power to the health districts and regional hospitals.

Tamaulipas failed to capitalize on the same opportunity to provide guidelines to the autonomous hospitals and health centers, to improve productivity or establish new delivery models to better meet the needs of the population, to control quality, and to curtail abuses of power. Instead, the Tamaulipas Health Secretariat used its new authority to centralize the autonomous hospitals. In the process, the hospitals' performance deteriorated. Instead of exploiting the small window of opportunity to improve the system, the Tamaulipas Health Secretariat closed it.

Interestingly, although these two states share a long border, there has been no official communication between the two State Health Secretariats. The two states have developed different strategies to respond to the challenges of decentralization, and neither is looking to the other to learn from its experiences or to coordinate efforts to provide tertiary or primary health services for inhabitants in the area where the states border one another. Both states would benefit from greater communication and collaboration, not only to share what they have learned after several years of decentralization but also because some of the issues affecting their ability to run efficient systems remain under the control of the federal Ministry of Health. The process of decentralization is still evolving, and there is much to be learned.

References

Cardozo Brum, Myriam. 1995. "La política de descentralización de servicios de salud: análisis de su proceso y evaluación de resultados." Unpublished report, June.

INEGI (Instituto Nacional de Estadística, Geografía e Informática). 2000. "Estadísticas de México." http://www.inegi.gob.mx.

Salud Pública de México. 2000a. "Recursos para la salud en unidades de la Secretaría de Salud, 1999," vol. 42, no. 3.

———. 2000b. "Información básica sobre recursos y servicios del Sistema Nacional de Salud," vol. 42, no. 1.

Secretaría de Salud. 2001. "Programa Nacional de Salud 2001–2006." México, D.F.: Secretaría de Salud.

SEGOB (Secretaría de Gobierno), Comisión para asuntos de la Frontera Norte. n.d. "Programa de desarrollo de la frontera norte, 2001–2006." http://fronteranorte.presidencia.gob.mx.

SSNL (Secretaría de Salud de Nuevo León). 2001. Gobierno del Estado. Servicios de Salud de Nuevo León. OPD. Junta de Gobierno, August 4.

Ugalde, A., and N. Homedes. 2004. "Venda de Serviços Públicos de Saúde: un estudo qualitativo." In *Pesquisa Qualitativa de Serviços de Saúde*, ed. M. L. Magalhães Bosi and F. J. Mercado. São Paulo: Ed. Vozes.

Zacarías Villarreal Pérez, J. 1999. "La reforma del sector salud," *Medicina Universitaria* 1, no. 3: 153–57.

———. 2003. "Visión estatal del proceso de descentralización del sector salud en México." In *Federalismo y políticas de salud: descentralización y relaciones intergubernamentales desde una perspectiva comparada*. Ottawa and México, D.F.: Forum of Federations and Instituto Nacional para el Federalismo y Desarrollo Municipal.

9

Decentralization at the Health District Level in Nuevo León

NÚRIA HOMEDES AND ANTONIO UGALDE

The decentralization effort in the state of Nuevo León included: (1) transferring administrative authority to the health districts; (2) granting administrative and some financial autonomy to regional hospitals; and (3) strengthening and expanding the role of municipalities in the health sector. Health districts are subdivisions within Mexico's state health secretariats and are officially defined as "technical and administrative units responsible for planning, coordinating, controlling, supervising, and evaluating the provision of medical services, public health activities, and social services within a given geographical area" (OPS 1990: 123). As mentioned in chapter 2 ., the health districts were created in 1984. Their geographical boundaries do not correspond with those of any other politico-administrative unit except in Tabasco, where municipalities and the health districts coincide. There is at least one regional hospital within the geographical boundaries of each district, with the exception of district 3, located in Monterrey.

The Local Health System program (SILOS) was the health-sector strategy promoted by the Pan American Health Organization (PAHO) to facilitate the implementation of primary health care in the spirit of the 1978 Alma-Ata International Conference on Primary Health Care—with equity, quality, and efficiency, and geared toward attaining "health for all by the year 2000" (PAHO 1993: 1). In Mexico, SILOS was executed through the health districts, and the terms "SILOS" and "health district" were sometimes used interchangeably in publications (OPS 1990: 123). SILOS was expected to: (1) coordinate resources from different sectors (political, economic, cultural, educational, and religious); (2) assume responsibility for enhancing health conditions in a given geographical area by emphasizing health promotion and environmental protection; and (3) include communities in decision making. This approach envisioned emphasizing primary care and avoiding the tendency to favor hospital care over primary care, leading decision makers to separate responsibility for the administration of health resources by levels of care. To this end, Mexico's health districts were made responsible for primary health care, and secondary-level hospitals became autonomous entities which reported directly to the state health secretariats.

SILOS did not yield the anticipated results; the program's success depended on the ability of health district directors to win the support of local political leaders and elites and the staff of other sectors of the public administration. In the 1990s, health district directors had very little autonomy; they were responsible only for implementing the policies and programs dictated by the Ministry of Health and state health secretariats, and under these constraints they could not advance the goals of SILOS.

In Nuevo León, the health districts gained some decision-making power in 1996 when Dr. Jesús Zacarías Villarreal, the newly appointed state secretary of health, decided to transfer responsibility for some functions of the State Health Secretariat to the health districts. By that time, PAHO, realizing that the health districts did not have the leadership or power to enlist the collaboration of other sectors in the attainment of better health conditions, replaced SILOS with the Healthy Municipalities (Municipios Saludables) initiative. Zacarías Villarreal supported the initiative but thought that the municipalities, especially small municipalities that did not have their own health offices, would be unable to carry it out and that the personnel of the State Health Secretariat could not support all the municipal projects. In his words:

> The municipalities do not have any public health infrastructure; it is going to take a while before we can decentralize to the municipal level. We first need to strengthen the health districts and the hospitals. The municipal governments are only responsible for a few sanitary regulation activities, such as rabies, dengue control, and regulation of restaurants and food establishments. [E:1]

In this chapter we present findings from a field-based study of decentralization of the health districts of Nuevo León. This study formed part of the research on decentralization in Nuevo León that was presented in the preceding chapter. Data were drawn from archival materials (program outlines and operational manuals, budgets, organizational charts) held at the headquarters of the Nuevo León Health Secretariat (SSNL), and from observations and information gathered during field visits to four of the eight health districts: two urban districts (districts 1 and 4) and two rural districts (districts 5 and 6). We conducted a total of eighteen open-ended in-depth interviews with high-level SSNL administrators and personnel in the health districts, including the district directors and heads of administrative units. In one health district where the director was unavailable, we interviewed the deputy director. Our field visits also included informal conversations with mayors and with users of SSNL services.

THE HEALTH DISTRICTS OF NUEVO LEÓN

The Nuevo León Health Secretariat comprises eight health districts, four in the greater Monterrey area (districts 1–4) and four in the state's rural areas (districts 5–8). About 80 percent of the residents of Monterrey are formally employed and have social coverage through IMSS, ISSSTE, or ISSSTELEON or have private health insurance. Two of the largest employers, a brewery and a glass manufacturer, created a separate network of services for their employees. Monterrey has two leading medical schools; one, the University Hospital, attracts physicians from several European countries who come to do their medical residencies there. The majority of specialists and hospital beds are concentrated in Monterrey. Health District 8 is the poorest and the largest; 94 percent of its population is uninsured. This district's population is scattered in 2,600 hamlets, of which 1,800 have fewer than 50 inhabitants. By decision of the governor, all SSNL medical services—including medicines—are provided free of charge in this district. Table 9.1 presents figures on the population, number of municipalities, and total number of physical and human resources available in each district (including social security, State Health Secretariat, and private sector).

The health districts are responsible for managing primary-care services and for all public health activities, including sanitation regulation. There are two types of health centers: basic health centers staffed by general practitioners (usually physicians and nurses completing their year of social service), and health centers that offer the four basic medical specialties

Table 9.1. Characteristics of Available Health Infrastructure within the Geographical Territory of Health Districts in Nuevo León (includes SSNL, social security, and private resources)

	Health Districts								
	1	2	3	4	5	6	7	8	Total
Population	727,869	972,283	724,436	970,264	71,325	123,611	203,567	100,611	3,893,966
Number of municipalities	1	9	3	3	9	13	7	6	51
Primary-level units	69	44	27	58	53	65	84	116	531
Secondary-level units	6	2	0	1	2	2	3	2	18
Tertiary-level units	9	0	1	0	0	0	0	0	10
Number of beds	2,855	468	60	177	28	57	76	60	3,801
Total number of physicians	1,755	309	121	102	100	178	171	183	2,919
Number of general practitioners	371	111	71	87	75	106	130	147	1,098
Number of specialists	816	169	43	10	19	64	24	30	1,175
Other	568	29	7	5	6	8	17	6	646
Total number of nurses in patient care	2,301	516	151	117	87	201	126	159	3,658

Source: SSA Information System.

(internal medicine, pediatrics, obstetrics/gynecology, and surgery). The health centers that provide care in the specialized fields are more frequently found in urban areas. In Health District 8, because of the region's remoteness and poverty, many cannot easily access SSNL services. To minimize the problem, the State Health Secretariat introduced mobile units, each staffed with a physician, nurse, and health promoter, and equipped to deliver the basic package of services. PAHO certified in October 1997 that 100 percent of Nuevo León's population had access to the basic package of services, but 6 percent live more than an hour away from a health center and are only served every two weeks by mobile units.

ORGANIZATIONAL STRUCTURE OF THE HEALTH DISTRICTS

Each health district has a similar organizational structure and its own administrative headquarters (see figure 9.1). The number of personnel reporting to the district director ranged between two hundred and five hundred in the four districts we visited.[1] The district directors are political appointees. They are responsible for managing the health centers, and they coordinate health activities with the municipal presidents and participate in the Healthy Municipalities Program.

Health District 4 exemplified the general functioning of a health district. District 4 is located in greater Monterrey and includes three municipalities (Guadalupe, Apodaca, and Juárez); it has 417 employees, 60 of whom work in the district's headquarters. The director is a general practitioner with a master's degree in public health. He, like all district directors, survived the state's political transition and was reappointed by the state's new secretary of health, Dr. Zacarías Villarreal, when the latter became head of the Nuevo León Health Secretariat. Such continuity, unusual in Mexican politics, facilitated the decentralization of decision making. Zacarías Villarreal understood the importance of retaining experienced administrators during times of change because they can apply their knowledge to ease the transition.

In August 2001, eight units reported to the director of Health District 4 (see figure 9.1). The unit heads met monthly in Monterrey with unit heads

[1] There were nearly 500 in District 1; 417 in District 4; 250 in District 5; and 261 in District 7.

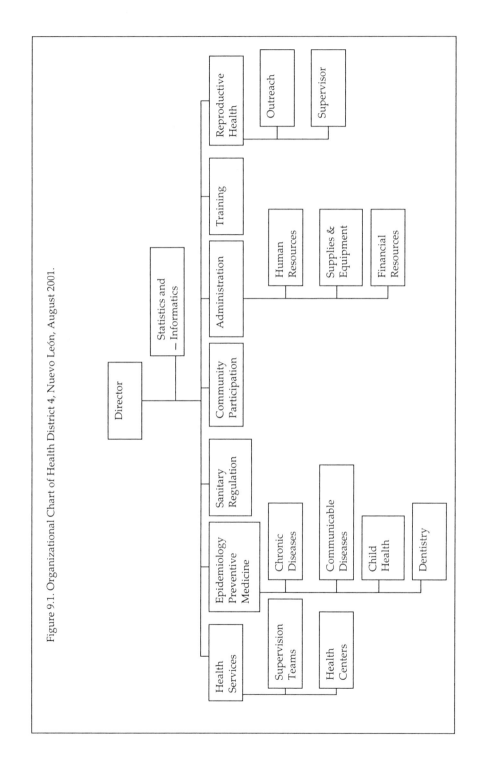

Figure 9.1. Organizational Chart of Health District 4, Nuevo León, August 2001.

from the state's other districts and with the various SSNL area directors (sanitation, health services, and so on). At these monthly meetings, the districts discussed the progress in their particular areas of responsibility; for example, the heads of information and statistics would discuss issues related to data collection, entry, and analysis. Participants also exchanged ideas and sought solutions to problems they had encountered.

The mandates of the various units are fairly obvious; only two warrant a brief description. The health services unit was responsible for supervising the health centers, coordinating the directors' visits to supervise the vertical programs of the State Health Secretariat and Ministry of Health (in reproductive health, child care, chronic diseases, and dentistry), and implementing the quality assurance program. Health District 4 had three supervisory teams, also called area supervisors, who regularly visited the health centers.

According to the director of the SSNL's quality assurance program, the indicators included in federal monitoring forms were not adequately measuring user satisfaction (there was no variance in responses) or quality, so his unit had been working with people at the federal level to improve the indicators [E:25]. According to the head of the health services unit of District 4:

> We are also responsible for implementing the quality assurance program. In our state we have used dummy patients to test the quality of services and the patients' satisfaction. The federal level is also tracking some "quality" indicators such as wait times, availability of medications, and number of prescriptions filled. [E:13]

The sanitation unit is responsible for ensuring that food markets and vendors, restaurants, other businesses (theaters, ballrooms, clubs), and public spaces (schools, parks, fairs, swimming pools) comply with all sanitary regulations. It is also responsible for recommending sanctions when sanitary regulations are violated. The unit is supposed to have three administrators: the unit head; the field supervisor who, with his/her workers, carries out inspections, collects samples, and responds to clients' complaints; and a third person who requests analyses of food and water samples, writes reports, informs clients of inspection results, and, if needed, issues warnings. However, in District 4 and in most districts, a single person carries out all of these functions.

THE TRANSFER OF DECISION-MAKING POWER TO THE DISTRICTS

Soon after taking office as state secretary of health, Dr. Zacarías Villarreal decided to transfer decision-making authority to the health districts as a way of increasing the efficiency of the State Health Secretariat. According to one interviewee, who occupied a high position at the SSNL, this limited decentralization has changed the culture of the SSNL:

> Before decentralization, people asked for large amounts of everything because they knew that they were not going to get everything they requested.... We have had to train the district directors to request what they need ... and then we had to prove that they could trust us. [E:3]

Such trust had to be earned. An important step in this direction was to include the district directors in the early stages of decentralization, incorporating their input in procurement guidelines and guidelines for treating dengue fever: "The SSNL produced a manual for the control of dengue, but we [district directors] told them that it would not work in practice ... and they changed it" [E:11]. Equally important was the SSNL's recognition that decentralization is a process and that, consequently, policies are implemented gradually and rules and regulations are corrected through trial and error. As will be seen in following paragraphs, this process involved the Nuevo León Health Secretariat, the health district offices, the National Union of Health Ministry Employees (SNTSSA), and the state government.

All district directors had monthly meetings with the state secretary of health to discuss the progress and problems of the SSNL and the new federal and state initiatives. These meetings seldom limited the district directors' decision-making authority; on the contrary, district directors were encouraged to use their resources in a creative manner.

District directors were authorized to reorganize their districts as needed (table 9.2). Because the State Health Secretariat has very limited control in managing human resources, there was little authority that could be transferred in this area, but district directors were allowed to move personnel from one location to another after negotiating the transfer with the union and the employee. In the financial area, districts were authorized to enter into contractual agreements with municipalities and communities; they were given flexibility in determining user fees and exemption policies; and they were free to decide how to distribute self-generated funds to meet their needs. The health districts' authority in sanitary regulation was increased slightly. The following paragraphs discuss each of these changes in some detail.

Table 9.2. Functions Decentralized to the Health District Level

Organizing the administrative offices of the health district
Negotiating the transfer of human resources with the National Union of
   Health Ministry Employees and with the employee
Levying funds from municipalities and from communities
Managing the budget
Determining the level of user fees and exemption policies
Sanitary regulation

Authority to Reorganize the Administrative Offices

Health district directors were authorized to modify their districts' organizational chart. For example, the director of District 4 intended to reduce the number of units from eight to four (information and statistics, health services, administration, and sanitary regulation) and expand the functions of the health services and the health information and statistics units. Under the new structure, the health information and statistics unit would conduct some planning activities; the administration and sanitation units would remain the same; and the units of epidemiology, reproductive health, community participation, and training of human resources would be merged under the health services unit. This change would represent a significant challenge for the head of the health services unit.

The decentralization of some decision-making power also facilitated problem resolution. At times, the Ministry of Health's supervisory visits to assess centralized programs created tensions, often because they put excessive pressure on health center personnel. After decentralization, solutions to an identified problem could be sought at the most appropriate administrative level, often at the point where the problems surfaced. Decentralization allowed district unit heads to search for solutions, and only when they were unsuccessful was the issue forwarded to the next level. According to the head of the health services unit in District 4:

> Sometimes the supervisors of the vertical programs are too demanding.... When this happens, the providers [physicians and nurses] come to me, and we negotiate.... In fact, I bring the problems to the attention of the district director, and he makes the final decision.... When problems arise, it is always the district director who is responsible for identifying and implementing solutions. [E:13]

Health district personnel felt free to point out flaws in programs designed at a higher level by managers who were sometimes not attuned to certain subtleties that were easily detected by those closer to the provision of services. One district director made the following observation regarding indicators that the Health Ministry selected for measuring quality:

> [Those who designed the quality indicators] did not take into account that sometimes a clinic visit does not result in a prescription, and so the "number of prescriptions filled" indicator is based on the number of medicines prescribed and not on the number of patients seen by the provider. [E:14]

Self-Generated Funds from Municipalities and Communities

As noted in the preceding chapter, the Nuevo León Health Secretariat used various strategies to raise money from the municipalities. Granting some control over self-generated funds to the health districts motivated the districts to seek out new sources of funding.

Twenty municipalities signed health coverage contracts with the health districts to provide medical care to municipal employees and their families. The beneficiaries received free care, including medicines; and when a patient needed a referral to a hospital, the health district paid for the services rendered in the regional hospitals. The SSNL's accounting system did not distinguish between the different types of self-generated funds (contracts with municipalities, user fees, contracts with the IMSS).

Municipal presidents supported the districts' medical services in a number of other ways. Some agreed to supplement physicians' salaries during their year of social service:

> Physicians [in their year of social service] earn about 1,000 pesos a month, but some municipalities supplement their salaries, so that some doctors are receiving about 3,000 pesos per month. [E:14]

One municipality committed to pay the difference between the salary of a general practitioner and a surgeon so that the health district could hire the latter:

> One of the municipalities in the northern part of the state [Anahuac] wanted to have a surgeon and [the municipality] offered to supplement the salary of a primary health physician (12,000 pesos) with 5,000 pesos. [E:6]

The municipality's generosity came about because patients were going to a hospital in Nuevo Laredo, Tamaulipas, for surgery, and when they returned there was no one to provide follow-up care. The health district director hoped that:

> If we can offer outpatient surgery for patients in Anahuac and Lampazos, they will not go to Nuevo Laredo. Now they go to Nuevo Laredo because it is closer [70 km distant] than the nearest hospital in Nuevo León, which is in Sabinas [140 km]. [E:15]

One health district director in the greater Monterrey area managed to secure municipal space for running a special program:

> The municipality will give us a building for an AIDS prevention program ... though we will need to obtain additional resources. [E:11]

Municipalities contributed cars and personnel for programs to control communicable diseases such as dengue, and they collaborated in renovating health centers or purchasing capital equipment:

> The municipality of Aldama paid for the renovation of the health center.... In many cases the municipality and State Health Secretariat share the cost of renovating a health center, of installing a radio communications system, or buying an ambulance. [E:16]

According to our respondents, it is easier to work with rural municipalities than with urban ones. In the words of one interviewee:

> It is easier to get rural mayors to collaborate and contribute to the health sector than to get a commitment from the urban municipalities; the urban mayors are arrogant and have to deal with too many problems. [E:14]

Personnel Management

Most rural health centers are staffed by personnel fulfilling their required year of social service, and the federal Ministry of Health assigns them to the specific health centers. Even though the health district directors have no voice in the assignment of these personnel, they tend to be satisfied with their performance. One director said:

> I prefer to deal with providers [physicians, nurses] doing their year of social service; they are devoted to their work. The civil servants have [developed] many bad habits and are more difficult to handle. [E:14]

On the other hand, physicians doing their year of social service were not always satisfied with the treatment they received at their postings:

> The director is never satisfied and keeps changing the targets. I usually see more patients than required, but they have never congratulated me. To the contrary, they raise the bar. At first I had to see 290 patients per month, and I went over

the target; I had 320 consultations.... Then they told me I had
to see 380. I had to put a stop to it because I could increase
the number of patients, but the quality of care would suffer.... Not all of us are treated equally.... They ask more of
those who are already performing better. [E:21]

The Nuevo León Health Secretariat allowed district directors to move
personnel within their districts (except those doing their year of social
service) if they could reach agreement on the change with the worker and
with the union:

We can make changes if we justify the need and can convince
the worker. It is not easy. You need really good negotiating
skills. [E:11]

The possibility of transferring workers from one clinic to another is an
important management tool and could be used effectively to increase efficiency. For example, if demand for services decreases in one clinic—as, for
example, the area loses population to out-migration—and increases in
another, the district director can exercise his/her autonomy to transfer
personnel. The district directors could use self-generated funds to contract
workers and pay overtime; and when a vacancy opened, they could suggest candidates though the final decision was made by the SSNL:

We cannot select people. We can propose them or refuse to
accept someone, but generally, if someone is recommended
for one of our positions, we can't say much. All we can do is
write poor evaluations so that the person is removed. [E:12]

The SSNL gave the district directors guidelines for distributing incentives to district personnel. For example, only health centers with a minimum of ten consultations per day can pay incentives to its good perform-
ers, but the guidelines allowed district directors a certain amount of
discretionary power. One director explained:

The allocation of incentives for administrators working in the
district office is discretionary. The district director decides

how to use these funds. I generally don't distribute them in my district because [the workers] are not productive.... I keep the funds, and I can use them to pay overtime or purchase equipment or medicines. [E:11]

Another district director distributed incentives to those working at the headquarters. Her preference was to pay proportionally more to those with low salaries:

It's different in our district office; we've decided to give a bigger incentive to the administrators because their salaries are very low. The administrators receive a bonus of about 400 pesos, and the physicians get about 200 pesos. In the health centers, incentives are distributed according to people's wages.... Those who earn more get more.... Physicians can make as much as 3,000 extra pesos per month on a base monthly salary of 11,000 pesos. [E:14]

Decentralizing Financial Management

Decentralization gave district directors control over part of the budget, though the Nuevo León Health Secretariat retained control over most of the little financial authority that the Health Ministry had transferred to the State Health Secretariats. All of the health districts' fixed costs—payroll of staff hired with state funds, electricity, water, gas, vehicle insurance, cleaning and security services, equipment maintenance, and major infrastructure investments—were paid directly by the SSNL. The districts were responsible for mail and transportation services, maintenance of vehicles and infrastructure, minor equipment repairs, and purchases of food, tools, supplies, and medicines. In 1997, in order to decentralize more financial responsibilities to the districts, the state secretary of health transferred the funds for purchases to the district directors, with no strings attached. In 1999 the state comptroller informed the SSNL that it was not following state procurement procedures and refused to reimburse it for purchases made outside of the regulatory framework.

In the beginning, the secretary of health let us make many direct purchases, but he got in trouble for it ... and since 1999

we've been gradually losing the ability to make direct purchases [with state funds]. [E:11]

Self-generated funds need not be spent in compliance with state procedures, which allows the districts some flexibility in their use. State regulations do require, however, that goods and services purchased with state
funds must come from state-approved vendors, a regulation that district
directors viewed as a constraint:

> We have to use providers approved by the state.... This
> means that we sometimes have to pay more than we would if
> we could contract with the people we know. [E:1]

> They want us to use the state providers, but they are more
> expensive.... We don't want to do that. For example, in one
> case the state-approved firm wanted to charge 70,000 to
> 90,000 pesos, and I could get the same thing done for
> 45,000.... I forwarded the quotes, and the issue is still under
> review. [E:22]

Additional providers could be added to the state-authorized list, but the
process was cumbersome.

State procedures required that all contracts for goods and services be
awarded through a bidding process; only if no one placed a bid (in about
10 percent of the cases) could the State Health Secretariat contract directly
with a provider. Complying with the state requirements required advance
planning and good coordination among the health districts.

In 2000 the SSNL prepared two documents to guide this process (SSNL
2000a, 2000b). In August of each year, district and hospital directors had to
submit their budgets in accordance with SSNL guidelines. Once the SSNL
had approved the various line items, the directors negotiated with the
procurement division of the SSNL to determine how the supplies, medicines, and services requested by each district and hospital would be obtained. If the amount the SSNL (central administrative offices and all districts and hospitals) planned to spend for any single line item (good or
service) exceeded 750,000 pesos (about US$83,300), the SSNL had to issue a
request for bids. If projected expenditure fell below this ceiling, the SSNL

and directors had to negotiate the purchasing process. The health districts and hospitals could buy some items themselves, but others had to be purchased by the SSNL. According to the SSNL guidelines, the health districts could not spend more than 20,000 pesos per line item per year using direct purchasing or direct contracting (up to 30,000 pesos if the SSNL had issued a request for bids and there were no acceptable responses). Once all the parties accepted the procurement plan, the SSNL executed the consolidated purchases, and services or items were delivered to each facility as previously specified. To cover the districts' operating expenditures, the SSNL sent funds on a monthly basis, specifying each expenditure category. The districts were also allowed to keep petty cash (up to 500 pesos) to be used at the directors' discretion and replenished as needed.

The purchase of pharmaceuticals followed a slightly different pattern. The State Health Secretariat had compiled an inventory of essential drugs, modeled on the national drug list, which contained about 350 products. Each year the SSNL's purchasing department asked the districts and hospitals to estimate their anticipated need for these drugs, and it then prepared tender documents specifying that: (1) the SSNL would purchase between 80 and 110 percent of the quantity specified in the tender at the price offered by the lowest bidder, and (2) the winning bidder would deliver the pharmaceuticals, when requested by the districts and hospitals, directly to their storage facilities. District and hospital directors were not obliged to participate in the tendering process, but they usually did because it allowed them to get better prices than if they purchased medicines at the retail pharmacies that were state-approved vendors. About 60 percent of medicines were purchased through the SSNL bidding process; the remaining 40 percent were bought in state-approved pharmacies.

There were instances when the proviso to purchase only from state-approved vendors could be waived:

> If we need to buy medicines, we can use suppliers not included in the list, but we have to prove that they charge us less than those on the list. [E:14]

And in cases of need, the districts could purchase medicines not included in the formulary:

> We can purchase medicines not included in the formulary for primary-care centers, but we have to buy them directly in retail pharmacies and we have to justify the purchase. These cases are treated as if they were emergencies. [E:11]

It was anticipated that the proportion of medicines purchased through the bidding process would increase as the districts and hospitals became better able to estimate their needs in advance. According to our interviewees, decentralizing the purchase of medicines allowed them to maintain a continuous stock and to save money. The SSNL secretary commented:

> We save money by decentralizing the management [of medicines] to the districts. Before, supplies and medicines were not distributed in a timely manner, providers and service users complained because they did not have the necessary supplies and medicines … or because the medicines they received were about to expire. Now we do not have this problem. If a distributor sends supplies and/or medicines that are to expire within three months, the district director can return them. [E:1]

According to one district director, "decentralization has allowed us to have the medicines we need within twenty-four hours" [E:14]. However, delivering them from the health district storage center to the clinics could take longer, as a clinic director noted: "When I request medicines, if the health district has them in stock, they send them within a day or two; but if they don't have them, it takes longer" [E:21].

User Fees

As mentioned in the preceding chapter, our interviewees were comfortable collecting money from service users and felt that users should pay as much as they could afford. The secretary of Nuevo León's Health Secretariat confirmed this: "There are national guidelines on the amount that we can charge as user fees, but we don't use it. In the end, those who can pay, pay; and those who can't pay, don't." One district director was quite explicit on this point:

> Our policy is to charge for all services, and to charge more than what the Ministry of Health suggests.... It is important to educate users and providers on the need to charge for our services.... Each health center decides how much they want to charge, and I approve the fee schedule. [E:12]

Another respondent expressed the rationale for charging fees:

> We need to charge user fees; if we don't, the system becomes unsustainable. Now we have better services. Not only are we able to deliver better quality of care, we also have better buildings. [E:14]

Our interviewees reassured us that no one went without care because of the fees. District directors reportedly had the authority to waive fees, and they often authorized physicians or other health providers to do likewise. However, we do not know how many people may be forgoing services because they are deterred by the user fees. Conversely, the extent to which health providers might be encouraging people to demand unneeded services is also an unknown, but if a provider benefits from offering a service, it follows that the provider may urge people to request services more often than is needed.

The new governor (1998) decided to refurbish all the health centers during his tenure, thus increasing the state's contribution to the health sector (see table 8.6 in the preceding chapter). However, in terms of operational expenditures, prior to 1999 the funds generated by the SSNL exceeded the state contribution and continued to increase after the decentralization effort. Unfortunately, the SSNL does not separate the self-generated funds by origin, including contracts with municipalities and social insurance programs. It is important to know if user fees are incrementally financing a larger portion of public health services for the poor, because these fees represent a regressive tax. In the case of the Nuevo León Health Secretariat, user fees went to finance salary supplements and could be considered a transfer of funds from the poor to the middle class. Other uses to which the fees were put—such as the installation of air conditioning and personal use of state vehicles—also benefited district employees rather than users of the services (for a detailed discussion on this topic, see Ugalde and Homedes 2004).

Sanitary Regulation

Each district had one sanitation unit. Fieldworkers conducted visits and collected food and water samples, and the district unit gathered the information and sent the samples to the state laboratory in Monterrey. When State Secretary of Health Zacarías Villarreal began the decentralization to the districts, the districts were allowed to issue violation warnings. After August 2001, these warnings had to be signed by the undersecretary of sanitary regulation because: "I think that this was illegal, and now they've told us that only the SSNL can issue the warnings" [E:13]. According to one respondent:

> The State Health Secretariat's legal department imposes the fines, which must be paid to the state treasury. Eventually the treasury returns the funds to the SSNL, and they are used to finance the sanitary regulation program. [E:18]

The district sanitation unit relied on the health centers for water quality control in the communities. The health centers only measured the level of chlorine (to make sure the water was potable). When a health problem arose that was attributable to the quality of water or food, the health centers reported the problem, which was then investigated by the health district. In addition to collecting information about such cases, the districts were responsible for taking samples of the material that presumably caused the problem and delivering them to the state laboratory in Monterrey. One interviewee felt that, after decentralization, "the number of inspections has increased; now we go to each and every municipality" [E:13].

One problem facing district sanitation units was a personnel shortage, especially given that unit staff had to travel constantly to Monterrey with samples for analysis and papers for signature by state health officials. To minimize this problem, the SSNL was about to change the organizational structure of the sanitation units, proposing four new regions, each with a state coordinator. The coordinators would be authorized to send official letters and warnings, and the new structure would presumably reduce the number of trips to Monterrey.

There were attempts to decentralize some sanitation regulatory functions to the municipalities, but only five accepted the transfer. These municipalities collect fines, but the system is not operating well:

> The mayors take on the responsibility, but they are not systematic. They don't communicate the norms [to owners of the establishments], and they are disorganized. The State Health Secretariat wants to decentralize, but in an orderly and incremental way. [E:15]

A second respondent also questioned the municipalities' capacity to shoulder the responsibility for sanitation controls:

> The municipality gives the permits for opening a restaurant, and the health district is responsible for sanitation regulation. Sometimes it's better if the municipality does not get involved. [E:12]

Corruption is one of the problems: "The SSNL is distributing a lot of information so that the inspectors do not overcharge" [E:15]. Another concern applies particularly in the smaller municipalities. Municipal presidents did not want to confront owners of local restaurants and businesses, who are generally members of the local elite (and voters). Mayors were reluctant to issue warnings or impose sanctions when these residents violated regulations.

THE HEALTHY MUNICIPALITIES PROGRAM

All of Nuevo León's fifty-one mayors received training in the Healthy Municipalities Program, which aims to encourage community participation, multisectoral coordination, and new local policies to improve health conditions. To participate in the program, a municipality had to organize a health committee and conduct an assessment of health conditions in the community, after which the health committee needed to set health priorities and select up to three projects that it considered important and feasible.

The program had a very small budget, and the health committees were responsible for fund-raising and program implementation. The health district directors' role was to advise the committees. In the summer of 2001, all of the state's mayors had attended meetings to discuss the Healthy Municipalities Program and the state's health priorities; forty-seven had established health committees; and forty-one had conducted a planning workshop. Several committees had selected projects (see table 9.3). Although we were not able to obtain full descriptions, some projects—such as personal hygiene for schoolchildren and control of street dogs—were concrete and relatively easy to implement, while others (such as addressing addiction and domestic violence) were very complicated and would require the assistance of experts.

Once projects were selected, SSNL personnel helped the health committees develop their implementation plans. The two Healthy Municipalities coordinators at the Nuevo León Health Secretariat felt that some of the projects were too technically complex for communities to manage with available resources. Nevertheless, the health committees saw these problems (alcoholism and drug addiction, for example) as critical and wanted to address them as soon as possible because the problems were escalating and the State Health Secretariat was not doing anything about them. One of the Healthy Municipalities coordinators expressed frustration:

> We do not have enough personnel trained in leading community participation processes or people who can assist in facilitating the work of the health committees and in coordinating activities between the municipality and the district. There are only two of us. [E:6]

Some of the projects that committees selected—such as prevention and treatment of dengue and diabetes—were initiatives that the health districts should have been leading; the fact that the problems persisted confirms that the districts' activities were insufficient to resolve the health problem. Whether problems such as domestic violence and alcohol and drug abuse should be the responsibility of the SSNL is a valid question; most health care systems only address the health impacts of such behaviors, not their causes. Information we obtained through interviews indicates that Nuevo León's Health Secretariat did not consider itself responsible for training

Table 9.3. Projects to Be Developed as Part of the Healthy Municipalities Program

Project Focus	Municipality
Accidents	Monterrey
Addictions	Monterrey, Ciénega de Flores, Hidalgo, Mina, García, San Pedro Garza García, Santa Caterina, Sabinas Hidalgo, Dr. Coss, Dr. González, General Bravo, Los Ramones, Marín, Melchor Ocampo, Allende, General Terán, Linares, Montemorelos
Alcoholism	Anáhuac, General Treviño, Lampazos de Naranjo, Villaldama
Alcoholism in teenagers	Agualeguas, Bustamante
Defecation in the open environment	Rayones
Dengue	Benito Juárez, Guadalupe, Pesquería
Diabetes	Salinas Victoria
Drug addiction	Anáhuac, General Treviño, Lampazos de Naranjo
Ecological culture	Galeana
Family problems	Higueras
Family violence	Montemorelos
Farms	General Zuazua
First aid (training)	Benito Juárez
Garbage disposal	Aramberri
Health education	Monterrey
Malnutrition	Los Herreras
Malnutrition in schoolchildren	Abasolo
Parent-child relationships	Parás
Personal hygiene for schoolchildren	Vallecillo
Sanitary regulation	Guadalupe
School health	Guadalupe
Street dogs	El Carmen
Street vendors	Guadalupe
Water	Hualahuises
Water contamination	Rayones, Aramberri
Welfare infrastructure	Monterrey
Wells (water potability)	Benito Juárez

Source: SSNL 2001.

personnel to solve problems that traditionally fall beyond the scope of services offered by health centers. Moreover, the SSNL did not have the resources to expand activities to resolve these kinds of problems.

DECENTRALIZATION'S IMPACT ON THE HEALTH DISTRICTS

By and large, our interviewees felt that decentralization to the district level had been very beneficial for the Nuevo León Health Secretariat and for the people. Some of the district directors and unit heads wished they had more control over two functions that remained centralized at the federal level: management of personnel fulfilling their year of social service and access to the media: "District directors cannot provide information to the public without consulting the SSNL, and the SSNL sometimes needs to request permission from the Ministry of Health" [E:12].

Administrators in the health districts felt that including the district directors in the SSNL's decision-making process and granting them some authority in managing their budgets were the most significant impacts of decentralization:

> Now we can make decisions and adapt them to local condi-
> tions. For example, before decentralization, if the SSNL asked
> us to promote a certain program, we had to do it, even if it
> was not suitable for our area. Now we just have to explain
> why the program is not applicable to our area, and they lis-
> ten to us. Also, if we want to purchase a medication that is
> not included in the formulary, we can justify the need and
> buy it. [E:14]

In practice, none of the directors made any significant changes to the health delivery system. What mattered was that they and the unit heads felt a sense of accountability and empowerment to quickly resolve problems that in the past had to be reported to Monterrey or Mexico City and took months to settle. According to one district director:

> The power to make decisions, to be accountable … means we
> have to justify our expenditures. The [state] comptroller vis-
> its the health district only once a year, but they [sic] do it
> without warning. [E:14]

According to the SSNL health secretary, decentralization opened a window of opportunity that enabled small but meaningful changes in the health system. One district director added that the outcome of decentralization depended on how the acquired power was used and on the leadership and creativity of the district director. Some districts used their new financial autonomy to improve infrastructure and to maintain adequate stocks in the health centers that, in addition to improving working conditions and health outcomes, allowed the health units to comply with the quality standards set by the Ministry of Health. Improved physical infrastructure and a reliable stock of supplies and medicines was, for another interviewee, decentralization's greatest benefit:

> [We have] greater technical autonomy; we still have limited autonomy to make direct purchases but sufficient to make enough adjustments to guarantee that the health centers have sufficient supplies and medicines. [E:11]

This opinion was reiterated by another interviewee:

> Decentralization has facilitated the refurbishing of the health centers, and we can also make direct purchases. Now we have the supplies and medicines we need. Before [decentralization] we did not even know what we were going to receive or when [it would arrive]. Now we have more vehicles and more mobile units for the rural areas. The vehicles we had before were broken down; now we have new cars.... Now the constraint is money; we do not have enough money to buy everything we need. [E:22]

While the outlook regarding decentralization was generally positive, district directors and other district-level administrators had some criticisms. One resented the minimal training they had been given before having to assume the new responsibilities: "decentralization increased our administrative and legal responsibility; we were not ready for this" [E:11]. Another interviewee saw the slow pace of bureaucratic operations as a constraint: "The major frustration is that the disbursement of funds is slow.... I think that the problem is with lower-level bureaucrats [at the

SSNL] who do not process paperwork expeditiously" [E:12]. The thought that decentralization could mean an increased transfer of responsibilities without the matching funds was also of concern to a district director:

> Decentralization is a positive thing. Now we have 30 percent of decision-making autonomy. I understand that we will not have 100 percent, but it seems that as we increase the amount of money we collect from user fees, the government decreases its contributions. [E:22]

DISCUSSION

The information collected during the fieldwork for this project suggests that decentralization facilitated the mobilization of municipal resources and improved health centers in terms of their physical condition and equipment. Decentralization also increased the retention of health professionals in rural areas and resulted in greater continuity of supplies and pharmaceutical stocks. Perhaps more importantly, it boosted the morale of district administrators and gave them the sense that they could resolve a number of problems which, before decentralization, had to be resolved in Monterrey or Mexico City. While these accomplishments are important intermediate measures, decentralization's success must be measured by its effects on equity, efficiency, and the quality of the health services offered to the population. At the time of this research, there were no studies that could answer these questions. Some very limited information that emerged during the study which is relevant to the aforementioned questions is presented in the following pages.

Efficiency

Prior to decentralization to the health districts, the efficiency of health clinics was very low, and this continues to be the case. In 1996, before decentralization, the average number of consultations per physician per day was 11; in 2000, after decentralization, the number had only increased to 13.5. One district director offered the following explanation for the low productivity: the doctors' work hours were not convenient for the users of the health services; the physicians were not willing to change the schedule, and the director could do nothing about it because the physicians were protected by civil service regulations and the unions:

> Productivity levels are low because of our work schedule: from 8 in the morning to 3:30 in the afternoon. The number of women who have jobs is on the rise, and most physicians have at least two jobs and are not willing to change their work schedule. [E:12]

This was the case despite the fact that the productivity of Health Ministry workers was below the levels negotiated with the union. Another district director was less concerned about low productivity. In her opinion, there were so few consultations because people did not demand them and she could not find other activities in which to engage the physicians and support staff [E:14].

The improved availability of supplies and medicines may have had a positive impact on the health centers' capacity to treat patients and may have reduced the number of referrals to other levels of care. However, if productivity remains low, system efficiency will not improve significantly. Understanding the reasons for the low productivity would be the first step toward reversing it. The contradictory explanations offered by the two district directors quoted above suggest that no assessment of this problem has yet been made. If there is no demand for services, then it would be reasonable to either reduce infrastructure and personnel or expand the services offered in the areas of public health or medical care. Two other strategies to raise productivity would be to increase the number of contracts to provide health insurance to municipal employees and to offer services to beneficiaries of social security institutes who, because of distance, may not be able to access the social security institutes' services.

On the other hand, if productivity is low because of inconvenient hours of service, because user fees do, after all, constitute a barrier to access, or because of some other reason, then the health districts need to direct their efforts toward identifying the cause and finding a solution. This may entail changing civil service/union regulations (a difficult but not irresolvable issue), reducing user fees or developing a system that more accurately identifies those who cannot afford to pay, or some other actions. Only after the underlying cause of low productivity is diagnosed can the SSNL define measures to increase efficiency.

Another cause of inefficiency is the duplication of supervisory visits to the health districts by the Ministry of Health and the Nuevo León Health Secretariat. Local administrators have to coordinate these visits, escort visiting supervisors, and prepare reports. The number of coordinating meetings in Monterrey may also be a cause of inefficiency because the time spent in travel means lost workdays in the districts. The frequency of such meetings may reflect the inadequate preparation that local administrators received for meeting the new responsibilities transferred under decentralization.

Equity

All of the people we interviewed concurred that the funds raised through user fees were very important for the delivery of health services. The use of these funds was not dictated by federal or state guidelines, and district directors could spend them at their discretion. The amounts charged for services varied by district, and district directors set the user fees and decided who would be charged and who would be exempted. Clinic directors or clinic staff could also waive all or a portion of a user fee. These decisions could be arbitrary and based on factors unrelated to the user's socioeconomic condition, making the system less equitable. But perhaps the most serious problem from an equity perspective was the allocation of funds raised from user fees. A large percentage was distributed to professionals and staff as "incentive" bonuses; and another portion was used, at the discretion of the district director, to upgrade infrastructure (including air-conditioning offices) or to purchase supplies and medications.

As implemented in Mexico, the system of user fees represented a subsidy that the very poor provided to medical professionals and staff. If user fees caused indigent persons to forgo needed health services, then decentralization's impact on equity may have been very negative indeed.

Quality

According to our respondents, investments in infrastructure and equipment that were decided upon at the local level and paid for with self-

generated funds improved work conditions in health districts. Our interviewees also agreed that there was a more reliable and steady provision of
pharmaceuticals to the clinics and that efforts were being made to attract
specialists to rural areas. The availability of drugs is an important factor in
attracting patients to public services, though it is not sufficient to improve
quality of care. A large percentage of pharmaceuticals are inappropriately
prescribed and used. If doctors and other medical staff benefit from pre-
scribing or dispensing drugs, this pattern may worsen. Our study did not
aim to analyze the quality of the care that was provided, but studies in
other countries have demonstrated that when providers benefit from the
sale of services, and especially from the sale of medicines, there is a tendency to create demand for unnecessary medical procedures and drug
prescriptions. Such a situation creates a potential for increases in medical
conditions inadvertently induced by a physician or medical treatment. The
health centers had not developed an independent system for evaluating
quality of care. Until such a system is in place, it will be difficult to determine decentralization's real impact on the quality of care.

Community Participation

Aside from increasing the availability of medicines, the districts did little to
improve the concordance between services and popular needs or to increase user satisfaction. They had not significantly modified the types of
services provided or made clinic hours more convenient for the users of
health services, and none of the interviewees mentioned incorporating the
community in decision making. The only avenue for communities to express their health needs and voice their concerns was through the Healthy
Municipalities Program, which was unevenly developed and was managed
as a vertical program coordinated by SSNL staff in Monterrey. The involvement of the health districts in the Healthy Municipalities Program
was limited, and the program functioned rather independently from the
health districts.

Pending Issues

Transferring authority from the top implies an assumption of responsibilities by those at lower levels on the administrative ladder. To transfer deci-

sion-making power while also creating controls to ensure that decisions taken at lower administrative levels are for the benefit of the users of health services is a very complex process. What upper-level administration considers a justified control mechanism may be viewed at the local level as interference in the use of the newly acquired authority. To find the perfect balance is probably impossible. Beyond abuses such as the personal use of public property (which one district director considered an acceptable practice, given the Mexican public administration context), there are other aspects specific to the health sector that need scrutiny in a decentralized context.

The setting of health priorities is one such aspect. Experiences in other countries suggest that when the allocation of resources is left to physicians, there is a tendency to invest in medical procedures and high technology rather than in public health interventions, health education, or health promotion. When asked which activities a district would implement if service provision was subcontracted to the private sector or to other public providers—as could happen under the structured pluralism model (see chapter 2)—a district director responded:

> We would be unemployed because we conduct very few regulatory activities.... Well, maybe we could do more public health activities, more disease prevention and health promotion ... but those are not being considered.... We do follow-up with patients with chronic diseases to make sure they take their medications ... but right now in my district we are only following up on about 30 percent of them. I would like to raise this to 50 percent by the end of the year. [E:14]

This district director could not identify specific interventions beyond medical care. In this case, decentralization had not improved decision making. How to overcome this type of problem is an issue that should be addressed before decentralization takes place.

The decentralization of responsibilities from the Nuevo León Health Secretariat to the district level has attracted interest from other states. At the time of this study, representatives from the State Health Secretariats of San Luis Potosí, Sinaloa, México State, Zacatecas, and Jalisco had visited Nuevo León to learn about the SSNL's experience. In Nuevo León, the decentralization effort had several very positive elements, but many important aspects of a successful decentralization project remained unrealized. Clearly, it would be impossible to have all problems resolved before deciding to decentralize, and decentralization may need to be implemented before all potential problems are ironed out. Because the decision to decentralize has already been made in Nuevo León, the issue of whether the State Health Secretariat was or was not ready for this transition is moot, but the issues of identifying problems, modifying behaviors, and learning from mistakes are not.

References

OPS (Organización Panamericana de la Salud). 1990 *Desarrollo y fortalecimiento de los sistemas locales de salud: análisis de experiencias.* Washington, D.C.: Organización Panamericana de la Salud.

PAHO (Pan American Health Organization). 1993. "Local Health Systems in the Americas." Communicating for Health Series, no. 4. Washington, D.C.: PAHO.

SSNL (Secretaría de Salud de Nuevo León). 2000a. "Manual de lineamientos administrativos para el ejercicio del gasto." Monterrey, Nuevo León.

———. 2000b. "Lineamientos para el ejercicio del gasto a través del fondo desconcentrado." Monterrey, Nuevo León.

———. 2001. "Avances en el proceso de organización de los comités municipales de salud." Subsecretaría de Prevención y Control de Enfermedades, Subdirección de Promoción de la Salud, Programa de Municipio Saludable. August 23.

Ugalde, A., and N. Homedes. 2004. "Venda de serviços públicos de saúde: un estudo qualitativo." In *Pesquisa qualitativa de serviços de saúde,* ed. M. L. Magalhães Bosi and F. J. Mercado. São Paulo: Ed. Vozes.

10

Conclusions

ANTONIO UGALDE AND NÚRIA HOMEDES

The twenty-three years of health services decentralization in Mexico (1983–2006) confirm that decentralization is a very complex political process. As in other Latin American countries, decentralization has not achieved the intended results outlined by its promoters. In Mexico, decentralization has encountered many obstacles, both in the policy planning stage and along the road to implementation. Our journey has covered four presidential terms and has allowed us to observe the ups and downs of the process during a relatively lengthy span of time.

Most researchers of Mexico's decentralization have concluded that it is only a limited deconcentration. Because deconcentration is poorly defined in the literature, this characterization is not very useful. One conclusion of our study is the need to define more precisely the terms used to classify the decentralization process, such as deconcentration, delegation, and devolution; otherwise, attempts to measure progress and conduct cross-national studies will be hampered. A starting point to overcome the limitation of a lack of precision in definitions could be the identification of functions that ministries of health perform. Then researchers could compare for each function the location of decisions before and after decentralization. One country may have achieved decentralization in human resources management, for example, but have advanced little in the decentralization of financial resources.

The identification of functions and the determination of which ones are to be decentralized are essential to planning and implementation. We suggest that Mexico's slow progress was in part caused by the planners' lack of precision in identifying the decision makers for each function before decentralization, and defining who would have the corresponding responsibility after decentralization. Planners also failed to foresee potential constraints, and they lacked a system of evaluation to check the process of implementation, to identify deviations, and to make the needed adjustments. A policy that is not carefully planned and does not anticipate obstacles and their solutions during the implementation has few chances of success. Without evaluation procedures and ways to steer the course when deviations occur, the policy is doomed to failure.

Planning also requires anticipating the capabilities of the administrative units that will receive the power to make decisions. Some functions are very technical and require training. Decision making has political dimensions, which also calls for advice and guidance. Transferring decision-making power is contraindicated if those who receive it are not technically and politically prepared. The case studies in this volume show that there was little training before beginning the implementation of decentralization. Dr. Zacarías Villarreal, the secretary of health in Nuevo León, understood the training needs when he took office, and his Secretariat spent considerable time and resources developing norms and guides that should have been available much earlier. In Nuevo León, the progress in decentralizing can be attributed in part to the efforts in preparing personnel for their new responsibilities.

In Mexico, according to official documents, health decentralization includes the transfer of health decision making to municipal authorities. There is a general acceptance among health personnel, however, that most municipalities are not ready, nor will they be ready in the near future, to take over the provision of health care. It is very fortunate that health services have not been decentralized to the municipal level in Mexico, but the contradiction between official pronouncements and policy implementation is indicative of poor planning and contributes to the politically unhealthy idea that government is not to be trusted.

THE PRICE TO BE PAID

It should be clear that decentralizing health services in countries with a history of centralism is extremely costly. The official estimate of the cost of Mexico's first decentralization is impressive. We have not found any yearly federal or state estimates of the costs of the second decentralization attempt. This by itself is very telling and reveals deficiencies in evaluation capabilities. Homologizing salaries and fringe benefits of state and federal employees required large outlays of federal and state funds. Transferring deeds for buildings, equipment, and other assets also requires funding, while personnel training and the preparation of policy and procedure manuals for the new functions are both time-consuming and expensive. It is true that some of these costs are one-time expenditures, but the money has to be earmarked and available. In addition, as some respondents indicated, there was no reduction of personnel at the federal level, and some functions, such as the supervision of a number of public health programs, continued to be carried out by the federal government, duplicating the activities of the states. It is to be expected that central civil servants will defend their turf and fight to keep power and job security; consequently, governments intending to decentralize need to resolve these problems in advance and prepare a plan to reduce the number of federal workers.

When advising governments, supranational and bilateral agencies should explain up front the large amount of money required for the successful implementation of decentralization. In the case of Mexico, to begin such a costly program during an economic crisis was a crass error. The World Bank promoted decentralization and provided loans for the reforms in Mexico and elsewhere, and it bears a major responsibility for the failure by not alerting governments to the perils of beginning a major policy change during economic recessions.

Throughout its postrevolutionary years, Mexico has severely curtailed the taxing powers of states and municipalities, and local decision makers found themselves without the financial means to pay for the newly acquired responsibilities transferred by the decentralization. The states had to depend mostly on user fees, which are considered to be a regressive tax. During the second attempt at decentralization, the federal government increased its allocation of funds to the states, but given the growth of the population and the additional responsibilities transferred, the states continued to lack adequate resources to implement the changes. The lesson is clear. Central governments should not transfer responsibilities to lower politico-administrative authorities until the latter have the required funds to pay for the services; otherwise, decentralization will not advance and the quality of care will suffer. It is in this light that respondents in our case studies viewed decentralization as a transfer of problems without the means to resolve them.

Our study confirms the loss of economies of scale in the purchase of equipment, medicines, and supplies. Although states with resources, such as Nuevo León, could organize a centralized purchasing system, it is doubtful that states with fewer technical and financial resources could do so. Besides, economies of scale at the state level cannot be compared to those that can be obtained by a national procurement system. To prepare international tenders requires technical know-how not available to most states, and corruption is more difficult to control at the local than at the federal level. Unfortunately, the decentralization in Mexico has created as many procurement offices as states. As of 2006, many health centers in Mexico, including those that serve the People's Health Insurance Program (SP), do not have a steady supply of medicines. Multilateral banks and the United Nations have advocated centralization of procurement of medicines, and countries wanting to succeed in decentralizing health services need to determine during the planning process the types of equipment, drugs, and sundries that should be procured centrally and the logistics of the procurement and distribution. The World Bank has prepared procurement manuals to help Ministries of Health in the preparation of international bids, and the manuals should be used.

POLITICAL SUPPORT

As a process, the implementation of decentralization requires time. Unless there is continuous political support, the success of implementation is doubtful. Mexico is one of the few countries in Latin America that has maintained a stable political system, with presidential elections every six years since 1934. The continuity in power of the same party until 2000 has also contributed to national stability. This condition is extremely rare in the rest of the region. But even Mexico's stability has not guaranteed continuity of policies. We have seen that President Salinas de Gortari failed to continue the decentralization that his predecessor began. Given the failure of the first decentralization, it is a moot question whether President Salinas's decision was the correct one. It was not correct, however, that he continued to proclaim that decentralization of health services was the policy of the country at the same time that he implemented an unwritten policy of centralization.

Laws, decrees, and agreements between the federal and state governments have not succeeded in securing continuity in the implementation of decentralization policy in Mexico. It is important to understand the characteristics of the legal and judiciary systems and to assess how they can support or impede continuity in the implementation of decentralization across changes of governments. In countries with unstable political systems, the problem is more serious. If a country cannot ensure that legal instruments such as laws, regulations, and contracts are binding for future regimes, it is unlikely that any policy requiring more than a single presidential term for its implementation (such as decentralization) will be successful. Before embarking on any major policy change, such as decentralizing the health system, policymakers and their international advisers need to identify the impediments that the legal and judicial systems may pose.

Another lesson learned from our study is the need to examine the compatibility of new laws with previous ones. When the government of President Vicente Fox had the new People's Health Insurance approved by Congress in 2003, legislators failed to see the incompatibility of continuing to decentralize while implementing a national health insurance program at the same time. The People's Health Insurance was conceived and designed at the center, with cosmetic inputs from the states that had to implement it. The federal Ministry of Health was aware of the contradiction, and it was not coincidental that the minister of health questioned in writing the wisdom of decentralization. The states are now encountering many obstacles in the implementation of the SP, and there are conflicts between the way the states are implementing the insurance program and the way the federal authorities had envisioned its implementation. The states argue that, since they are decentralized, they can decide how to proceed, while the Ministry of Health feels that a national program must be implemented as designed or it will not succeed. The lesson from the Mexican experience suggests that, before policymakers send a bill for legislative approval, they should first examine the incompatibilities with previous laws and make the necessary modifications. If they fail to do so, then the legislative body should assume responsibility for the outcome.

Policy contradictions can also take place at the state level. Tamaulipas is a good example of the difficulties of settling local conflicts of interest when decentralization is imposed from the top. Workers in the decentralized hospitals opposed their centralization, which was carried out in the name of "decentralization." When a policy goes against the vested interests of key stakeholders, it is to be expected that they will oppose it. Political leaders need to negotiate with stakeholders, modify the policy, or wait for a more politically propitious moment to seek policy approval.

THE NEED FOR TRANSPARENCY

The case studies of Sonora and Baja California Sur show that the staff and physicians of their respective state health secretariats were poorly informed about the nature of the decentralization. Because the meaning of decentralization is poorly defined, it is understandable that health workers were apprehensive, particularly when authorities failed to explain the objectives and stages of decentralization. Fears of job loss, changes in work environment, and bureaucratic interference in their medical practice are legitimate. Predisposing health workers to oppose a policy, not so much for its content but because of fears born out of the failure to explain the nature of the changes, makes the implementation unnecessarily more problematic. Even when policymakers foresee opposition to decentralization, including potential strikes, policymakers are ill advised to avoid explaining clearly to workers the intent and characteristics of the policy. It is difficult to accept that one of the goals of decentralization is the strengthening of democracy when the policy process is carried out secretly and hidden from those workers whose jobs are affected. It can also be expected that a lack of transparency has a negative impact on the quality of health care.

COMMUNITY PARTICIPATION

Community participation has been presented as one of the main goals of decentralization, but Mexican federal and state health authorities never considered fostering community participation as one of decentralization's objectives. The only official political space for community participation provided by decentralization in Mexico was the presence of one or two community leaders on the health councils. But even this token participation was a travesty, as we learned from the interviews in Guanajuato. In a democracy, community participation takes place through elected officials. If the elected officials in any nation do not work for the welfare of their constituencies, it is deceptive to refer to such nations as democracies. It is naïve to believe that a policy such as decentralization can strengthen democracy when institutions that are supposed to guard it do not function properly, and even more ingenuous that this be the case in countries under authoritarian regimes, military strongmen, or dominant oligarchies.

While community participation and the strengthening of democracy are worthwhile goals in themselves, it is difficult to understand why supranational and bilateral agencies consistently include them as decentralization goals. Perhaps the leadership of these agencies thought that it would be easier to sell decentralization if it was linked to such attractive concepts. Once community participation and strengthening democracy were made outcomes of decentralization, governments, health ministries, nongovernmental organizations, and aid groups accepted this as a matter of fact, without questioning such a nonsensical idea. Whatever the reasons for the inclusion, Mexico officially accepted community participation as one of the goals of decentralization and paid lip service to it.

As discussed in the various chapters of this book, promoters of decentralization expected that the active participation of the community in decision making would make local political leaders more responsive to the needs of their constituencies. Given that community participation did not take place in Mexico, it is not possible to verify whether the hypothesis is correct. Nevertheless, the case studies show that moving the location of some decisions from Mexico City to the states made little difference regarding the adequacy of decisions to meet the needs of the local population. Preference continued to be given to hospitals over primary care and public health. Would involvement of the communities have changed the decisions? Probably not, because many health decisions are very technical and complex, and the users of services do not have the necessary information to make the best choice. Many decisions are better left to those with expertise, but expertise by itself does not guarantee the best choice for a community. Physicians exercise influence in the health sector, and their interests do not always coincide with those of their patients. Professional expertise has to be tempered by judicious political leaders. The lesson to be

learned is that if a country lacks sufficient professionals and political leaders who seek a greater good than self-interest, there are few possibilities
that decisions will be made on behalf of the welfare of the community.

THE IMPACT ON EQUITY

There is unanimous agreement that one of the most serious social problems
in Latin America is the profound wealth difference between social classes.
Decentralization was considered to be one strategy to reduce the gap between the poor and the wealthy. The comparison of the results of decentralization in Oaxaca and Guerrero shows that the opposite occurred during the first attempt to decentralize. During the second decentralization,
the study of Nuevo León raises questions about the equity impact of charging user fees to the very poor and using them mostly to increase the salaries of the staff and professionals of the state health secretariat. In Guanajuato, decisions by state health authorities benefited urban populations
over poorer rural dwellers.

There are also deep geographical wealth differences in Mexico. The
federal government's attempt to replace the historical budget allocations to
the states with an allocation formula based on the states' health needs was
too timid and insufficient to improve equity. Wealthier and politically
more powerful states were not willing to share part of their historical allocations. There are also technical difficulties in determining the allocation
formula, namely, the many variables that have to be included and the uncertainty regarding the weight that each variable should be given.

Decentralization required states to increase their financial contributions
to their own health secretariats. On a per capita basis, poor states have not
been able to contribute as much as the wealthier states, and the latter can
collect more in user fees than can the former. The result is an increasing
regional gap in accessibility and quality of services.

If governments want decentralization to decrease class inequities, it is
imperative that they define a budget allocation formula that takes into
account differences in regional economic and epidemiological profiles,
infrastructure and human resources availability, population dispersion,
health status and wealth, and the ethnic composition and degrees of accul-
turation of the population. Otherwise, decentralization inevitably will
increase inequity.

National policymakers also have to consider that devising an equity formula for budget allocations to states is necessary but not sufficient. Without oversight, health authorities in each state or province could allocate the additional resources to wealthier cities and towns and, within the centers of population, to more affluent neighborhoods. Ensuring that state authorities distribute resources equitably is not easy in societies whose political system is dominated by an entrenched upper class that has successfully rejected a progressive tax system.

THE FUTURE ...

The findings from Mexico question the feasibility of decentralization as a policy for achieving equity and improving efficiency and the quality of care. History has shown that decentralization is successful when the impetus to carry it out springs from nationalistic and religious causes, and less so when the justification comes from economic demands. The timing of Mexico's decentralization during an economic recession reaffirms that the main force behind decentralization came from the interests of the World Bank and the International Monetary Fund to free up funds of the central government to meet debt payments. This was accomplished by asking the states to increase their contributions and by attempting to privatize health care. Both attempts failed, and the future of decentralization in the country remains in doubt.

In sum, the failure of decentralization goes beyond the embarrassment of the political leaders who promoted it. It carries enormous economic losses for countries that have few resources. The decision on such a policy cannot be taken lightly. Additionally, if decentralization fails, future administrations may have to revert to previous or new organizational forms, which will also require large allocations of funds.

There is an urgent need to solve the administrative inefficiencies that plague centralized health systems, inefficiencies that have been recognized for many years. It is irresponsible, however, to continue to follow the same road of decentralization without first finding solutions to the constraints that have been uncovered previously, and now in this study of Mexico.

Acronyms

BCS	Baja California Sur
CFE	Compañía Federal de Electricidad / National Electric Power Company
CIS	Commonwealth of Independent States
CONAMED	Comisión Nacional de Arbitraje Médico / National Medical Arbitration Commission
CONASUPO	Compañía Nacional de Susbistencias Populares / National Commodities Company
COPLADE	Comité de Planeación del Desarrollo del Estado / State Development Planning Committee
COPLAMAR	Coordinación General del Plan Nacional de Zonas Deprimidas y Grupos Marginales / National Planning Group for Depressed Zones and Marginalized Groups
CTM	Confederación de Trabajadores de México / Confederation of Mexican Workers
CUD	*convenio único de desarrollo* / consolidated development agreement
DDF	Departamento del Distrito Federal / Federal District Department
DIF	Desarrollo Integral de la Familia / National System for Integral Family Development
EAP	economically active population
EU	European Union
FASSA	Fondo de Aportaciones para los Servicios de Salud y Asistencia / Health Care Savings Fund
GDP	gross domestic product
IMF	International Monetary Fund
IMSS	Instituto Mexicano del Seguro Social / Mexican Social Security Institute
INI	Instituto Nacional Indigenista / National Indigenous Institute

ISSSTE	Instituto de Seguridad y Servicios Sociales de los Trabajadores del Estado / Social Security Institute for State Employees
ISSSTELEON	Instituto de Seguridad y Servicios Sociales de los Trabajadores del Estado de Nuevo León / Social Security Institute for Employees of the State of Nuevo León
ISSSTESON	Instituto de Seguridad y Servicios Sociales de los Trabajadores del Estado de Sonora / Social Security Institute for Employees of Sonora State
NAFTA	North American Free Trade Agreement
NGO	nongovernmental organization
OECD	Organisation for Economic Co-operation and Development
OPD	*organismo público descentralizado* / decentralized public agency
PAC	Programa de Ampliación de Cobertura / Program to Expand Coverage
PAHO	Pan American Health Organization
PAN	Partido Acción Nacional / National Action Party
PBP	Patronato para la Beneficencia Pública / State Welfare Agency
PBPF	Patronato para la Beneficencia Pública Federal / Federal Welfare Agency
PEMEX	National Oil Company of Mexico
PNR	Partido Nacional Revolucionario / National Revolutionary Party
PRD	Partido de la Revolución Democrática / Party of the Democratic Revolution
PRI	Partido Revolucionario Institucional / Institutional Revolutionary Party
Progresa	Programa de Educación, Salud y Alimentación / Education, Health, and Nutrition Program
Pronasol	Programa Nacional de Solidaridad / National Solidarity Program
PT	Partido del Trabajo / Labor Party
SEDESOL	Secretaría de Desarrollo Social / Ministry of Social Development
SEMESON	Servicios Médicos de Sonora / Sonora Medical Services

SEP	Secretaría de Educación Pública / Education Ministry
SHCP	Secretaría de Hacienda y Crédito Pública / Ministry of the Treasury
SIFs	Social Investment Funds
SILOS	*sistema local de salud* / local health system
SNTSSA	Sindicato Nacional de Trabajadores de la Secretaría de Salud / National Union of Health Ministry Employees
SP	Seguro Popular de Salud / People's Health Insurance Program
SPP	Secretaría de Planeación y Presupuesto / Ministry of Planning and Budgeting
SS	Secretaría de Salud / Ministry of Health
SSA	Secretaría de Salud y Asistencia / Ministry of Health and Welfare
SSBCS	Secretaría de Salud de Baja California Sur / Baja California Sur Health Secretariat
SSG	Secretaría de Salud de Guanajuato / Guanajuato Health Secretariat
SSM	Secretaría de Salud de Morelos / Morelos Health Secretariat
SSNL	Secretaría de Salud de Nuevo León / Nuevo León Health Secretariat
SSS	Secretaría de Salud de Sonora / Sonora Health Secretariat
SST	Secretaría de Salud de Tamaulipas / Tamaulipas Health Secretariat
UDE	*unidad de descentralizacion estatal* / state decentralization unit
USAID	U.S. Agency for International Development

About the Authors

Raquel Abrantes Pêgo is a lecturer and researcher at the Centro Interamericano de Estudios de Seguridad Social and a PhD candidate at El Colegio de Michoacán. She has an extensive record of researching health policy in Mexico and Brazil, and has recently given attention to issues of social security. She has published book chapters on health systems, as well as articles in such journals as *Revista de Saúde Pública*, *Salud Pública de México*, and *Cadernos de Saúde Pública*. She has collaborated in projects with the United Nations Population Division, the Pan American Health Organization, El Colegio de Sonora, and El Colegio de México, among others.

Sofía Arjonilla Alday received her undergraduate training at the Universidad Nacional Autónoma de Mexico and her doctoral degree at the Universidad Autónoma de Madrid. Her research interests include the study of international migration and of health policymaking. Her publications have appeared in academic journals including *Revista de Saúde Pública*, *Cadernos de Saúde Pública*, and *Salud Mental*. From 1988 to 2002 she was chair of the Department of International Health and Political Analysis at the Instituto Nacional de Salud Pública (Cuernavaca) and has been a visiting researcher and professor in several Mexican and Spanish institutions.

Anne-Emanuelle Birn is Canada Research Chair in International Health and associate professor of International Development Studies at the University of Toronto. Her scholarly work explores the history of public health in Latin America and the history and politics of international health policy. Professor Birn has published widely in public health, medical, and history of medicine journals. Her recent article, "Gates's Grandest Challenge: Transcending Technology as Public Health Ideology" (*The Lancet*, August 2005), has sparked a lively debate in international health circles; her forthcoming book is *Marriage of Convenience: Rockefeller International Health and Revolutionary Mexico* (University of Rochester Press, 2006).

Miguel González-Block is associate director of the Health Systems Research Center (CISS) of Mexico's National Institute for Public Health (INSP). His advanced degree work in social anthropology and sociology at the University of Cambridge and El Colegio de México centered on the sociology and politics of health services in Mexico. Later research focused on the reorganization of Mexican health services in the face of economic crisis and the evolving relationship between the federal and local levels of government. He has published over 80 works on social epidemiology, health systems and health policy, and the strategic development of public health research.

Núria Homedes is associate professor at the University of Texas School of Public Health-Houston. She is a medical doctor and holds a doctoral degree in public health. She has worked for several international agencies and has extensive fieldwork experience in Africa and Latin America. Dr. Homedes is the author of forty articles in leading journals, including the *American Journal of Public Health*, *WHO Bulletin*, *Health Policy and Planning*, *Health Policy*, and *Social Science and Medicine*.

René Leyva is currently a senior researcher at the Center for Health Systems Research at the National Institute for Public Health in Cuernavaca, Mexico. A medical doctor, he also holds a master's degree in social medicine and also a doctorate from the University of Barcelona. Dr. Leyva, a specialist in international health, conducts research in the areas of health policy, essential drugs, and migration and AIDS.

Ricardo Loewe is a medical doctor, currently active in Acción de los Cristianos para la Abolición de la Tortura (Christian Action for the Abolition of Torture).

Lucila Olvera Santana received her M.D. from the School of Medicine of the Autonomous University of Coahuila in Torreón and her master's degree in public health from the National Institute for Public Health in Cuernavaca, where she received honorable mention for her thesis, "Análisis de la implementación de la descentralización en Mexico." Areas of particular interest to Dr. Olvera Santana include health-sector reform and health services organization. She is currently the director of planning and development at the Baja California Sur Health Secretariat.

Antonio Ugalde is emeritus professor in the Department of Sociology of the University of Texas at Austin. He is the author of five monographs and the guest editor of several issues of *Social Science and Medicine* and *Studies in Third World Societies*. His publications include more than eighty articles in professional journals and numerous technical reports for the World Health Organization and other international agencies. His fields of interest include the sociology of health, health policies in developing countries, and global studies.

Óscar Zapata is a graduate of the National Autonomous University of Mexico (UNAM), where he did research in the field of public education. His professional interests include health economics and health policy.

Index